Books of Stone

Books of Stone

TRAVEL TO 13 MAYA PYRAMIDS IN THE YUCATÁN PENINSULA

BY VICTORIA THOMAS ▲ PHOTOS BY DAVID ALEXANDER BJÖRKMAN

Zone 913 Press, Inc.
Niwot, Colorado, USA

Books of Stone, Travel to 13 Maya Pyramids in the Yucatán Peninsula
By Victoria Thomas
Photographs by David Alexander Björkman.
Copyright © 2001 by Victoria Thomas and David Alexander Björkman
Photographs © 2001 by David Alexander Björkman

Cover photos by David Alexander Björkman. Front cover: *Rainbow over Chichén Itzá.* Back cover: *Spring equinox sunrise at Dzibilchaltún*

Published by Zone 913 Press, Inc.
P.O. Box 516, Niwot, Colorado 80544 USA
Phone and Fax: 303.652.8179, E-mail: zone913inc@aol.com
Website: www.Zone913.com

Zone 913 Press, Inc. titles may be purchased for business or promotional use or for special sales.

Grateful acknowledgment is made to Red Crane Books Inc., Santa Fe, New Mexico, for permission to reprint
"Recado Colorado" from *Yucatán Cookbook, Recipes & Tales* by Lyman Morton. Copyright © by Lyman Morton

Cataloging-in-Publication Data
Thomas, Victoria, 1949-
    Books of stone : travel to 13 Maya pyramids in the
  Yucatán Peninsula / by Victoria Thomas ; photos by David
  Alexander Björkman. -- 1st ed.
    p. cm
    LCCN 2001094915
    ISBN 0-943289-03-3

    1. Mayas--Mexico--Yucatán (State)--Antiquities.
  2. Pyramids--Mexico--Yucatán (State). 3. Maya cookery.
  4. Yucatán (Mexico : State)--Description and travel.
  1. Björkman, David. II. Title.

  F1435.T46 2002   972'.65

Table of Contents

Map of the Yucatán

Good Going...

THE YUCATÁN PENINSULA of Mexico reaches up like a thumb between the waters of the Gulf of Mexico on the west and the Caribbean on the east. Situated south of New Orleans, it's closest neighbor is Cuba, and then Miami at 400 miles away. Most people know its famous tourist resort, Cancún. About the size of Ohio, it has three states, Yucatán, Campeche, and Quintana Roo, and is safely and easily traveled by public bus, tour, taxi, or rental car. From Cancún, the ancient Maya cities of Tulum and Cobá are ninety minutes away by car. Muyil is another thirty minutes beyond Tulum. Chichén Itzá is a three-hour drive inland, as is Ek Balám. The ancient sites on the side of the Peninsula opposite Cancún are easily reached from the charming colonial city Mérida. First-class and deluxe buses travel non-stop in four-and-a-half hours from the Caribbean to Mérida, where taxis and rental cars are for hire. Dzibilchaltún is thirty minutes north of Mérida. Izamal is thirty minutes east. (Both are accessible by bus.) Ak'e is close, but is an out-of-the-way site requiring a car or taxi. Oxkintok is sixty minutes southwest and requires a car or taxi. Uxmal takes about an hour to reach and is accessible by bus. Mayapán requires a car or taxi. Edzná is best reached from the city Campeche. Travel is safe and comfortable if one carries bottled water and stops in village stores for snacks. ▲

1. Dzibilchaltún

Dawn...

IT'S THE HOUR before dawn on the first day of spring, and David and I are about to link our creative future to the ancient past as we begin our journey to the Maya pyramids in Mexico's Yucatán Peninsula. The charcoal night has burned down to ashes when Fernando squeezes the taxi into a crowded parking lot at the archaeological site of Dzibilchaltún. He points down a gravel road to a visitors center barely visible in the dusky light. I pull on my backpack and David slings his cameras over his shoulder, and we fall into step with hundreds of sleepy people heading into the ancient Maya city. It's spring equinox, and we've come to witness the phenomenon of the dawning Sun rising up into the doorway of a thirteen-hundred-year-old temple. It's a memory we'll cherish—waiting for the sunlight to fill the temple as we begin our journey armed with a hungry notebook and expectant rolls of film.

Everyone is wearing white—the women in blouses and flowing skirts, men in trousers and wide-sleeved shirts. In the dim before dawn, they look like bits of tree fluff bobbing along on the breeze. It didn't occur to me to wear white, but even if it had, the clothing I've packed for this year-long odyssey is mostly black while David has brought serious khaki.

At the visitors center, we follow a hall past locked stores and out onto a dirt path leading into a dark tangle of trees still wrapped in the night. Forward-motion abruptly stops. People strain to see what lies ahead in the dark, "what's-happening?" appearing on their faces until "it's-too-early-wait-a-little" floats back from the front of the line and soothes the worry.

David is impatient. He's eager to get on site and scout the best place for shooting photos of the Sun lifting up into the temple doorway. He checks his cameras like a pilot monitoring the instruments of a cockpit. Batteries: strong. ISO: appropriate. Black-and-white film: on exposure 8. Color film: on exposure 2. He studies the brightening sky and wonders aloud how many minutes before let-there-be-light puts the night to rest.

I'm in no rush. The air is lazy, the wind still asleep in its nest. The fragrance of dew wafts from the damp foliage. I pull my green notebook from my pack and turn to the first virginal page. I uncap my pen. But then I hesitate—it seems that I should write something Really Important on it, and nothing important is occurring to me. But determined to begin my account of our journey in this hour

Dzibilchaltún's Temple of the Seven Dolls was built in about 700 CE over a much older temple.

before dawn, I flip to the second page and scribble a few words about standing where ancient people once waited for the Sun to be born-again into spring.

"Your first time here?"

The woman ahead of us has turned around. Her straight, dark hair stops short of touching the lime-green collar on her wrinkled, white satin dress.

I nod. "And you?"

"I came last year," she says. "A group of us actually, the same people I'm with today. We're going to Chichén Itzá this afternoon. To watch the seven triangles of light come down the pyramid. Dawn here, sunset there. It'll be a good day."

"Yes," I say.

"I keep a journal, too," she says, and she bends over my notebook to read what I've written:

The path eats the sound of our footsteps
in this sliver of time when the Earth twirls like a ballerina
between the tuxedoed night and the gossamer light of day.
Dawn, the hermaphrodite.

"I've just started," I say, suddenly self-conscious about the scrawled words that have leapt half-cocked from my brain to gestate in my notebook. I'm glad there's nothing for her to read about our trip barely six months ago to the ancient ruin of Teotihuacan near Mexico City where David and I climbed the Pyramid of the Sun and suddenly decided to quit our long-standing jobs so we could write and take photos. I'm not ready to talk about that. Nor to admit that like countless pharaohs, kings, and adventurers before us, we see in the pyramids the powerful potential for change. Thankfully, there's no mention in my notebook of my desire to write from my heart. Nor of the photos David envisions but hasn't yet taken.

This odyssey—both the career move and our journey—runs counter to family wisdom, which condemns it as sheer folly. A bird in the hand—a good job—has been Released. Recklessly. Wrong-headedly. My father wants to know when I'll be looking for "gainful employment," and gives me a look of disappointment (always stronger than his disapproval). Never mind that the bird in hand was stuffed and as dry as dust. To parents who came of age during the Depression, a bird is a bird is a bird. To be held on to, at whatever cost, until Retirement. I imagine that they silently wonder whether they'll be asked for money if another bird doesn't appear on cue.

I have my own quiet doubts about this major shift in our lives for which we have no real plan. Over the years that I worked a job that didn't touch my real interests, I hadn't noticed my creative fire dwindling until now I wonder if the embers have grown too cold to spark a new flame. I hadn't realized that the personality I developed to handle Work had crystallized into thick glass that now keeps me from experiencing the world with the sensitivity I desire. For years I squelched Intuition and put Analysis on a pedestal, and now I'm afraid I can no longer touch my authenticity. I'm afraid I've become a glass eye.

Standing on the path in the darkness, I become aware of the expectancy in the woman's brown eyes—she must have asked me something I didn't hear. But Time saves me from answering. The line lurches forward. The woman turns away.

The path takes us through shadowy tree shapes, past a sign prohibiting visitors from bringing candles, incense, drums, and conch shells into the archaeological zone, past guards looking to confiscate these tools of ceremony. Ahead of us, a boy of about ten is carrying a small drum. A guard tells him to leave it behind.

The boy's mother protests. "It's just a toy," she says.

The guard doesn't relent.

"Why can't I have it?" the boy whines.

"Because ceremony *scares* some people," his mother tells him. "Because they just can't *handle* it that these ancient centers are being reactivated by rituals."

BEYOND THE TREES, the path delivers us to a wide boulevard elevated four feet above the forest floor. It's an ancient Maya *sacbé,* literally translated as white road, that once connected the different sectors of this large city. We scramble up onto it and turn in the direction people are looking.

"That's it," a man says, pointing to a little temple a quarter of a mile or so down the *sacbé.* "That's the Doll House."

At this distance, the Temple of the Seven Dolls resembles a little cottage in a fairy tale. Made of gray stone and not much larger than a big, square living room, it sits atop a squatty pyramid. It has two little windows like sad-sack eyes on either side of a little front-door mouth that aligns with a back door to give a straight-through view. On its top is a short, square tower like a party hat, making it look like a sleepy baby at a birthday party.

From what I've read, the temple's tower and windows baffled archaeologists restoring it in the late 1950s. Maya workmen clearing debris from it reported finding windows in its front and back walls. The archaeologists scoffed—Maya buildings in the Yucatán Peninsula were not thought to have windows. But then someone pointed out its similarity to ancient structures in Guatemala having windows, and further digging in other sectors of the site revealed pottery indicating that the city's early inhabitants were probably from Guatemala's northern Peten region. According to the Maya's own account of their history, the temple was constructed between 692 and 731 CE (our Common Era) on the base of a much older pyramid. For centuries, the Maya conducted rituals in the temple, but then they buried it, carefully stuffing it with big stones then covering it with another structure that still overlays it in places like a stone cloak. Centuries later, their descendants tunneled into the earlier temple and meticulously removed the stones. They cut a small shaft in the floor over which they placed an altar incised with hieroglyphs. At the bottom of the shaft, they placed the seven clay dolls that give the temple its name.

The dolls are crude little figures. If you were to find them in the cellar of an old house, you'd toss them without a second thought. Hand-made from solid clay, they're unpainted, rough, and scarcely more than five inches tall. Each has a strange physical feature—two are hunchback, one is a dwarf, one has a swollen stomach, another has an oversize, erect penis. So far, no one has offered a suitable explanation of their purpose.

THE SKY IS brightening, but the night is in no hurry to move on.

During spring equinox, the night claims the sky for twelve hours and refuses to give up even a minute to the coming day. Someone—anticipating the sunrise—starts to chant in a self-conscious voice but stops when no one joins in.

Guards have strung a rope across the *sacbé* to block access to the pyramid and temple, and people jockey for space near the rope. A small, blonde woman kneels beside it, holding her elbows akimbo to keep from being crowded. Some people who can't get close to the rope climb up onto a low stone structure beside the road to stand above the crowd. I follow David up onto its walls, but after a few minutes I jump down—while he needs room for the camera between him and the subjects of his photos, I want nitty-gritty. Down here on the road, people make themselves small to fit into the spaces between bodies until we're crammed-jammed together and deodorant soap meets morning breath.

Still people pour in until the crowd swells to a couple of thousand. They clamor up onto the road, and then finding no room to stand, move to the rear of the crowd. A boy of about sixteen with coal-black hair slicked back above coal-black eyes complains loudly about having to go to the back.

"What does it matter?" a man says affably. "The Sun shines on us all."

"Yeah, you can say that," the boy retorts, "you're standing in front."

"Okay, then, you come up here and take my place," the man says. "I'll go back."

The boy doesn't answer.

"Really," the man says, "I mean it. Come up here in front."

But the boy puts his head down and pushes like a bull toward the rear, and I wonder what causes us to stop ourselves from having what we want. (And why we ask for what we aren't prepared to have.)

Just when there seems to be no room for more people, a group of thirty people climbs up onto the road. Several of the women are wearing white *huipiles*, the traditional dress of Maya women of the Yucatán. Others have woven clothing in the brilliant colors of the Guatemalan Maya. Still others are Americans with red bandannas tied across their foreheads. A large man who appears to be a Native American from the United States wears a brown flannel shirt and new jeans. Space miraculously opens for the group, and they form two lines facing the Doll House.

Above the trees, the eastern sky flushes with rosy light. The wind has awakened and whipped two clouds over the horizon into long, slender eyebrows arched in red surprise.

A low tone sounds. At first, it's barely audible, like the subtle hum of electricity running through high wires. But then it swells as individual voices pick up the note and strengthen it. Someone blows a conch shell smuggled into the park, and the sound cleaves the air. The conch sounds again, raising its note to the sky, and when the vibration begins to waver, another conch lifts the note and offers it up.

A tall man with long, thin, gray braids lifts a silver bowl and strikes it with a wooden mallet, and notes like silver rods go flying. The human-voice-conch-shell-silver-bowl vibration swells as the Sun lifts above the horizon, an orange in the bird-blue sky.

The Sun appears to rise up into the pyramid's temple, and the Temple of the Seven Dolls becomes the sacred vessel for the great solar fire that shines from its window-eyes and front-door mouth.

"*Kin, kin,*" sing the Maya women and men, uttering their name for the Sun, which they believe to be a sacred manifestation of divine spirit. "*Kin, kin,*" they sing until they've repeated it twenty-one times.

As the chant fades, the big Native American man strikes a match and holds its flame against sage leaves cradled in an abalone shell. The sage ignites, and he fans its smoke with an eagle feather onto those who step forward to receive it. Bathing them, purifying them, blessing them in its smoke.

Maya women lift goblets of water and yellow flowers toward the Sun. People raise their palms to the light and then make motions of spreading the light over their faces and bodies as though it were butter.

People celebrate the sunrise on the first day of spring as the rosy light of dawn fills the Temple of the Seven Dolls.

Then as the phenomenon of the Sun in the doorway begins to fade, people who have witnessed the dawn together grin and greet strangers like friends. A man with a long, dark ponytail catches me up in a hug—he smells of wood smoke. A thin, young man with matted sandy hair places his palms together and bows to me. An older woman flashes a smile of yellow chipped teeth and pats my arm. The joy of the day shines in their eyes, and I hope mine mirror it.

David is motioning me to come up onto the low structure where he has been taking photos. I squeeze through the crowd and climb the steps, where he hands me a camera and tells me to look through the lens at the Doll House.

"What do you see?" he asks.

Keeping the camera at my eye, I walk a few feet to the right until I face the Doll House straight-on.

"The Maya angled the temple to face this structure," he says, "not the *sacbé*."

It's well known that the Maya were astute astronomers who positioned hundreds of temples and pyramids throughout their realm to align with the Sun's rising at spring equinox. They also aligned some buildings to the Sun on winter solstice and others to its position on August 13, which they believed was the first day of the current cycle of creation in 3114 BCE. In this way, their sacred structures marked the Sun's journey through the year, and also linked the people themselves with the solar disk.

I try to remember what Mrs. Wheeler, my junior high school science teacher, taught us about the spring equinox. At equinox, which means equal night, the Sun is midway in its journey between its farthest rising point in the south at winter solstice and its farthest rising point in the north at summer solstice. On spring equinox on March 21 and again on the autumnal equinox on September 22, it rises due east and sets due west.

"So if the temple's rear door faces east, the door we see faces west," I say, turning to look at the high wall of a structure behind us in the west.

"What if the temple's builders positioned it so it directs the light of the spring Sun into another part of the city?" David asks.

"But where?" I say, and we laugh, realizing we've been caught up in a journey that will take us who knows where. ▲

2. Dzibilchaltún

The Pure Sea...

WHEN THE GUARDS remove the rope barrier from across the *sacbé*, the crowd surges toward the Temple of the Seven Dolls, and David and I follow along wanting to get a closer view of the pyramid. When we arrive, some people are chanting at the foot of its stairs while others are taking snapshots. The Sun has risen so that those having cameras must now lie on the ground to frame it within the temple doorway, and their friends kneel in front of the camera posing so they seem to be balancing the golden orb on their head or having it come out of their ear.

Another rope across the pyramid stairway keeps us from climbing, and so with the Sun still low in the eastern sky, David and I turn and walk away from the temple using a small compass to align our path with the last rays coming through its doorway. The course takes us off to the left of the *sacbé*, where we walk in ankle-high grass covering the foundation stones of ruined structures. Walking among them, it occurs to me that history is the redistribution of stones. If ceremony serves as an expression of the human soul, then buildings mark the course of the human ego. Men construct temples and palaces according to their vision of the world, then die. Later men reconfigure the buildings according to their values and die. Even later men demolish the structures. Only the stones remain. Pressed into the service of transitory masters, the stone knows: These people too will pass.

Dzibilchaltún's stones have been reused countless times during the three thousand years that people have inhabited the site. When Tutankamen was king of Egypt around 1500 BCE and Moses hadn't yet been born, settlers from northern Guatemala were beginning to build council houses and small ceremonial temples in Dzibilchaltún. Located on the northwestern side of the Yucatán Peninsula just three miles from the Gulf of Mexico, Dzibilchaltún came of age in the years between 600 to 800 CE under the name *Ichkantihó*, translated as "five in the sky." It prospered from selling salt from its outlying evaporative salt beds, and in the glow of wealth, it grew to 40,000 citizens who constructed its magnificent pyramids and palaces and a *sacbé* sixty feet wide. In the year 790 CE, it was of such high prestige that it hosted a summit of Maya leaders who forged the Itzá alliance that divided the land of the northern Peninsula like a piece of venison.

In fact, the history of the Maya has been greatly revised since the early 1970s when ethnographers were able to decode the name

Pacal, the name of the great Maya king of Palenque, and from that stellar success began to be able to read Maya inscriptions carved in stone. Most researchers now accept that the ancient Maya lived in the area that is now Honduras, Guatemala, El Salvador, Belize, and southern Mexico as early as 9000 BCE. By 3000 BCE, they had formed agricultural communities, and by 1500 BCE, they had kings. From 300 BCE to 200 CE, which archaeologists call the late Preclassic period, the Maya were already building small, stone ceremonial pyramids in their city centers. From 200 to 600 CE, the Classic period, Maya civilization was flourishing, and cities such as Dzibilchaltún, Izamal, and Oxkintok were the power centers of the northern Yucatán. During the late Classic period from 600 to 910, these old cities had reached their apex and had been superceded by newer powers such as Chichén Itzá and Uxmal. In the Postclassic period from 910 to 1200, even these newer cities faltered and declined, and during the late Postclassic period from 1200 to 1524, Mayapán became the last new Maya city to be built in the Yucatán before the Spanish *conquistadores* arrived and changed the course of history.

Dzibilchaltún itself was a major player until 1000 CE when most of its people moved away, even though it was never completely abandoned and was occupied even when the *conquistadores* rode in. During the 1600s, its pyramid stones were carted off to become the building blocks of churches and governmental palaces. During the 1800s, most of its grand *sacbé*, estimated to have 700 million pounds of stone, was hauled away to build seven haciendas and two towns.

By the 1950s, the Age of the Auto demanded the building of roads, and each day, a fleet of trucks roared into Dzibilchaltún to get stones to feed the gravel crushers laying the road from Mérida to the port city Progreso. The price for the road was the ancient temples.

Even the site's human stones—bones—are subject to redistribution. The skeletons of an old man and two young women companions once buried beside the city's grand palace now molder in a box in a museum.

Now, with interest in Times Past pulling tourist dollars into the Peninsula, Dzibilchaltún's stones are being re-redistributed, and its once grand structures are being rebuilt. For Mexico, revenue from tourism is second only to that of oil production, while revenue from Nationals who work outside the country and send their money home is in third place. Now Dzibilchaltún sports a new museum exhibiting artifacts from the ancient Maya to the colonial period to lure tourists.

As David and I forge a path westward from the doorway of the Doll House, the rising Sun becomes intense, and we bake in its heat like loaves of white bread. The first structure we encounter is the one where David stood and watched the sunrise. It's a low building with the barest remains of a doorway that seems to us to align with the Doll House doorway and possibly funnel the dawn light behind it into a grand plaza. Walking on into the plaza, we see a majestic palace on one side and a reconstructed pyramid on the other. In the center stands a Catholic chapel, now in ruins. Constructed from pyramid stones, the solid wall of its east-facing altar appears to block the first rays of sunlight rising into the Temple of the Seven Dolls—whether by design or by accident.

Using the compass, we continue on the path the sunlight might take were it not blocked by the chapel. In a few hundred feet, we arrive at a modest, old pyramid. At its feet lies Dzibilchaltún's large *cenote* (pronounced c-no-teh), a natural pool of water bubbling up from one of the underground rivers that flow beneath the surface of the Peninsula.

"Look!" I say, delighted with the pool. "Maybe this is where the temple doorway was meant to funnel the sunlight at equinox."

"BUENAS DIAS," SAYS an old man sitting on the small pyramid. Good morning. He beckons to us, pointing to oranges he has lined up beside him on the step. "Very sweet."

The thought of quenching our thirst with a juicy orange sounds good, and we climb up and sit on a step beneath him, the crystal pool at our feet.

The man gives each of his oranges a little squeeze, making a show of selecting the best for us. His hands are dark with age spots—liver spots, my grandma called them when she was alive. His face is a canyonland of wrinkles beneath a sweat-stained Panama hat. His ears are long and lush like the ears on a statue of Buddha, their fleshy lobes dangling almost to his jawbone. He holds out an orange to me—its dimpled skin is warm in my palm. He hands another to David.

"What do we owe?" I ask.

"Four little pesos. But eat first," he urges, "in case they're no good."

He's smiling, he knows they're good.

I sink my fingernails into the skin, and oil sprays into the air like fragrant shrapnel. I smile. The fragrance of orange is at the heart of many precious floral perfumes. Aromatherapy uses it to help clear a dull complexion, mouth ulcers, obesity, colds, and constipation. In perfume, it evokes a mood of cheer, uplift, and balance. It brings back happy memories of a good childhood—maybe that's why I'm suddenly thinking of my grandma, who lived with us from the time when I was a toddler until she died more than thirty years ago. I remember her preparing the "fixins" for supper and feeding me slices of apple and raw potato. Now, the skin of the orange in my hand slips off the succulent fruit, and as I tear the sections apart, juice trickles down into my palm. David, who keeps his fingernails short, takes a knife to his. When we finish, we return the empty peels to the old man for disposal and turn our attention to the pool below us.

This cenote called *Xlacah*, Maya for Old People, with the "x" pronounced as "sh", is as oval as an eye. Nearly a hundred feet long and sixty feet wide, it was created when a portion of the Peninsula's limestone surface collapsed into the underground river and opened a window into the watery Underworld. The ancient Maya called the subterranean water the Pure Sea, and revered it as being sacred.

The Yucatán Peninsula once lay at the bottom of an ancient ocean. Over the eons, it received the shells and skeletons of dying ocean creatures, which slowly hardened to become limestone. With the passage of Time, the Earth's temperature fluctuated, the level of the oceans rose and fell, and the ancient seabed that would become the Yucatán Peninsula slowly emerged from the tepid sea. Now, the Peninsula is a primarily flat limestone shelf that juts from mainland Mexico like a thumb reaching up toward Florida between the waters of the Gulf of Mexico on the northwest and the Caribbean on the east. Most of its surface is only two to seventy-five feet above sea level with its small hills reaching an elevation of only about three hundred feet.

About 65 million years ago, a meteorite slammed into the Yucatán near the little town of Chicxulub not far from Dzibilchaltún, making a crater sixty-five miles wide. The resulting sulfuric gases and debris changed the Earth's atmosphere so dramatically that science now considers it a factor in the extinction of the dinosaurs, along with an estimated 90 percent of all other species on Earth at the time.

Now, during the summer rainy season, the rain trickles through the porous limestone, feeding vast underground rivers and transforming them into raging black monsters. In places where the limestone crust is thin, it may weaken to the point of collapse and fall into the river below, making a portal into the Maya Underworld. The Xlacah cenote, or *dz'not* in Maya, is one such portal.

From where we look down on it, the pool seems like a watery blue eye through which the Earth silently watches the heavens. At its shallow end, the water is the clear blue of a baby's eyes. Pebbles on the bottom shine like magnified jewels, and the white flowers of floating lily pads rocket skyward like happy thoughts. In the deeper water toward the center, the blue becomes indigo, then becomes black at the deep end—mysterious, treacherous, unfathomable. A dragonfly skims its dark surface in pursuit of a smaller insect, which it eats, and then itself becomes lunch for a swooping bird.

On the surface, the cenote reveals nothing of its inner self. But explorations into its depths have shown that it holds eons of secrets in a sloping gallery tunneling underground for more than one-hundred-forty-feet. In the depths are the mementos of a slow rain of history: old bones and pottery and the new bones of drunken young men who stole into the site on a Saturday night and dove into the water on a dare, never to emerge.

In 1958, divers probing the cenote's ooze brought up ancient Maya pots and gourds, jade figurines, bone tools, and the bones of tall and small men, women and children. Divers found so many artifacts that it became apparent that Dzibilchaltún's cenote was a very special Cenote of Sacrifice where the Maya came for centuries to offer treasures in petition for favors from their gods.

A wealth of carved stones still rests in the dark mud—limestone now returned to its watery origin. To explain this cache of stone, locals tell this story. A petty ruler of Dzibilchaltún once built a pyramid on the lip of the cenote. One day, his mother came to him, asking for water. "I have no water!" he told her, and sent her away. The old woman left, but as she departed, the ground fell out from under the ruler and his pyramid, and both tumbled into the cenote.

In other stories, the old Maya claimed that the spirit of the cenotes took mercy on them during the Killing Time of the Conquest. It is said that many warriors outwitted the murderous *conquistadores* by jumping into one cenote, then swimming downstream to emerge from another one. Even today, the Maya say that if you shout into one cenote, your voice can be heard emerging from another.

Mysterious sounds reportedly come from Dzibilchaltún's cenote on the feast day of St. Ursula. According to locals, the statue of St. Ursula, a legendary British princess martyred with eleven thousand virgins, once watched over the now-ruined chapel at Dzibilchaltún. When her statue was moved to a church in town, her image manifested in the cenote. Now, they say that on St. Ursula's day, the music and fireworks set off on land in her honor can be heard rising up out of the cenote.

AS WE WATCH, people emerge from the shade of the trees on the far side of the cenote and walk toward its shallow end. As they near the pool, we can see the reflection of their faces in the water as though the Earth's eye is appraising them. There are three men and four women— I recognize one of them as the dark-haired woman who stood on the path ahead of us before dawn in the wrinkled white satin dress with the lime-green collar. Now she stands on the edge of the cenote, removing her shoes while the others put eyeglasses and watches aside for safekeeping, but leave thick purple crystals, silver ankhs, and gold crosses hanging against their chests.

One of the men—rail thin and shorter than the others—strips off his white shirt and steps into the water. He slowly wades into the cenote until the water reaches his chest. He motions the others into the water. The dark-haired woman is the first to follow, her dress swelling with trapped air until it becomes a white balloon beneath her arms.

In the water, she and the others form a line facing the thin man. The thin man asks them something I can't hear, and then lifts his arms and holds them palms up and wide, as though he's holding a beach ball. He raises his face to the Sun.

"Honor your Father Sun," the man says loudly, his words bouncing across the water and up the pyramid steps.

The people lift imaginary beach balls and say, "I honor you, Father Sun."

David picks up one of his cameras and holds it in his lap, struggling with the urge, I suppose, to raise it to his eye and click off a dozen photos of the people in the water.

"What are they doing?" I ask.

"It's an initiation." says the old orange vendor.

"Initiation!" I say. "But into what?"

The man shrugs. "People often come."

The thin man ducks under the water and comes up with a bit of

People come to the Xlacah cenote at Dzibilchaltún to swim.

mud in his fingers. Water races down his back in its swift return to the cenote.

"Honor the body of your Mother Earth," he says.

The others duck under the water to collect a small bit of dark ooze.

"We honor the body of our Mother Earth," they say.

The thin man smears mud on his cheeks and forehead.

"Clean your karma away. Be as little children."

The others smear mud on their faces. They look way too serious for people who probably haven't had mud on their faces since they were three years old.

"The water is the fluid of your mother's womb," the thin man says, and leaning over, splashes water on his face. "Let this water wash away all negativity."

The others splash water on their faces.

The thin man walks forward until he stands in front of the dark-haired woman. She bends her knees a little, keeping her back straight. The thin man places his hands on the top of her head, pushes her beneath the surface, and holds her down for a few seconds. Beneath the water, her white arms and her fingers are like the delicate fronds of an albino fern. The man removes his hands from her head, and the woman rises, gasping, in a cascade of water.

"Be as new," the thin man says, and moves to the next person.

As he repeats the gesture on the others, I study the dark-haired woman, searching for a clue to her desire to be initiated by this man. I open my notebook and write:

> *Initiation, reverser of the past*
> *undoer of a path undertaken*
> *thwarter of unconsciousness.*
> *Would I participate if asked?*

The fragrance of an orange breaks my reverie. The old man is peeling one.

"You know," he says, "every moment you're alive is an initiation. Because each moment leads to the next."

TWO YOUNG COUPLES are approaching the cenote. The girls carry a heavy, orange plaid shopping bag between them, food and soft drinks visible through the mesh. The boys break into a run. They race toward the black waters at the deep end of the pool and jump in with a great splash. The water leaps into the air. Some of it makes it back into the cenote, but more ends up on the sun-warmed rocks to be evaporated. The boy's bodies are milky in the depths before they rise sputtering.

"Oh, it's so cold," one says.

"Help, I can't swim," the other shouts. "Help!"

The ceremony people look at him with alarm.

"Just kidding," he says.

The ceremony people dry themselves and leave. The kids turn from swimming in the cenote to necking on blankets under the trees. The old man takes our pesos in payment for the oranges and pulls at one of his lush earlobes.

"I'll tell you a secret," he says. "The way the ancient Maya made their buildings to shine the light of the Sun and Moon into the *dz'not*—that was their way of connecting with their gods."

I hadn't considered that the rising full Moon would also show its bright face in the doorway of the Temple of the Seven Dolls.

David and I climb down off of the pyramid and lie down on our bellies on the rim of this portal into the Pure Sea. We wash our hands in the water, giving it a little taste of orange juice. With the Sun now overhead, the water's surface becomes inscrutably metallic—platinum, really—as the Earth's eye turns its gaze inward. ▲

3. Mérida

Heaven-born...

THE STONES THAT make up the stark face of Mérida's main Cathedral are old-bone white in the mid-morning Sun. This church in the heart of the Peninsula's largest city is said to occupy the ground where a great Maya pyramid once stood, and we're examining its exterior walls for stones carved with hieroglyphs like the ones we saw in the ruined chapel in Dzibilchaltún.

"See any?" I ask.

David shakes his head. "I think you'd need someone to point them out."

We've taken a room in a small, charming, colonial-style hotel half-a-block north of the Cathedral, wanting to be as near as possible to any remnants of the city's ancient Maya past—however covered over they might be. On this sunny Sunday morning, the plaza in front of the Cathedral is bustling with people coming and going to Mass and vendors setting up portable stalls for *Mérida en Domingo*, the Sunday market where vendors offer handmade wooden toys, embroidered dresses, handmade Panama hats, jewelry, and countless other items of the Peninsula, including food.

Kids in front of the Cathedral are raising money for orphans and have outlined a cross on the sidewalk with masking tape. Whenever someone puts a peso on the tape, they do the macarena, giggly and self-conscious. David begins taking photos of them.

I drift into the Cathedral with the people going to Mass. The crush of bodies presses me against a receiving line of little old ladies asking for pesos. They push their hands and plastic cups into my arm and ribs, and I distribute coins as the crowd pushes me on.

Inside, the immense Cathedral is made entirely of stone. Stone columns as thick as old trees support the high, domed ceiling where vaults look like open parachutes drifting to Earth. Its stone walls are eight feet thick (allowing God's house to double as a fortress) and telescope down to small windows. Yet the interior is surprisingly light as sunlight streams through the windows of a high dome. The altar is spare, and above it a very thin Crucified Jesus, more than twenty feet tall and carved from honey-colored wood, hangs on a dark wooden Cross, nailed through the wrists.

This is not a carpeted sanctuary of Silent Reverence, but worship in motion. Of the thousand people present, hundreds are on the move in any given moment—walking, talking, kneeling, leaving,

Mérida's Cathedral is immense and made entirely of light-gray stone illuminated by sunlight streaming through the windows of its high dome.

coming. There's none of the self-consciousness of the spring equinox ceremonies at Dzibilchaltún. The white clothing of that celebration is here replaced by dresses in a riot of red roses, purple pansies, blue stripes and green polka dots. The bottom tenth of the church (which the people occupy) looks like busy static on a color TV. Babies babble, old people pray aloud, high heels tattoo a staccato rhythm on the marble floor. For these people, church is an extension of home.

I make my way down a side aisle and slip into a dark pew midway down. Beside me in the aisle, people are lined up to pray beneath an image of the Virgin of Guadalupe, Queen of Mexico, Empress of the Americas (as proclaimed by Pope Pius XII in 1945 and repeated by John Paul II in 1999). When the kneeler at her feet becomes crowded, people lower old kneebones to the cold marble floor and lift their faces to their adored Celestial Mother. A young man lays a bunch of white chrysanthemums before her. An old man, his face as weathered as driftwood, lifts his eyes to her, battered hat over his heart, lips moving in whispered prayer.

I open my notebook to write my impressions. It has become the cache for my observations, and as I try to rekindle my creative fires, I find that writing anchors me in my senses. I make note of what I see, hear, and feel without censorship. I set down my thoughts without judgment, letting them flow onto the paper while remaining as neutral to them as possible, although I can't help but be aware that some seem exceedingly simple while others are overwrought. Yet in putting my thoughts and feelings in black-and-white in my notebook, I find that I can have them and at the same time let them go. Watching people pray to the Virgin, I write:

> Where is the wellspring of these people's faith?
> Is it a gift born into their soul
> or does it grow like a sturdy flower
> when watered by happy outcomes?

"What's a mother to do?—everyone needs her," says a voice beside me in the perfect, flat English of an Iowa farmer. A small man smiles at me from the aisle. "Peace be with you."

I stifle the impulse to flash him a peace sign, and instead allow a polite half-smile to cross my lips. "Yes, and with you," I say, and turn back to my notebook.

"Do you want to buy a hammock?" the man asks.

It's an all too familiar pitch posed by the dozens of men on the street trying to herd you into tourist shops. I'm suddenly annoyed—his apparent kindness has only been a prelude to a sales pitch.

"No, I don't," I say too loudly.

People turn to look at me. These are people who value civility. Their forefathers saw strife enough to last forever, and in turn, they strive for the resolution of small transgressions without confrontation. When Méridians describe their city, they always say that it's *tranquilo*, safe, and that its citizens are *contento*, unafraid. My raised voice draws curious stares from people turning to see who has failed to master the Art of Overlooking.

The small man sinks into the pew beside me. My hopes sink, too—even if he were to leave me alone, anger has now knotted my stomach like a hard nut. I reach for my backpack.

"I can give you a tour of the Cathedral," he quickly says. "I'm an official guide."

I make no attempt to hide my impatience, and he quickly reaches into his pocket and withdraws a white, plastic, hospital-style name tag, which he pins on his shirt. Etched in black, Helvetica-narrow letters is the name "Herman Needleman, M.D." There's a deep scratch through the M, which probably caused the real doctor Needleman to toss it into the trash in Miami or Houston, after which it somehow fell into this man's hands.

He's small—tiny, really, and thin. His shoulders are a wire coat hanger under his shirt. His body seems more suited to a ten-year-old boy than a man who looks to be more than fifty. His head is too large for his frame, as though some disease arrested his growth at an early age, leaving him with a stick-figure body to support a melon-sized head. A thick shock of unruly brown hair cuts across his forehead, and his nose is flat, probably from being smashed and never fixed. His brown eyes are large and edged in red where the lower lids droop away.

He waits without self-consciousness while I study him. I sigh. It's a gift to allow oneself to be so seen.

In the aisle, the faithful still stream toward the Virgin of Guadalupe. A man with a large gasoline can kneels at her feet. A young mother shows her little boy how to kiss his fingers and put the kiss on the altar. I sigh again. What nurtures such faith?

"Many miracles come through the saints if you pray," says the Herman-Needleman-MD-name-badge man.

"Really," I say without enthusiasm.

"Please, I've interrupted you, let me apologize by telling you a story," he says and leans toward me to deliver his words.

A long, long time ago, he begins, there was a young monk who had a great talent for writing the truth in a simple way that ordinary people could understand. Even though he lived cloistered away in a monastery, all of the priests from the parish churches came to ask him to write their sermons. He obliged, and this went on for several years, until one day the young monk became confused in his writing and stopped it altogether.

In the monastery, all the monks prayed constantly and passionately for God to open their hearts. When their hearts did open, they sometimes thought they were having a heart attack. Since the young monk's days were no longer spent on writing, he did nothing but pray very, very hard for God to open his heart.

One day while he was praying, he had a vision that he was in the presence of Jesus and an old priest. The old priest was asking God's blessing on all of the living and all of the ancestors, and yet every time the old priest mentioned the young monk's name, Jesus tilted his head and listened very closely.

Finally, the young monk interrupted the old priest. He said, "Excuse me, Father, but can I ask Holy Jesus a question?"

Jesus himself answered, "Yes, of course."

The young monk said, "I want to know, did you inspire me to write those sermons?"

Jesus said, "Do you remember the day you saw many doves flying around you? Some flew so near that you could touch them, while others flew too high for you to reach."

The young monk nodded. "Yes, I remember."

Jesus smiled. "The doves you could touch were the teachings I allowed you write—they are the lessons that people can understand now and put into practice. The others that were too far away are the teachings that people aren't yet prepared to have. For the truth is, people become responsible for what they know—they must put what they know into practice and suffer the consequences if they do not. So out of my love for my people, I kept you from writing those teachings that people aren't yet ready for."

As the small man finishes the story, tears sting my eyes.

"Oh," he says, "it's a gift to allow oneself to be so moved."

Meanwhile, the Mass has ended, and while people are leaving the Cathedral, others are coming in for the next one.

"Come back in an hour," urges the Herman-Needleman-MD-name-badge man, "and I'll show you the Cathedral."

I can't promise, I don't know what David wants to do.

"No charge," he says.

Outside, David is watching a blind man sitting on the sidewalk playing a guitar for coins. The man sounds like a bad Jimi Hendrix. No one is contributing. I tell David about the man in the Cathedral and his preposterous Herman-Needleman-MD name tag.

"He's actually Herman Neutic," David says.

"What?"

"Herman Neutic," he repeats, "for hermeneutics."

I laugh. *Hermeneutics*: the science of interpreting sacred build-

A Maya grandmother collects alms by one of the front doors of Mérida's Cathedral.

ings in terms of their function in relation to religious beliefs. Named for Hermes, the Greek messenger of the gods.

"So, will you go on a tour of the church?" I ask.

David hesitates. As a man, he subscribes to the male code of behavior that equates hiring a guide with asking for directions—while it can be helpful, it's rarely done, and then only at the insistence of a woman.

"No charge," I say, teasing him. "Almost free for you today."

He doesn't smile. But he does agree to go.

WE HAVE AN hour before we must meet our guide. It's nearly noon, and the sunlight is too harsh for photos. We consider going back to our hotel, but then we see a fellow guest from the hotel eating a piece of homemade pecan pie and we sit down with him on one of the benches that line the wide, shady sidewalks of Mérida's central park.

Called the *zócolo*, the square park is the heart of Mérida. Based on a grid put in place by the Spanish *conquistadores*, it serves as the anchor for the Cathedral on its east side, city government buildings on the west, the state government on the north, and the house of the first Spanish *conquistador* on the south. It establishes the order and pattern, cycle and rhythm that repeats in the streets beyond.

In reality, Mérida's feet were already wide with age before the *conquistadores* rode in. Preconquest, the Maya lived here according to their own established order and cycles, which they kept track of with their ritual and civil calendars, the *Tzolk'in* and the *Haab*. From the few Maya ruins still visible in the city, it appears to have been settled as early as 100 CE. Over the centuries, it became an ample metropolis with at least five large pyramids and some 10,000 inhabitants. It was called *Ichkantijo* (confused now with the old name for Dzibilchaltún), shortened to *T'jo* or *Tiho*, which has been translated as "Heaven-born."

By the time the Spaniards arrived in the 1500s, Tiho's pyramids were already dishelved, their stones tumble-down and sun-bleached,

and its citizens paid tribute to Chakán, one of the nineteen Maya chieftancies that ruled the Peninsula at that time.

It was the Spaniard Francisco de Montejo y Leon who kick-started this current cycle of Mérida's history. Part warlord, part entrepreneur, it was he who secured the right to become *Adelantado*, or first promoter, of the Yucatán from Emperor Charles V. A minor noble from Salamanca, he had grown rich in Cuba, and with entrepreneurial ambition, had gained experience as a warrior on an expedition with Hernán Cortés, subduer of the Aztecs. The Peninsula was the New Frontier, and Montejo invested considerable wealth in a high-risk, semi-private enterprise wherein he agreed to underwrite the cost of men and ships in exchange for receiving the first pick of the spoils of conquest and the title and salary of Governor-for-Life of the Peninsula.

Montejo's ships first reached the island of Cozumel on the eastern coast of the Peninsula in 1527, then sailed on to the mainland to establish the first Spanish settlement in the territory beside the Maya village of Xel-Ha, now a popular water park for tourists. Leaving fifty men behind in Xel-Ha, Montejo sailed on around the Peninsula. He tried to put in at several points but was repelled by the Maya. Finally, returning empty-handed to Xel-Ha, he discovered his men reduced in number to a handful and withdrew from the settlement.

Four years passed before the sting and cost of defeat faded from Montejo's memory enough to allow him to try again. He still held valuable rights to the development of the Yucatán and decided to try again to get his enterprise off the ground. This time he took with him his illegimate son, a skilled soldier bearing his name but called *El Mozo*, the Boy. In 1531, these soldiers of fortune tried to settle an area west of Tiho, but met fierce resistance that wounded the elder Montejo. Angered by the defeat, El Mozo took a small detachment of men and pushed through to Chichén Itzá, the ancient Maya city in the center of the Peninsula. But the Maya,

Don Legg, a Canadian traveler known for his fondness of pies, cruises the food stands during Mérida's Sunday fair.

who often fought among themselves, banded together to fight for their land and preserve the sacred Cenote of Sacrifice at Chichén Itzá. El Mozo was forced to retreat. Again the elder Montejo had no return to show for his investment.

It wasn't until 1540 that the elder Montejo delegated his authority to El Mozo for another try at conquering the Maya. Pumped up by his new-found authority, El Mozo took with him another Montejo, *El Sobrino*, the Cousin. The men and their troops landed west of Tiho and fought off the Maya's sustained resistance. Then El Sobrino made a daring push to Tiho and held it long enough for El Mozo to join him with reinforcements. The Maya fought mightly, but they were seriously depleted by drought and disease (the Spaniard's unintentional biological warfare), and were no match for Spanish firepower. Disheartened, they returned to their homes, and when in June 1541, the Montejos still held Tiho, they took it as a sign of God's favor.

The victorious El Mozo stood in the city of the Heaven-born, surveying the pale limestone pyramid-ghosts that reminded him of the Roman ruins in the city of Mérida, Spain.

"We will build our Mérida here," he said.

Reborn Mérida was founded on January 6, 1542.

Finally, the Maya leader Tutul Xiu, Lord of Mani, approached the Montejos and offered to accept Catholicism and the rule of the Spanish king. With the Maya forces divided, the Spaniards killed off Tutul Xiu's leading enemies and converted their followers.

In 1546, the elder Montejo believed that the city was stable enough for him to take over, but a cruel trick of fate awaited him—when his men rode the whole of the Peninsula, they realized that it held no precious metals nor any other riches. Even its soil was too thin to support large-scale crops. Its only wealth was the Maya themselves (of whom 25 to 50 percent had perished), and the Spaniards pressed them into service providing food and labor for the colony. Luckily for the Maya, the demand for food in the colonial city allowed them to continue their village farming, and as a result, a traditional way of life continues to exist in part today.

In Mérida, the Spaniards grafted their fragile settlement onto a hardy Maya root. They drafted Maya men to strip the worked stones from the pyramids and then reuse them in the construction of the foundations and walls of their new governmental and religious buildings. Montejo's grand home was begun in 1549, but the Elder barely got to enjoy it—he was stripped of his authority and recalled to Spain in 1551, never to return to the Yucatán.

Now Montejo's former palace is home to Banamex bank, where an ATM machine spits out pesos. Painted a delicate shade of coral, its facade is adorned with elaborate stone carvings that look like frosting soldiers on a military cake. Two larger-than-life warlords (El Mozo and El Sobrino?) stand in full suits of armor, their metal feet crushing the throats of natives, whose eyes bulge with terror. Pigeons nest on their shoulders, strewing gray feathers on them like dirty boas.

A carved image of the elder Montejo also overlooks the *zóloco*. If he could see it now, he'd probably be pleased—the pattern the Spaniards established more than four hundred years ago still endures, and the city has grown to 750,000 inhabitants. But the ancient Maya lords of Tiho, the Heaven-born who peer down on the city in the guise of headdress-wearing clouds, would probably also be pleased. Mérida isn't "new" Spain, nor is it "old" Maya—rather, it's a city of New People synthesized from the melding of cultures and blood. Mérida has ascended a few loops on the spiral of Time making it still ever new, ever expanding. Ever old. ▲

4. Mérida

Phallus of the land...

HERMAN IS WAITING for us outside the Cathedral, dwarfed beside its massive facade.

"Mucho gusto," David says, using the shortened, traditional greeting of "my pleasure" as he offers his hand.

"I'm glad to meet you, too," Herman says.

"You speak English very well," David says.

Herman nods in acknowledgment of the compliment. "Like most people in Mérida, I'm part Maya, part Spanish, but my parents sent me to school for many years to learn English." He tells us that he never married but cared for his aged parents until they died—his father first, then his mother a year ago on Christmas Day. "I'm a full-time guide to the Cathedral now."

The tour begins at the Cathedral's front door. Construction began in 1562, Herman tells us. The bishop of the Yucatán blessed the cornerstone, and then generations of Maya laborers laid course after course of stone until the structure was consecrated in 1599, the first Cathedral of such large proportions to be built in the Americas. Its facade—as sober as a military judge—is a departure from the ornate Gothic-style churches of Europe. Its only ornaments are a central triumphal arch and statues of the Saints Peter and Paul. A two-headed Hapsburg eagle representing the Spanish monarchs once adorned the face, but this hated symbol of colonial rule was effaced in 1822 and replaced by the eagle and serpent of the Mexican Republic. The Cathedral's two towers reach one-hundred-twenty feet, nearly as tall as the tallest Maya pyramids in the Peninsula.

"But is it true that the Cathedral was built over a pyramid?" David asks.

"It's true that a colossal Maya pyramid once occupied one side of the *zócolo,*" he says. "It was dedicated to *Baklum Cha'an,* which translates as Phallus of the Land, for potency, power, and father."

We've seen examples of the stone phallus—unsheathed, erect, eternally excited. Five-feet tall. The generating god, who is infinitely potent in his creation and re-creation (with the goddess) of the universe.

"But the Spaniards dismantled the pyramid," Herman says. "They wanted to erase the memory of Maya power. But there's also another reason for covering one ceremonial structure with another . . ."

He pauses as an elderly man in soiled clothes totters toward us, his hand out for a coin. We make a contribution, and Herman leads

A calesa, or horse-drawn carriage, passes in front of Mérida's main Cathedral on a Sunday afternoon.

us into the Cathedral, now empty except for a few people praying in the front pews.

"Like everyone and everything in Mexico, the Cathedral has several names," Herman says, his voice echoing in the vast interior.

Originally the Cathedral was dedicated to Saint Idelfonso because it was on his feast day that the Maya leader Tutul Xiu agreed to accept Catholicism and support the Spanish crown, thus ending Maya resistance. An oil painting in the church commemorates the alliance.

But over the centuries the locals also came to fondly regard it as the church of the *Cristos de las Ampollas*, or Christ of the Blisters. We follow Herman into a small chapel off the sanctuary, where a handful of people are praying under an image of the Crucified Jesus carved from black wood. About four feet tall, the image of Jesus has a long mane of thick, wavy, brown hair topped with a golden crown. A brown handmade cloth covers his loins.

"The black Christ came to the people under mysterious circumstances," Herman says, his voice softening as he begins the story.

Many centuries ago, he tells us, a tree in a farmer's field was struck by lightning. But instead of burning, its wood turned black and became as hard as stone. When the farmer found the wood, he believed it must be very special and took it to the priest of Ichmul. The priest put it away and kept it for many years.

One day a stranger came to town. He was dusty and hungry, so the priest took him in and saw that he got something to eat. The priest was taking the man to a room where he could sleep when the man noticed the black wood.

"I could carve it for you," the man told the priest, patting the small bag he carried. "I have my tools right here."

The priest hesitated but then decided to accept.

"Well, then, go to it," he said.

Early the next morning, the stranger left town, and the priest shook his head, thinking that he had known the man was all talk. But then the housekeeper came running, and when the priest went to the room where the man had slept, he found a beautiful carving of the black Christ. He took it to the church, where it stayed for many years.

In 1645, the church at Ichmul caught fire and burned. It was a horrible loss for the people, but to their amazement, the black Jesus survived. The fire further blackened the wood, but had not burned it. Instead, it had raised blisters on the wood. The people were touched— the Crucified Jesus had blistered in the heat just as a human would. They took it as a sign of Jesus being their ever-present companion who shared their sorrows. When the Cristos de las Ampollas was moved to this Cathedral in Mérida, even more people came to love him.

But even the black Jesus couldn't survive angry men. On September 24, 1915, a revolutionary mob of machete-wielding railroad workers and port stevedores rode their horses into the Cathedral, looking for trouble. They tied their animals to the organ in the choir loft and pulled it down. They burned paintings and statues, and the black wood that had survived lightning and fire was reduced to ashes.

"But they couldn't destroy its spirit," Herman says. "The tender mercy of the Christ of the Blisters still lives on in this replica of that extraordinary carving. The people's faith in him survives."

Leading us back to the center of the Cathedral, Herman tells us that the church has a third name. He points to an oil painting showing a young Maya woman carrying a banner of the Virgin.

"Unity is the third name," Herman says. "For forgiveness. For all that has gone before."

I wonder whether he sees the *conquistadores* as heroes or oppressors.

"Montejo was a Spanish soldier," Herman says, "and he did what he was trained to do. Tutul Xiu was a Maya leader, and he did what he believed was right for his people. Neither man could foresee all that his actions would set in motion. You see, it's hard to know when you're acting alone, according to your own desires, and when you're an instrument of a future that wants to be born."

David speaks. "You mentioned two reasons for building on the ground where a pyramid had stood—to erase the memory and . . . "

The stones in the Catheral have overheard the prayers of people's grandparents and great-grandparents, going back to the year 1599. Here a man prays to the Virgin of Guadalupe.

"The other is something the Maya call *chu'el*," Herman says, "which essentially means the sacredness of a place. The Maya still believe that part of your ancestors' spirits remain in the place where they once prayed, and as generations of people pray in a place, great power builds up, making it very sacred. That's chu'el. "

"And the Spaniards wanted to capture the power of the pyramid?" David asks.

Herman shrugs one thin shoulder. "Surely the ground beneath the Cathedral was consecrated before construction began," he says. "But now people have prayed here in the Cathedral for four hundred years—much longer than rituals were held in the pyramid, I suspect. These stones here"—he places a hand on a column—"have overheard the prayers of these people's grandparents and great-grandparents on back to the year 1600. People and God—together they create faith."

HERMAN STAYS BEHIND in the Cathedral as we prepare to leave. We say goodbye, and David gives him a "Boston handshake," something we learned when we were at a trade show in Boston and trying to get union electricians and movers to set up our booth. In Boston, a bill—folded small, tucked into the palm, and transferred in a handshake—got us the extra extension cord we needed. Here in Mérida, it's a quiet way of giving a gift.

At the rear of the church, I turn to look at Herman. His tiny shoulders are hunched in prayer as he kneels at the altar, and a woman in a *huipil* stands beside him, her dress lily white, a blue shawl over her head. I turn to tell David, but when I look again, the woman is gone.

IT'S NEARLY DARK when we sit down to dinner in the courtyard restaurant of our hotel. Outside in Hidalgo Park, a band is playing on

Generations of families are memorialized on the Cathedral's marble floor.

a stage that's been set up for the weekly Sunday celebration, and loudspeakers pound the Latin beat through the lobby and restaurant.

We're not hungry enough for a big meal, having eaten at a food stand in the *zócolo*. I order eggs scrambled with *chaya*, a spinach-like leaf, and accented with *xnipek* (pronounced sh-nipek), a Maya salsa made from diced tomatoes and onions, fresh cilantro, lime juice, salt and habañero pepper. The heat from a very little bit of the pepper flames in my mouth, imparting a welcome zing to the fluffy eggs. David has *sopa de lima*, a hearty chicken-vegetable soup flavored with lime. Among the generous chunks of tender white meat are pieces of diced lime peel that can be eaten or not, although locals claim that eating them discourages casual parasites. We share the steaming, thick corn tortillas that Grandmother Lupita hands us hot from her *comal*, or griddle.

After dinner, we climb the stairs to the roof with its little jewel-blue swimming pool that is open to the night sky. Built around a traditional open courtyard in a century-old building, the hotel's three floors are open to the sky, with only the bedrooms and bathrooms enclosed. We rest our elbows on the balcony rail and look out over the city. The overcast sky is a luminous blanket of clouds colored violet by the city lights. Directly below us is a parking lot, now locked and quiet. Ahead of us a hundred yards or so is the Cathedral, the windows of its dome now dark, unseeing eyes. In the night, the structure seems even larger than is does during the day—nearly half a block wide, and a block long, with its spires reaching into the purple sky.

"If there was a pyramid where the Cathedral stands," David says, "then I'll bet this hotel stands near its ceremonial center."

WE GO TO our room and lie in bed in the dark, listening to the sound of footsteps in the broad, courtyard corridor outside our open window. The whisper of rubber soles, the click-clack of hard heels, and the metallic jangle of a cane all drift in through the shutters. We catch snippets of passing conversations spoken in English with a southern accent, the up-and-down lilt of Wisconsinese, the flat twang of the Rockies, and then Spanish and German. People wearing hard heels mostly speak Spanish and chatter late into the night without lowering their voices. We fall alsleep to the soft whir of the ventilator fan.

It's after midnight when we wake and sit up in bed.

"I was dreaming," David says.

"Me, too," I say.

"It was night," David begins, "and I was in a shopping center parking lot, and there was a big billboard advertising a Nikon F5 camera. I was sitting in the passenger seat of an old pickup truck with my cameras. The driver had gotten out to talk to somebody. I could see him talking to a man, and I knew they were calling the cops on his

cellphone. I knew there was going to be trouble, so I got out of the truck and ran away. The men were coming after me, and I hid in the shadows behind a tree. I could see that one man had an M 16 assault rifle. So I woke up."

My dream was different in details, but similar in feeling. I was in an old, old city. It was night, but there were people everywhere. Some strong, nice-looking young men wearing gray pants and shirts were armed with long, thick sticks painted black. They were patrolling—they seemed like police—but there was something evil about them. David and I were on a balcony, and we saw them beat a boy with their sticks. We saw them bring someone into a parking lot and beat him senseless. A man was lying in the street covered with newspapers, and I knew that if they saw him, they would beat him, too. It was awful. I was shouting, telling people to run. The uniformed men with sticks saw us and put a ladder up to our balcony. I pushed the ladder over, and they fell down into the parking lot. David ran away and told me to check out of the hotel. I remember that our bill was $150.

"Why are we having such violent dreams?" I say.

"Maybe we're somehow picking up on the old fear and violence that once happened in this city," David says.

I remember my first sensation upon waking. That we should go slow in opening ourselves to any energy—chu'el was what Herman called it—that might still be present in the pyramids we're planning to visit on this odyssey. It occurs to me that there are powers or forces—whatever one might call them—beyond what we've ever dealt with or can even imagine. I'm suddenly aware that we'd be nâive to think of any residual power or chu'el in the ancient sites as being benign or beneficial to us in any way. Sure, we're curious about the powers exhibited by the ancient Maya shaman-kings during their rituals as they surfed between the dimensions. But now I wonder, what did that power cost them?

I can't answer my question, and we lie back down to sleep. ▲

5. Chichén Itzá

Serpent Mountain...

CHICHÉN ITZÁ IS barely open for business when we arrive at the park at just after eight in the morning. We made the two-hour trip from Mérida by bus the day before and have spent the night in a nearby hotel so we can climb the pyramid before busloads of tourists begin arriving from Cancún in the mid-morning. At the visitors center, we present our pesos to ticketsellers who begrudgingly stop stamping today's date on the tickets to take our money. At the turnstile, a guard ambles over to punch our tickets and send us down the path into the park.

The day has dawned gray, and the sky is pregnant with the overdue Sun, the borning-one still wrapped in its watery membrane. Beneath the canopy of intertwining branches, the path is dark, and as we walk, thick arms of fog drift out from between the trees to caress us with cool, damp fingers.

It isn't until the path dumps us out onto a large grassy plaza that we can finally see Chichén Itzá's great pyramid. Stark against the sky. Gray-stained from dew. Reaching nearly a hundred feet into the clouds. All angles and corners. Nine stacked platforms with a temple on top. A mountain made by man.

I take out my notebook and write:

A tidal wave of stone, frozen in Time
a huge stone birthday cake
a stairway connecting Heaven and Earth.
Power.

Some part of me longs to race up it and claim its summit with pride and possession as though David and I have just discovered it. But there's another, stronger feeling in the pit of my stomach—something about the pyramid scares me, aside from my reluctance to put myself too far above the ground. It's as though it were never meant to be climbed by those who don't know its potential, or be climbed only purposefully by the few who do.

But for now it's a non-issue because David is immersed in taking photos of the pyramid. The light is subtle and without shadows, and he's engrossed in his view of the pyramid through the camera lens. I imagine his mind processing angles and perspectives, his brain flooding with impressions that he alone experiences. It's a marvel to

me that people experience the same scenes and events so differently, never perceiving the colors or shapes in exactly the same way as they filter them through their unique perspectives. I watch as David strides from one point of view to another, shooting photos of the pyramid from here, from there. Intent. Silent. As focused as the lens on his camera. Alone in his relationship to it.

At this early hour, we're alone in the park except for the guards coming to work on bicycles. Gliding slowly across the grass, their bikes carve thin, black tire tracks in the silvery dew. A sleepy dog suddenly plops down on the grass as though his battery has run out, and David takes a final photo.

"You ready to climb?" he says suddenly.

"Okay," I say.

"Then let's climb the front."

We bypass the pyramid's west stairs and walk around to the north side. Here, the heads of two huge stone serpents keep watch over the stairway leading to the entrance of the temple above. Carved to have feathers instead of scales, they represent *K'uk'ulkan*, or the Plumed Serpent, literally the merging of bird and serpent, which the ancient Maya viewed as the union of Heaven and Earth, spirit and matter, the reconciliation of opposites beyond the forms of sensibilities inherent in creation.

The staircase itself has ninety-one stairs that rise at a very steep angle. As I look up, fear of climbing it makes itself known in my stomach in the image of a startled moth fluttering its wings. My desire to climb the pyramid pales.

David puts a sandaled foot on the first step and begins to ascend in a slow, zigzag course across the staircase as though he's traversing the switchbacks of a steep mountain. The steep stairway is more than twenty feet wide, with nothing at all to break a fall down it, and yet David climbs higher and higher.

"Come on, people are coming," he urges, glancing at two couples emerging into the plaza from the path.

I put my foot on the first step and follow, hunched over, keeping my uphill hand on the stair above for balance. I try to keep my eyes on the stair straight ahead, but I can't resist a glance at the ground that's getting farther and farther below me (in only a few tall steps).

"Just count the steps," I tell myself. "Seven, eight, nine, ten."

I move feet and hands in my effort to climb, but the niggling feeling of fear has grown large in my stomach as though it's alive. It's the moth, like a giant Moth of Fear, that threatens me. My breathing has become rapid and my heart is pounding, and I seize on the unreasonable fear that it will cut off my senses and reason and then extinguish my very consciousness. I stop counting the steps, and sit down hard, burying my face in my hands. An ironic thought flashes across my mind—I've given up the financial security of a steady income to leap across the great abyss of a mid-life career change and yet I can't force myself to climb these ninety-one steps of the pyramid.

"Here, give me your hand," David says from above.

"Come down, then," I say in a very tiny voice.

He walks back down the steps—I see in his face that the height is no picnic for him either—and offers his hand.

"I've got to be above you," I say, wanting his strength between me and the ground.

He descends to the step below me.

"Okay, ready?" he asks. "Don't look down."

My hand gripping his, I let him lead me back and forth across the stairway. He controls our ascent, I try to control my eyes. Then within a few minutes, we're at the top. We step onto the platform at the summit, breathless and exhilarated.

"We're here," David says. "The first people of the day."

The clouds have thinned to tissue, and within seconds, the Sun burns through them and floods the day with light. A forest of trees covers the land like a lush emerald robe that spreads as far as the eye can see. Where the Earth meets the sky, the horizon is luminous, an unbroken circle from this mountain top, and we are at its center.

Chichén Itzá guards bicycle across the early-morning plaza on their way to work.

But then the ground seems to buck before my eyes, and I back away from the edge of the pyramid and sit down heavily to lean against the wall of the Itzá's sacred temple.

CHICHÉN ITZÁ'S HISTORY is being revised as archaeologists learn more from its ancient structures. Early on, it was thought that the Itzá were aggressive "Toltecs" who marched into the Peninsula from central Mexico, squelched the placid Maya, and put their new-fangled great pyramid on the north side of an established city. Support for this theory arose from the similarity between the structures of Chichén Itzá and Tula, a Toltec city north of present-day Mexico City.

But new discoveries have shown that Tula was built long after Chichén Itzá, and that, in fact, all of Chichén Itzá's main structures were built within a one-hundred-and-fifty-year period along a network of roads in place since its inception.

Yet, oddly, it's an old road through the site that has lent psychological credence to the old theory: The old highway that still connects Mérida with Cancún and the Caribbean coast once ran within a few feet of the pyramid's south side, and people conveniently designated the structures on the north side of the road (including the pyramid) as "big-new" Chichén and the structures on the south side as "little-old" Chichén.

And because the Toltec theory has found its way into books, it refuses to die.

Now one accepted theory is that the Itzá were actually Maya from the Lake Peten region near Tikal in northern Guatemala. They entered the Peninsula just before 700 CE, and traveled up the Caribbean coast during an eighty-year migration from their home, possibly fleeing the war zone where Maya engaged in stunning battles fought for the purpose of capturing slaves and the victims of future sacrifice. Monuments and pottery found near Tikal show that people calling themselves Itzá lived there during the early Classic period, and people known as Itzá still live there today. The name *Itzá* has been translated as water witch or sorcerer, although linguists suggest that it could have derived from the name Itzamná, one of the Maya's principle gods.

Once on the Peninsula, the Itzá grew powerful in the land. They aggressively sought to establish themselves in the new territory that was by no means empty but occupied by successful cities such as Cobá to the east and Izamal to the west. In 790 CE, they called for a summit to take place at Dzibilchaltún to divvy up the northern territory of the Peninsula. They took for themselves a place with a huge, nearly round cenote, which gives the city its name—*Chichén Itzá* means mouth of the well of the Itzá.

The Itzá were enterprising merchant-traders and artisans who thrived on the business of selling salt gleaned from their evaporative pools at the tip of the Peninsula and importing valuable raw materials such as obsidian from central Mexico and jade from Guatemala and fashioning them into exquisite, precious commodities. The Itzá city became a true Mesoamerican capital that grew to cover fifteen square miles and was home to more than 50,000 inhabitants. It was a city of industry. It was the Big Apple of the old New World, and its great pyramid was like Rockefeller Center—the symbol of power, influence, affluence, and the solemn manifestation of Maya values.

Innovators, the Itzá brought to the Peninsula the design for the radial or four-sided pyramid, the pronounced imagery of the Plumed Serpent, and the *multepal* form of government whereby a council presided over the city rather than a single king.

But sadly, they dropped the tradition of carving their history on monuments and thus shrouded their lineage and origins in mystery.

They constructed or renovated most of the buildings we see in Chichén Itzá proper between 800 and 948 CE. The High Priest's Tomb, a smaller version of the great pyramid, was dedicated in 842. The great pyramid itself was erected over the smaller pyramid in about 850. The city's great ballcourt was dedicated on November 16, 864.

Then by the mid-900s, it was over. In the strange way the Maya have of suddenly abandoning a city then returning to rebuild it after two to three centuries, people abruptly left Chichén Itzá. Latter-day people twice resurrected the city—in about 1050 CE and again in 1200, but nothing much came of it, although Itzá descendants still occupied the area when the Montejos tried to establish their first capital here.

But even though the city of Chichén Itzá lay dormant, Maya pilgrims continued to travel here over the centuries to toss jade offerings into the Cenote of Sacrifice and pay their respects to the pyramid. The Franciscan monk Friar Diego de Landa, who undertook the mission of converting the Maya to Catholicism, wrote that the people called their great pyramid K'uk'ulkan, for an entity who was variously described as a great leader, a mythic teacher, the wind, the Plumed Serpent, and the planet Venus.

But the Spaniards called the pyramid what it most resembled from their frame of reference—*El Castillo*, or the castle.

DAVID AND I watch as a young man and woman storm the pyramid, running straight up its steps, their shoes making a sound on the musical stones like water filling a crystal vase. Other people climb more slowly, commanding reluctant thigh muscles to lift them stair after stair after stair and feeling the burn.

"This is better than any Stair Master," a woman says.

"Climb this every day," her companion says, "and you'll never have to go to the gym."

A man and woman are about halfway up the ninety-one steps when the man stops cold. "I don't know if I'm up to this," he says.

"Well, it's no Mount Everest," the woman tells him.

"It might as well be," the man says, as he turns to go back down, "because I couldn't climb that either."

For the Maya, the pyramid symbolizes a Place of Origin where the creator gods placed the first four True Human men on Earth. And then their wives. This serpent mountain, which once wore red paint, is where the Itzá came to contact the divine. It's an instrument of devotion. And power (because men who have the ear of God can also command men). Even now, it's commanding. Dynamic. Raw. It's a four-hundred-pound wrestler entering the ring in a red cape. It's a red neon sign that reads High Voltage. It's Eden with an attitude.

Watching hundreds of people arrive at its summit, I remember what Herman Needleman MD said about chu'el—residual spirit—and wonder how much power the pyramid retains from the ceremonies and rituals performed by Itzá shamans. Does its power, like that of a volcano, lay dormant? Or is it still fully evident for those who have eyes to see? I don't know yet although I do have a feeling that my fear of heights is somehow amplified by its latent power.

It was to this temple on the great pyramid that Maya shamans of old came to perform the ritual of self-sacrifice, and leaning against the temple where the act was performed, I think about that ceremony.

Long ago, on a day chosen by astronomers who predicted the movements of the planets, a lone shaman slowly climbed the steps of the K'uk'ulkan pyramid to summon the Vision Serpent, his link with the ancestors and gods. For days he had made himself ready for the ritual by purifying himself in the sweat bath and suffering through many days of fasting and sleeping alone, for the Maya believed that a man's blood, sweat, tears, and semen are sacred and must be used wisely. Slowly the shaman ascended the holy red mountain to offer his precious blood to the Mystery—to sacrifice to the gods as they had once sacrificed for humankind. In return for his offering, he hoped to receive a vision that would transport him from this world of Time-Place into the unseen dimensions of spirit.

With drums and rattles echoing up from the plaza, the shaman entered the sacred temple to perform his ritual. It was dark inside except for a single torch, and the air hung still and heavy with the

Afraid of the height of the pyramid, people cling to its temple walls.

smoke of incense. On a small woven mat on the stone floor were the bowls and gourds and awl-like sea-spine he would need for his sacrifice. Sitting down on the mat, he lifted a gourd of *baalché,* a meadlike liquor made from honey fermented with tree bark. He sipped it, deliberately taking on the essence of the alcohol.

When he was ready to perform the ritual, he grasped the long, needlelike blood-letter and plunged it through the foreskin of his penis. His face contorted with pain, but as the blood flowed from the wound, he suffered gladly for it was his sacred right and duty to give birth to the ancestors through his gift of blood.

The shaman caught the precious blood dripping from his penis on paper made from the felted bark of a tree. When the paper became saturated with his blood, he placed it in a bowl containing nodules of copal resin and lit the incense The blood and sap burned together, their sweet smoke rising, writhing, curling into the air.

Altered by pain and blood loss, alcohol, and other substances, the shaman let his consciousness drift through the portal between this world of form and the Otherworld of spirit. As his awareness expanded beyond Time-Place, the Vision Serpent that rose on his burnt-blood offering spoke to him of things to come.

Down in the plaza, men stood looking up at the temple. In other temples and in their homes, they too had offered their blood to the gods, piercing their tongues and ears and the flesh of their arms. Under the influence of sacred alcohol and the shock of blood loss, they waited amid lighted torches and the beat of drums until they too saw the Vision Serpent rise.

Now, sitting beside the temple, I consider how extreme (and unnatural) it would seem today to wound oneself and offer blood in a ritual.

Today, the power of the pyramid is said to be inert. Supposedly, before the ancient Maya shamans abandoned Chichén Itzá, they ritually decommissioned its great pyramid, as though cutting the telephone line between it and the ancestors and gods. Since then, Maya elders, concerned for the safety of tourists climbing the pyramid without permission from the spirits, ritually "capped" it—in effect switching off its power.

Still, the very height of the pyramid is enough to blow climbers' circuits. An Australian woman—thin and athletic-looking—climbs about two-thirds of the way up the pyramid before she stiffens with fear. She sits down and scoots back down the steps on her rear.

Friends at the top coax her to try again.

"No way," she says. "I'm not crazy."

"What're you going to tell the folks back home?" a friends asks.

"I'm going to tell them the truth," the woman says, "that I'm a *chicken* Itzá."

Those with braver hearts pit their will against their fear. But while will might win the battle and get them to the top, fear wins the

The brave-hearted pit their will against their fear and marshal their forces to climb the pyramid.

war—when it's time to descend, and the ground is nearly ninety feet below, terror sets in. Stricken, they become Wall Huggers who press themselves against the temple walls, digging their fingernails into the joints between the stones and staying as far from the stairs as they can. One woman hugging the temple wall resists her husband's attempts to help her down.

"I can't go down," she says, grimly.

"You must," her husband says.

"But I can't," she says. Tears run down her cheeks.

"Which would be better," her husband asks, "you take my hand and we go down? Or the guards have to come up and carry you?"

She doesn't answer.

"Come on," he says, gently. "The bus is waiting. And lunch."

The terrorized kneel on the platform far from the steps and crawl slowly backward until their feet dangle in space and they slowly lower one foot to the top stair. They descend the steps in Full Contact, sliding down backward on their bellies.

Others descend in the Grapevine, twining arms and legs around the rope that runs the length of the west steps, offering some psy-chological comfort. Others do the Butt Warp, scooting down on their rear.

People try to mask their fear with humor.

"Where's the elevator?" a man says.

"I'm waiting for my helicopter to come," says another.

They make jokes about being sacrificed and role-play scenarios in which they sacrifice each other.

"Anyone still up here at the end of the day gets sacrificed," a man says.

They pretend to lop off each others' heads and cut out each others' hearts. It seems naive to me—my guess is that they'd all say that life demands enough sacrifice from them without their volunteering for more.

One man grabs a woman and tries to drag her into the temple. "Each group has to give up one person to be sacrificed," he says.

The woman angrily pulls away, saying, "Then you go."

As I watch, several middle-aged American women arrive on top of the pyramid and take a quick peek into the temple.

"Is this where they sacrifice virgins?" one asks.

"Well, not to worry," another responds. "*We're* safe." ▲

6. Chichén Itzá

Chakmool...

BY NOON THE Sun is a blowtorch. People who have arrived in Chichén Itzá in tour groups and dutifully followed their guides from the site's cenote to its ballcourt to its observatory are being released from their groups to climb the pyramid. On top, people stand shoulder to shoulder, and we decide to descend. Petrified at simply stepping off the summit onto the first step, I scoot to the edge of the platform on my rear, then take David's hand and let him guide me down. He descends on a zigzag course, dodging people coming and going. On the ground again, we find that we each have a little, bleeding wound—David's on his shin, mine on my knee—that neither of us were aware of getting.

"I guess that's our little sacrifice," David says, as I get little antiseptic towelettes from my backpack to blot the blood.

Standing at the foot of the steps, we see several people pausing for a Kodak moment with the huge head of the Plumed Serpent. A sunburned young woman stands near the giant head while her boyfriend trains his camera lens on her. She shakes her hair so it tumbles free, and lifting her skirt up to her panties, puts her foot on the serpent's jaw. A guard sees her and blows his whistle.

"*Por favor,*" he says. Please.

The young woman moves away, but resumes her pose when the guard turns his back.

"Too bad," says a woman, standing beside us. "If only people knew how sacred the Plumed Serpent was to the ancient Maya."

She's about thirty, small and slender, the pale skin of her face framed by a close-fitting black bonnet that ties under her chin. Her black dress has a tight bodice and its long skirt reminds me of clothing from the late 1800s. At first, it seems that she might be one of the Mennonite women who farm large, productive acreages in the Yucatán and Belize with their husbands and children. We've seen them in Mérida, the men in bib overalls, long-sleeved shirts and straw hats, the women fully covered in long dresses—even when it's a hundred degrees in the shade—sitting in the bed of a pickup truck while their men go into the bank.

"Oh, let me introduce myself," the woman says with a smile. "I'm Alice Le Plongeon." She offers David the tips of her fingers in a dainty Victorian handshake and nods at me. "Perhaps you've heard of my husband? Augustus Le Plongeon."

"Do not touch" signs posted at the giant stone heads of the Plumed Serpent don't deter tourists.

Augustus Le Plongeon was an eccentric explorer who delved into Chichén Itzá's secrets in the last decades of the 1800s—sometimes with dynamite. Accompanying him was his young wife, Alice Dixon. I assume this woman must be portraying her—it's such a clever idea, people dressing in the costume of a particular period to present a novel view of history. I glance around for someone dressed as old Augustus himself, or as Edward H. Thompson who came later, sponsored by the Peabody Museum of Anthropology, and dredged treasures from the Cenote of Sacrifice. Or as Earl Morris, from the Carnegie Institute, who discovered an ancient temple under the Warrior's Temple in 1928. Or as the Mexican archaeologists who reconstructed the K'uk'ulkan pyramid in the early 1930s. But I see only tourists.

The first modern tourists to see Chichén Itzá and other ancient Maya cities were the American lawyer John Lloyd Stephens and British artist Frederick Catherwood, who traveled the area together in 1839. Their book, *Incidents of Travel in Central America, Chiapas and Yucatán*, went through ten printings in three months as readers devoured news of the mysterious Maya. The young Augustus Le Plongeon—who would later become an adventurer, engineer, surveyor and spiritual seeker—read their work and became intrigued by their romantic view of the (seemingly) peaceful, simple Maya.

"Augustus was in his mid-forties when we married—I was just twenty-two," Alice says. "When we set sail from New York in 1873, I never dreamed we'd spend twelve years here in the wilds."

In the Yucatán, Alice contracted yellow fever, and while nursing her, Le Plongeon learned to speak Maya. When Alice recovered, the couple moved to Chichén Itzá and set up housekeeping in one of the ancient structures. Le Plongeon's gentle nature won the Maya. They called him Great Black Beard and because he spoke their language, confided many stories and myths while he poked around the ruins. Le Plongeon later wrote that he found the Maya to be "respectful, honest, polite, unobtrusive, patient and brave." He reported witnessing their *h'men*, or shamans, being able to cloak themselves in a cloud and materialize and disappear objects. They sometimes appeared to glow in a bright light, and they could make flames appear from nothing.

"He glimpsed their world of spiritual reality that was of indescribable beauty," Alice says, "and inexpressible horror."

Through careful measurements and observations of Chichén Itzá's structures, Le Plongeon came to believe that the ancient Maya had built them as astronomical observatories. He believed the ancient Maya to be astute mathematicians and navigators with a working knowledge of plane and spherical trigonometry that enabled them to compute the dimensions of the globe and understand latitude and longitude.

"Augustus thought outside of the box," Alice says with a laugh. "But this went against the grain of the establishment. Scholars who called the Maya 'primitives' just shook their heads over my husband's notion that the Maya not only knew how to build pyramids but also calculate the cycles of planets and stars. But by far his most radical theory was that the Maya had visited Egypt."

Le Plongeon cited similarities in art and language—Maya is the name of the Buddha's mother, and the Egyptian concept for order is Ma(y)at—as indicating that the Maya possessed knowledge of Asia, Africa, and Europe. He theorized that the Maya had traveled west across the Pacific in ocean-going canoes, going to Polynesia and Indochina before crossing the Indian Ocean to the Indus River, going north to Kabul, then continuing on to Syria and Egypt before returning home. He believed the contact occurred as early as 9,500 BCE.

David and I laugh a little.

"Of course, this theory was unthinkable," Alice says, "for scholars in the late 1800s, who believed the world began in Eden only five thousand years before Christ."

After years of exploring Chichén Itzá, Le Plongeon had a hunch that a figure lay buried in the ancient ballcourt where the Maya played their ritual game. He directed his Maya helpers to begin digging in its center. They had descended twenty-four feet and were about to give up when their shovels struck something hard. It turned out to be a huge, stone figure of a man. The stylized figure had been carved so that it half-reclined on its back with its knees bent, its head up and facing right, its hands encircling a little dish on its belly. Le Plongeon dubbed the figure a "Chakmool." Decades later, another Chakmool was found in the temple of a smaller pyramid entombed inside the great pyramid, and now the figure is thought to depict a sacrificed warrior staring into the Otherworld, with the little dish on its stomach intended to hold the heart of a sacrificed human, a ceremonial fire, or both.

"Augustus wanted to take the Chakmool to Philadelphia for the 1876 centennial ceremonies," Alice says. "It weighed more than a ton, but he drug it by oxcart to Mérida. But then, authorities there seized it and shipped it to Mexico City where I believe it remains today."

In the end, Le Plongeon never received much credit for his work.

When authors mention him at all, they usually call him "eccentric and ecletic." During their years in Chichén Itzá, he and Alice took more than five hundred photos of its structures and made twenty sheets of mural drawings and dozens of molds of glyphs and carvings. When Le Plongeon couldn't send the Chakmool to the States, he sent photos. But most were archived and never saw the light of day. He traveled to New York with the intention of going on the lecture circuit to talk about the Maya, but that never materialized either. Frustrated, he lobbied for funding to continue his research in the Yucatán, but no one would back him. Great Black Beard was blackballed by academia. He died in 1908, without ever returning to the land of the Maya. His wife died in 1920.

"I think that science will find a common root for the world's peoples," Alice says. "Maybe it's already happening—traces of cocaine and nicotine, which are only in the New World, have been discovered in Egyptian mummies more than four-thousand years old. Someday we'll learn that ancient peoples were in contact and that something happened to isolate them, after which their art and architecture evolved differently. Just as birds in different areas adapt differently."

DAVID AND I walk across the plaza to stand under trees facing the Itzá's great pyramid. We overhear a guide explaining how it counts Time.

"Its nine levels are for the Moon," he says, and the nine months we spend in the watery "Underworld" of the womb before being born.

Its steps count the solar year—each of its four stairways has 91 steps, which when added make 364 steps, "with the top step making 365," he adds, "a year's worth of days."

The fifty-two stone panels on each of the pyramid's faces count the return cycle of the Pleiades and the New Fire ceremony.

"Its most famous count, though, is from spring to spring," he says. On March 21, spring equinox, seven triangles of sunlight descend the pyramid from its temple to the ground in the form of a serpent, with the seventh illuminating the huge Plumed Serpent's head.

"Okay, folks," the guide says. "We're going to try an experiment."

He raises his hands and claps his open palms together. The pyramid echoes the sound of the concussion.

"Now I'm going to clap my hands again," he says, "and this time I want you to count the echoes."

He smacks his palms together sharply. "Nine echoes, hear them? Nine echoes for the nine levels of the pyramid. Here, I'll do it again."

The echoes come too fast to count, but his people smile and slap their palms together too, and the sound of clapping splashes against the pyramid until the air seems to ring with applause. The guide takes off his hat and bends low in a sweeping stage bow. Everyone laughs.

"Now, listen once more," he says. He hits his cupped palms together, and the stones repeat the small, hollow noise. "That's the cry of a baby eagle."

His people giggle.

The guide smacks his flat palms together again, and the stones return the fierce cracks.

"That's the eagle grown big," he says.

His people clap their hands until it sounds like a frenzy of eagles.

When the group moves on, David and I sit on the thin grass in front of the pyramid. I lean back on my elbows and enjoy the peacefulness of the plaza. The sky is a force here—this is Big Sky country, like the blue expanse above the Great Plains of Nebraska and Wyoming, punctuated with fast-moving clouds. I pull my notebook out of my backpack and write:

The clouds fly by like fast trains, driven by locomotive winds.
They combine and disassemble and recombine,
clotting and flowing like blood.

Ahead of us, a couple is posing for a photo in front of the pyramid. "Say cheese," the picture-taker says. The couple moves on, and other people of different nationalities come to pose in front of the pyramid. "Say Pizza," their picture-takers say. "Say Sushi."

Twenty years ago, Chichén Itzá was an exotic destination. Now its great pyramid gets more than 500,000 people each year. The pyramid's unique shape has led it to become the unofficial symbol of Maya Mexico as tourists show their photos to the folks at home, and advertisers—certain of consumer recognition—put pictures of the pyramid in their magazine ads and television commercials. According to Maya elders, there's a prophecy foretelling that people would return to Chichén Itzá's pyramid in what's called the "Time of Quickening," the years before this current cycle of creation ends on December 21, 2012. I jot in my notebook something from William Faulkner:

The past isn't dead,
it isn't even gone.

BACK AT THE hotel, I head for the shower. The water is cool, the shower stall narrow, and I keep my movements small as I launder my hair and skin so as not to touch the tile or the clammy plastic shower curtain, which shows dark streaks of mold.

"You know," I holler out to David in the bedroom, "Thor Heyerdal crossed the Pacific from Peru to Polynesia on a raft. And I also read somewhere that some six-thousand-year-old pottery discovered in Ecuador matches pottery made in Japan."

I listen for David's reply. None comes.

"Did you hear me?" I call.

Suddenly the cold, slimy shower curtain is plastered against my body. David has grabbed me through the curtain. I scream. Now I know why Janet Leigh started screaming in the Bates Motel in the original movie *Psycho*. The shower curtain was cold. ▲

7. Ek Balám

The Ballplayers...

THE ANCIENT MAYA city of Ek Balám is about an hour's drive northeast of Chichén Itzá, and wanting to set out early the next morning, we keep our room near Chichén for another night. While David is putting the rolls of film he'll need for the day into the pockets of his photo vest, I open the door of our room and step out into the morning

The day is bright and clear, the Sun already up over the trees. Exuberant bougainvillaea flowers make strings of gleaming, scarlet rubies. Yellow-breasted birds adorn the trees like Christmas bulbs. Fallen leaves from the flowering almond are a red mandala on the grass.

At my feet, ants are transporting a dying wasp. They carry him along the edge of the step, belly up, like a trophy of war, still kicking. A little gray gecko, transparent as a vinyl toy lizard, races up and strikes the squadron of ants. The frenzied ants scatter, letting the wasp fall. The gecko claims the prize. But the victory is hollow. He tastes the wasp, rejects it, lets it fall, then scurries away. Finding himself suddenly free, the wasp makes a feeble attempt to right himself, but the ants quickly regroup. They gather him up and carry him off, intent on recycling his life into theirs.

At that moment, a fragment of a dream appears behind my eyes: I'm sitting on a big, flat wooden raft or maybe at the end of a long pier. The ocean is churning around me, its waves washing up over the wood. I'm wearing a yellow rain slicker, and God is standing a few feet from me watching the storm. Suddenly, the waves deposit a fish on the wooden floor beside me. Out of water, it's beginning to die when another fish is washed up and lands beside me. Another comes, and another until there are four different kinds of fish in a row beside me. They're gasping for air, frantic, and I'm beginning to worry about whether I should try to save them. God laughs at me. "What a silly sentimentalist," he says. "Do you think they care if they die? Only humans think they're separate."

I have a hunch to check my notebook for today's date and its corresponding date from the Maya ritual calendar, the *Tzolk'in*, which I've copied into my notebook, trying to get fully into all things Maya. I see that the Maya sign for the day is *Kimi*, the god portrayed as a fleshless skull. Death.

Then David is ready, and we head off to breakfast beside the hotel's round swimming pool. The smiling waiter sets plates of fresh

fruits in front of us. Nestled among slices of cantaloupe and honey-dew, pineapple and papaya are half-moons of sapote from the hotel's own trees, a soft fruit with orangish flesh reminiscent of a pear mated to a melon. Next comes a basket of warm baguette rolls with pale butter, then golden honey, then scrambled eggs as fluffy as small pillows. Finally, there's a Diet Coke for David and coffee for me, which turns out to be hot, thin Nescafe. A man at a far table is complaining about the coffee, but to me it seems preferable to the usual brew served in Mexican restaurants—bitter, black water that has stood so long in an aluminum pot that it could strip the enamel from your teeth.

David and I turn our attention to our dilemma: When we first arrived in Pisté, the town just half-a-mile from Chichén Itzá, we spoke with a taxi driver about taking us to Ek Balám. We really just wanted to get an idea of the cost, and he quoted an amount that seemed fair to us for the round-trip and his time. At the time, we didn't know for certain when we'd be going—or whether we'd go at all. But eager for the fare, the *taxista* insisted on giving us the phone number of his son Donatu, the family member with a phone. We casually agreed to call if we decided to go.

"This is my taxi number, 103," the driver said, getting out of his car to show us stenciled black numbers.

Now we've misplaced the little slip of paper with the phone number, but since we've decided to go to Ek Balám, we've looked for his taxi among those pulling into the hotel. Number 128, 122, and 118 have come. Number 126 has come twice. But no 103. Over breakfast, we reason that the man must have given up on us—after all, we spoke with him three days ago, an eternity in Tourist Time when most people spend only a day or two at an attraction.

"But we said we'd call," David says. "That's the rub. We gave our word."

We linger at the breakfast table watching the pool man vacuum floating leaves from the water with a long, white, accordion-pleated serpent.

"Let's say this," I say. "If he's meant to have the fare, then we'll find him this morning. And if he's not, we'll find his equivalent."

David considers the suggestion, then nods. We agree and let it go.

WHEN WE ARRIVE at the taxi stand beside the entrance to Chichén Itzá, it's empty. But within seconds, a taxi pulls in. It's 103.

"Taxi?" says the driver. He looks barely more than twenty, with a pie-round face and dark, thick hair.

"Are you Donatu?"

He nods, a look of puzzlement clouding his eyes.

"We spoke to your father about taking us to Ek Balám," David says.

"What did he say the fare would be?" Donatu asks cautiously.

"We agreed on four-fifty," David says.

"Yes," he says, and as knowingness floods his eyes, it's apparent that we've passed some kind of test.

We take our places in the rear seat of the taxi. The blue upholstery is slip-covered in clear vinyl that soon radiates our body heat back to us like a steam iron. Newspapers placed on the floor to catch dribbles and gravel from passenger's feet are a rumpled mess. A dusty green air freshener in the shape of a Christmas tree swings from the mirror, a dizzy pendulum.

Donatu needs gas and heads toward the Pemex station on the other side of town. On the main street of Pisté, Maya women in white *huipiles* are scrubbing the night's grime from the sidewalks with buckets of water and brooms. Little boys chase after a ball. Old men sit on the low walls and benches in the town's center *zócolo* getting their daily dose of chitchat.

Donatu pulls up hard behind a slow-moving pickup truck loaded with squealing pink and gray pigs.

"They'd be making even more noise if they knew where they were going," he says.

The truck ahead begins a slow turn, and the taxi pulls out to pass it. Just ahead, a very crippled black dog is slowly creeping into the street, his spine so broken or deformed that his back legs curl up uselessly under him and drag along the pavement. David and I recoil from the expected impact, but at the last moment, the animal pauses, and the taxi passes by, inches from crushing his head. Donatu honks the horn.

"Poor little thing," I say.

At the Pemex station, a young dog is curled up on the pavement, mostly hairless from mange—a ball of pink skin tormented by the Sun. Another little dog has a badly herniated navel and his intestines hang out and swing below his belly with every step like a pendulum counting the minutes of his life. A mother dog is drinking from an oily puddle. She's bone thin, her raw teats flat and empty. Her puppies are thin and skittery.

"Do you have a cracker?" David asks.

I dig a package of Ritz out of my backpack, and getting out of the taxi, David offers the crackers to the puppies first, and then the mother. But they're unaccustomed to kindness and keep their distance. Even when David tosses the crackers close to them, they barely give them a sniff.

I wonder what sad spark of spirit volunteers to inhabit the dogs in Mexican villages. Poor animals born to misery. Gentle creatures who've linked their destiny to humankind only to be abandoned. Skin-and-bone ghost dogs. Do they somehow echo the sorrow the people themselves have endured? Or is the poor animal's misery due to the lack of a low-cost spay-neuter clinic to stop the flow of unwanted dogs?

Donatu turns the taxi back through town toward the highway on the far side of Pisté. The crippled black dog is still dragging himself across the street. His haunches are a massive, oozing scab from the constant abrasion.

"Someone should shoot him," I say.

David is silent, sorrow darkening his eyes.

"Why doesn't someone do something?" I say.

I can imagine myself feeding the dog ever so nicely and petting him ever so tenderly. I'd take him to a vet, and if he couldn't be helped, I'd have him put to sleep. Put out of his misery. I'd do *something*.

Yet I do nothing but pass by in a taxi. I find a smidgen of comfort in thinking about our own big, fat dog, Theo, at home, eating chunks of boiled beef mixed in with his Iams dog food.

"Lucky boy," I say.

David looks at me.

"Theo," I say.

He smiles. "He's probably dreaming of us right now."

EAST OF PISTÉ, the highway curves around Chichén Itzá, veering left from where it once ran within feet of the site's great pyramid. Beyond the driveways to the hotels Mayaland, Hacienda Chichén, Club Med, and the smaller Dolores Alba, it makes a straight-arrow shot through the scrubby jungle on its way to Valladolid. Unlike the four-lane, divided *cuota*, or toll, highway that connects Cancún and Chichén Itzá, this *libre*, or free, road is a narrow ribbon of asphalt through the jungle. Cement trucks, double-long tractor trailers, and second-class buses grind up its hills, then roar down its inclines, rumbling past pedestrians and men on bicycles. At its edge, crosses strewn with plastic flowers mark a Place of Sudden Death, where the give-and-take of the road broke down, and a human life was extinguished by a chrome bumper.

Half an hour more and the highway enters Valladolid, the colonial town built on the foundation of the ancient Maya city of Zaci. Valladolid, famous for its *longaniza,* or sausage. For its beautiful cenote Dzitnup. For the bloody slaughter of its "white" citizens during the Maya uprising in the mid-1800s called the War of the Castes.

Donatu threads the taxi through Valladolid's busy streets, then turns north at its *zócolo*. Beyond the city limits, he crosses over the toll-

Navidad shows us the great pyramid of Ek Balám.

We walk single-file on the path without speaking, distant strangers, uncertain of the purpose of our togetherness, a group without any groupness. When we reach a low, wide wall that abuts the path, the boy scrambles ahead of us.

"This is Ek Balám's *muralla*," he says about the wall. "Sometimes a wall was built around a city for defense, other times it was a boundary that enclosed the ceremonial part of the city. This one is three meters (nine feet) wide and five meters (fifteen feet) high at its tallest. Walls like this one can be found in Uxmal, Chichén Itzá, Mayapán, Ak'e, and other cities."

The boy's voice is oddly flat as though he's reciting facts that hold no meaning for him. He looks at the ground while he speaks like he's reading a script among the pebbles. I wonder how many archaeological tours he's hung around to get the rap down.

He points to a nearby arch.

"This is an example of a Maya arch," he says. "It's called a corbelled arch or a false arch because it doesn't form a true arch. Instead it uses a cap stone at the top to span the distance between two sloping walls. The disadvantage is that it doesn't allow for very much distance between the walls."

We climb up onto the platform and examine the arch. It seems strangely placed, with no path or road now leading up to it, although it undoubtedly once connected with a *sacbé*.

"An arch to nowhere," I say.

"That's why it's called a false arch," David says.

I laugh. Donatu smiles, probably more at my laughter than at the joke, and seeing Donatu's smile, the boy smiles, too. Our groupness is coming together—tourists, *taxista*, and boy guide. I ask the kid his name. It's Navidad. For the nativity, and Jesus born in a manger at Christmas.

We walk on, and Navidad points to two side-by-side structures that share a single base.

"These are the *Gemelas*, " he tells us. The Twins. "At equinox,

highway to Cancún and heads on north until he comes upon a sign pointing the way to Ek Balám down a one-lane road. In the parking lot, a few German tourists are getting into a van, the only vehicle.

We pay the small admission, and a guard points us down a path lined by small, newly planted bushes. Donatu comes with us, and a boy trails behind us. The boy is about twelve years old, with quiet eyes and a buzz cut overgrown into a black bush. His T-shirt has holes that have stretched and run so they make a design like the fancy, expensive, pulled-thread designs usually done in linen, not the polyester-cotton blend of a T-shirt. His trousers are shiny turquoise as though fashioned from a scrap of material left over from the making of a woman's dress. Unhemmed, the trouser legs end in a tangle of threads. On his feet are plastic jellies yellowed from age.

when the Sun makes the triangles of light on the pyramid at Chichén Itzá, the Sun shines right here in the space between them."

"Really?" I say, becoming interested. "At the same time as in Chichén Itzá?"

He nods.

"Gemelas," Donatu says. "Twins—like the Minnesota Twins baseball team."

It seems that sports talk is the common language of the men of the world. And television its dictionary. Every man is bilingual—speaking his primary language, and also football-, baseball-, or soccer-ese. Games bring men together in the (televised) stadium where they cheer Our Team and forget for the moment their differences in the Big Three Issues—economics, religion, race. In its way, sports talk is beginning to repair the confusion wrought at the Tower of Babel.

"You like baseball?" David asks.

"It's okay," Donatu says with a shrug. "I like soccer better."

Navidad steps forward, his eyes bright. "Me, too," he says. "Soccer."

NAVIDAD LEADS US into what appears to be a big courtyard. There's the remnant of an altar ahead and an eroded *stele*, an upright carved monument. On the far side is the broad terrace of another ancient building. Navidad draws our attention to a small rounded pyramid on our right, which he says is the site's observatory. Then stopping us, he dramatically turns and points to the left where a huge pyramid stands at the far end of a plaza.

"Amazing," David says. "They're rebuilding the pyramid."

Navidad smiles proudly.

The enormous pyramid is the pinkish-yellow of newly cleaned and reset stone. Still undergoing reconstruction, it's so large that the men working on it seem as small as figurines. Measuring nearly five hundred feet across the front, the pyramid is much larger than that of

Ek Balám's huge and complex pyramid recently revealed a wealth of stucco statues.

Chichén Itzá, and seems more sophisticated. If Chichén Itza's pyramid is a four-hundred-pound wrestler, Ek Balám's is a tuxedoed tenor—a pyramid-mansion with dozens of governmental or residential rooms opening onto the plaza. In its center is a long, narrow staircase that ascends to the as yet unrestored summit, which sports a blonde crew-cut of yellow grass.

"How tall is the pyramid?" David asks.

"Over a hundred feet so far," Navidad says, "with 107 steps, although there might be more."

The name *Ek Balám* has been translated as Black Jaguar (although locals also call it Bright Jaguar because *ek'* can mean star). Archaeologists have known about the city since the late 19th Century, but serious research has been undertaken only during the past fifteen

Workmen finish repairing stonework on an elaborate scene showing the deceased king of Ek Balám entering the mouth of the Earth monster.

years. So far more than a hundred structures have been discovered at the site, the oldest indicating that people lived here as early as 500 BCE.

The ceremonial plaza has three vast structures. In addition to its grand pyramid, the eastern structure of the plaza measures 300 feet long, 150 feet wide, and 75 feet high, while its counterpart on the west is almost as large. A few feet from them is a traditional Maya ballcourt.

Structure 1, as the site's great pyramid is known, is a six-level structure covering at least four earlier buildings. A tomb inside it recently gave up the remains of the king Ukit-Kan-Lek, whose name means Serpent Gourd, who ruled the city from about 790 to 835 CE. Twenty-two ceramic vessels were found in his tomb along with jade pieces, obsidian blades, and inscribed conch shells.

Now workmen are resetting stones thrown down by centuries of aggressive trees and bushes. They're removing roots and rubble bit-by-bit to expose the ornate mountain underneath. Like a plastic surgeon restores the face of an aging woman, they're turning back Time.

A rope barrier across the stairs closes them to climbers during construction (I'm initially relieved), but then Navidad asks the archaeologist on duty if we can climb, and she allows us to go up under his care. I feel the Moth of Fear begin to make itself known in my stomach, but not wanting to expose that phobia to Navidad and Donatu, I manage to hold it down. It helps that the steps open at intervals onto adjoining platforms where I calm myself by examining the pyramid's minutest details (carvings, grain, and mortar).

On the first platform, twin serpents adorn the pyramid—heads flung back, jaws unhinged to reveal massive tongues that roll out like a red carpet to display hieroglyphs. Higher up, bits of pyramid-red stucco still cling to the stones. It's orangey-red, like venal blood in a test tube. It's the red of dawn during spring. The east-facing wall of our bedroom at home wears paint of this color (painted before we ever saw the pyramids), and we wake each morning to the coral hue of Valencia 1616 from Sherwin-Williams reflecting the dawn's early light.

Details on the ancient sculpture show costumes that look like angel wings.

But it's the platform near the top of the pyramid that has the most intricate statues. These stucco figures held their pose for twelve centuries beneath a cover of dirt, and now freed from the soil, they again preside over the plaza of Ek Balám. They are stunning, intricately fashioned men and a woman—their arms, hands, and fingers making delicate gestures—adorned for all eternity with sculpted necklaces and earrings and capes that look like angel wings.

Workers redoing the pyramid must have been surprised to see the figures emerge from the rubble. *Brush, brush,* and the rounded crown of a head appeared. *Brush, brush, brush,* and the forehead became visible. *Brush, brush, brush, brush,* and eyes, nose and mouth emerged. Within weeks, wonderful figures that were buried more than a millennium ago by the ancient Maya arrived in the 21st Century.

"Just like a ghost suddenly appeared," Navidad says.

"Or the Maya kings coming back," Donatu says.

I open my notebook to write:

When the sacred things of the past reemerge,
do the old gods come back, too?
The gods—forever old, forever young.

DOWN ON THE ground again, David is engrossed in figuring out how to take a photo of the huge pyramid, and I sit down on the low wall of a *temscal,* or ritual sweat bath, choosing to sit on it rather than the structure Navidad says is an altar to the site's *dueno,* or care-taking spirit. Navidad and Donatu sit down beside me.

It's quiet in the plaza. The workmen are eating lunch under the trees. The bugs and birds are snoozing through the mid-day heat. A subtle fragrance plumps the still air. Sweet yet tangy. Like the aroma of star-gazer lilies. Perhaps it's a little too quiet—Navidad picks up a pebble and taps it rhythmically on a stone.

"Does your father work here?" I ask.

"My brother," he says.

"Where's your father?" Donatu asks.

Navidad answers him in Maya, shutting me out. When their conversation winds down, I ask how much his brother earns in a day. The weekly pay, he says, is 420 pesos for a skilled craftsman, less than ten U.S. dollars a day, with a helper getting roughly half that. In comparison, white-collar workers in Mexico City make slightly more than 500 pesos a week.

"Is that enough?" I ask.

Navidad smiles. "*Bastante,* enough."

"Yes, it's enough," Donatu says. "They're glad for the work."

As the workers finish their lunches, the older men lie down to nap while the younger men bring out a white-and-black soccer ball and form two teams. A couple of the men warm up by kicking the ball across the grass between the pyramid and the ballcourt. When they're ready, the game begins in earnest.

It's a fast game and furious as the players hustle the ball. The men race back and forth across the grass after it. They holler and grunt in exertion. Their feet pummel the ground as they run, then connect with the ball with a sharp smack. One of them kicks it hard, and it crashes against the stones of the ancient ballcourt, and once again the sound of a ballgame rings from its walls.

Ek Balám's ballcourt is smaller than that of Chichén Itzá, which is the Super Bowl of courts in Mesoamerica. But while this ballcourt is modest in size, it has all of the same elements found in ballcourts in the Maya realm. The playing alley is I-shaped with two angled benches on either side that abut vertical walls having vertical stone rings near the top. So far, the oldest ballcourt discovered is an earthen structure in Chiapas, Mexico, dating to 1400 BCE, while the farthest flung is in Chaco Canyon in northern New Mexico. The newest ballcourt graces the tourist park Xcaret south of Cancún, the first to be built in seven hundred years.

The Maya *pitz,* or ballgame, wasn't a game but a deadly serious ritual that symbolized the astronomical events that the Maya believed led up to the beginning of this Fourth Creation in 3114 BCE. The *pitzlawal,* or ballplayers, were the heroes who ritually prepared the way for the new creation to begin, and in the end, one of them lost his head.

While there's no ancient manuscript explaining the ballgame, it's thought that the seven ballplayers on each team represented Venus and the other planets, with the eight-pound rubber ball as the Sun. On the court, the men kept the ball in play with their hips and legs (or on some courts with sticks), their objective being to lob the ball through the stone rings representing a portal to the Otherworld. The game went on for days, with the city's nobles watching from the grandstands.

At the end of the ritual, one of the ballplayers was sacrificed. Carvings in the Chichén Itzá ballcourt show the captain of one team holding the severed head of the captain of the opposing team—no one knows whether the sacrificed man was from the winning or losing team. The headless man is shown kneeling on the ground with seven streams spurting from his neck. The six streams of blood represent the six directions, while the seventh is a squash vine symbolizing the regeneration of life through sacrifice.

Whether winner or loser, the headless ballplayer died a hero.

THE MEN'S LUNCH-TIME soccer game reminds me of the Maya story of creation told in the book, *Popul Vuh*. In it, two young men ballplayers—the Hero Twins—set out to defeat the lords of Death and prepare the way for the coming humans.

The story begins with the boys' father and uncle, One and Seven Hunabk'u, who are sons of the old Grandmother and Grandfather who existed even before the first dawn. One and Seven Hunabk'u (also spelled Hunahpu) were avid ballplayers, and one day they were noisily playing ball in the celestial ballcourt, when the lords of *Xibalba*, or the Underworld, heard their footsteps and grew angry.

"Let's challenge the ballplayers to a game, and we'll slaughter them," exclaimed the Death lords, who ruled over pus and jaundice and sudden accidents on the road. And they sent their owls to summon the ballplayers to the Underworld.

"Very well," said One and Seven Hunabk'u, accepting the challenge, "but wait while we go tell our mother."

Going into the house, they hid their rubber ball in the loft under the peak of the roof.

Once in the Underworld, One and Seven Hunabk'u suffered many tests. At a crossroads, they mistakenly stepped into a river of pus. When they saw wooden dummies dressed up as lords, they foolishly greeted them. When the Death lords invited them to sit down, they mistakenly sat on a hot rock that burned their backsides.

The Death lords laughed themselves silly at the mistakes.

When it was time to sleep, One and Seven Hunabk'u were led into the Dark House where they faced the hazards of darkness, cold, jaguars, bats, and razor-sharp stones. When they were given two cigars, they made the fatal mistake of smoking them.

"Give us back our cigars," the Death lords demanded.

"We can't," One and Seven Hunabk'u said. "We finished them."

"Then you will die," the Death lords declared.

The Death lords sacrificed One and Seven Hunabk'u and buried them at the Place of the Ballgame Sacrifice. As a trophy of their victory, they hung One Hunabk'u's head in a tree at a crossroads.

When the tree received One Hunabk'u's head, it suddenly blossomed and brought forth gourds as big and round as a head. Fearing that it was a sign, the Death lords forbade anyone to go near the tree. But Blood Woman, the young, pure daughter of the lord Blood Gatherer, was overcome with curiosity and visited the tree. As she sat beneath it, the severed head of One Hunabk'u spat into her hand.

"It's a sign," the head told her. "When a man dies, his son is like his saliva. Death doesn't destroy him if he leaves daughters and sons, for they always remember him. So it is with me. Now go up onto the face of the Earth and find my mother."

Blood Woman remained in the Underworld, and six months after she received the head's spittle, she was obviously pregnant. Her father was enraged and commanded the owls to take her into the woods and cut out her heart. But in the woods, the maiden explained to the owls how the life in her belly had generated all by itself when she visited the head of One Hunabk'u. The owls believed her, but they were afraid to return without her heart.

"Then this is how it shall be," the young woman said. She gathers red sap from a copal tree and shaped it to look like a heart shiny with clotted blood. "From this point forward, Death shall have only nodules of sap to burn, not hearts."

And with that, she went up onto the face of the Earth.

Blood Woman immediately went to find Xmucane, the mother of One and Seven Hunabk'u. Blood Woman explained how she came to be pregnant, but Xmucane didn't believe her.

"I don't want you," said Xmucane. "My sons are dead."

But Blood Woman persisted, and so Grandmother Xmucane decided to test her. She instructed the young woman to go into the field and pick a netful of corn. Blood Woman obeyed, but in the field she could find only one cornstalk, and it was bare. She cried with self-pity, but then thinking of her unborn sons, she called out to the guardians of food to help her. Suddenly the stalk produced corn.

When Xmucane saw the corn, she was amazed.

"Well, you really are my daughter-in-law!" she said. "My grandchildren that you carry are already showing signs of genius."

In a few months, Blood Woman's twins were delivered on a mountain, and she named them Hunabk'u and Xbalanque. The Twins grew up quickly, and one day they found the ball their father and uncle had hidden in the loft before going into the Underworld. The Twins swept out the ballcourt and began to play ball.

Again the Death lords heard the noise and grew angry. Again they summoned the ballplayers. Again the old Grandmother was heartbroken.

"Wasn't it to Xibalba where my sons went to die?" she asked.

The Twins knew that it was their destiny to go, and yet they wanted to leave their grandmother with hope. So they each planted an ear of corn in the patio of her house. They told her: "When the corn dries up, you'll say, 'Perhaps they died.' When it sprouts, you'll say, 'Perhaps they live.' The corn is the sign of our Word."

In the Underworld, the Twins were much more clever than their forefathers, and they outwitted the tricks that defeated One and Seven Hunabk'u. The boys stepped over Pus River, not into it. They sent a mosquito on ahead to bite the Death lords so they could distinguish the lords from the wooden dummies. They refused to sit on the hot stone bench. And when they were led to the Dark House and given cigars, they only pretended to smoke them by placing fireflies on the tips.

They overcame the treachery of Razor House, Cold House, Jaguar House, and Fire House, but in Bat House, they met their fate. The bats had snouts like knives, and one of them cut off Hunabk'u's head. Xbalanque mourned his brother, but then he determined to save the day and summoned the Earth's animals.

When the Death lords called for the ballgame to begin, they tossed Hunabk'u's head into the court as the ball.

"We've already won! You're done!" they shouted.

But Xbalanque hit Hunabk'u's head hard. Following it down the ballcourt, he hit it far out into the oaks. In the chaos, Rabbit pretended to be the ball and jumped into the ballcourt. The Death lords became confused, and Hunabk'u got his head back.

By their wits, the Twins survived all of the tests of the Underworld, but in their hearts they knew the Death lords were going to sacrifice them for it was their destiny to prepare the way for the future human beings. So they devised a plan to defeat Death.

The Death lords had built a big oven in which to burn the Hero Twins. But to their surprise, the Twins jumped into the fire. Wanting to be rid of them, the Death lords ordered their bones to be crushed and thrown into the river. But the Hero Twins reappeared in the form of fish men. They realized that to defeat Death once and for all, they must use the power of their wits. So dressing themselves in the rags of vagabonds, they returned to Xibalba to perform magic tricks for the citizens.

The disguised Hero Twins set fire to a house and brought it back. They killed each other, then brought each other back to life. They sacrificed a dog and brought it back to life.

Hearing about the miracles, the Death lords sent for the magicians, and the magicians performed for them, too. Xbalanque cut off Hunabk'u's head, then dug out his heart and smothered it in a leaf. Then Xbalanque shouted, "Get up!" and Hunabk'u came back to life.

The Death lords were amazed, and they commanded, "Do it to us! Sacrifice us!"

The ballgame is played on the first ballcourt to be constructed since the Conquest at Xcaret Park, near Playa del Carmen, where players lob the ball through the rings using their hips.

The Hero Twins obligingly sacrificed the chief Death lords, but they didn't bring them back to life. Seeing the defeat of their leaders, the other lords slunk away. In time, the citizens of Xibalba failed to remember the Death lords, and in this way, Death lost its power to destroy and was confined to the watery Underworld.

Victorious, the Hero Twins went to the Place of the Ballgame Sacrifice to find their father and uncle and restore them. But sadly, their forefathers couldn't remember how to speak and couldn't be resurrected. Still, ever respectful of them, the Hero Twins promised that One and Seven Hunabk'u's sacrifice would always be remembered in the Place of the Ballgame Sacrifice.

"You will be the first to be remembered by those who will be born in the light," the Hero Twins told them.

With their destiny fulfilled, the Twins ascended into the sky to become Venus and the Full Moon, companions of the coming Sun. And then, when the first day dawned on Earth, the creators (with the help of the Grandmother Xmucane) made the first four human men (and then their wives) in the light of day. This is how the Hero Twins defeated Death and prepared the way for humans beings on Earth.

HERE IN EK Balám, the lunch break ends, and the sweating ballplayers put away the soccer ball and pick up their tools. The old men stiffly unfurl from their naps, and the men all go back to resetting the stones placed by their ancestors.

Remembering the carved panels in the ballcourt in Chichén Itzá, I wonder whether the ballplayer who lost his head was the winner or loser. It's a cruel premise—dying to play and playing to die.

"Clearly the winner was killed," Navidad says. "For the honor of it."

Donatu nods. "The sacrificed ballplayer went to heaven."

As Navidad and Donatu discuss this in Maya, I listen to the cadence and rhythm of their speech, thinking that as modern Maya,

they are truly the inheritors of this revival of the ancient cities.

"It's a proud and complex culture," Donatu agrees. "But we never forget that our ancient grandfathers were enslaved and forced to leave their homes."

I wonder how the modern Maya feel about the rebuilding of the pyramids.

"It's good," Donatu says. "It's the reclamation of our ancestry."

And with work to be done on them, men like Navidad's brother can earn money without having to leave their villages for the cities.

But what about the impact that tourism is having on the villagers?

Donatu shrugs and says nothing.

Some Maya still talk about the *Kuxan sum*, an umbilical cord of energy or spirit that once connected them to the heavens. They say that the cord was cut by the Spaniards—that the blood ran out and separated the Maya from the ancestors. But some believe that the Kuxan sum lies coiled in the ballcourt at Chichén Itzá, waiting, waiting, waiting. That one day it will be restored and reconnect them with that heavenly *sacbé*, the Milky Way, and a Maya king will emerge at the Right Time.

Maybe a hero will come. Maybe a ballplayer.

IT'S LATE AFTERNOON when we leave Ek Balám. The slanted Sun is orange, and vertical clouds seem to form mighty columns in the bright blue sky. I turn to the boy guide.

"How much do you want for your guide service?" I ask.

He kicks at a pebble with his plastic shoe and mumbles. "However much you want to give."

"Okay, but what do you think is fair?" I say.

Navidad looks at Donatu. Earlier, I overheard them discussing how much the boy should charge, with Donatu coaching him in what to say. This intelligent boy—who has memorized a thousand facts about Ek Balám but has barely been outside his village, who has never had much money except for a few *pesitos* for a Coca-Cola—is having to learn the art and science of international negotiation.

"How much does he want?" David asks me.

"You can decide," Navidad says shyly. "But I would take thirty, or forty, or fifty."

Donatu smiles. His protégé has done well.

David laughs. "Oh, I have a choice, do I? Let's see. Which shall I choose?"

I know which he'll choose.

He reaches into his pocket, pulls out a fifty-peso bill, and hands it to Navidad. It's more than a helper at the site makes in a day.

"What will you do with so much money?" I ask.

"Give it to my mother," he says.

"Your mother is lucky to have you," I say.

He walks with us to the taxi, where Donatu gives him a couple of rolls to eat.

DONATU TURNS THE taxi back toward Valladolid, and beyond Valladolid, he takes the old, free highway to Chichén Itzá, and then Pisté. In Pisté, the crippled black dog is still dragging himself alongside the street not far from where we first saw him. The scab on his raw haunches is oozing, and gravel is stuck in the fluid.

Women and children on the street pay no attention to him. Donatu makes no allowance for him either, keeping the steering wheel straight and his foot on the gas as the taxi barely clears him.

But seeing the dog again, I notice that he's kind of pudgy, with well-developed shoulders—like a man on crutches develops big arms and shoulders. His coat has escaped the mange that has ravaged other animals and even has a little shine. Someone must be feeding him— he's not agile enough to scavenge food.

I glance at my open notebook, and the sign for the day—Kimi, or Death—catches my eye. It makes me wonder. As maimed as this poor dog is, would he go quietly into death? Or would he struggle against the knife?

The dog pauses, tongue out, panting from heat and exertion. In the light of the dying day, he looks a little noble. A little handsome, from the shoulders up at least. I recall a saying—I don't remember its source—"he also serves who only stands and waits." Maybe this black dog reminds those of us who see him of our blessings. Maybe we consider his plight and say, "Thank God!" Maybe in this way he helps to redeem us.

I suddenly recall bits of an old tale about a dog, although I don't seem to know its source. Once there was a man who was always in a bad mood and who never missed a chance to kick his poor old dog. One day, the Tempter, who is always present in every moment, approached the dog, believing that he could take advantage of the anger the dog must surely feel.

"Come," the Tempter said. "Tell me your problems."

The dog replied, "My master beats me whenever he wishes."

"That is so cruel," the Tempter sympathized. "Why don't you leave him?"

"Because he's my master and I must be loyal," the dog said. "I would not leave him for anything."

But the Tempter knew an opportunity when he saw one and kept goading the dog to rise up against his master. Finally, the dog tired of it and felt he had to do something to get rid of the Tempter.

"You might have convinced me," the dog said. "Tell me what I must do."

"Give me your soul," the Tempter said.

"And what will you give me in return?" the dog asked.

"Whatever you wish," the Tempter said.

The dog thought for a minute, then said, "Then give me a bone for every hair on my body."

The Tempter agreed to the deal and began to count the dog's hairs. Just as he was counting the last hairs on the tail, the dog remembered his loyalty to his master and gave a shake, and the Tempter lost count.

"Why did you move?" the Tempter asked irritably.

"I cannot help it with all the fleas that plague me," said the dog.

"Please start again."

A hundred times the Tempter began his count of the dog's hairs, and a hundred times he was interrupted when the dog shook.

In the end, the evil one said, "I will count no more. You have deceived me, but you have also taught me a lesson. I now know that it is easier to buy the soul of a man than the soul of a dog." ▲

8. Chichén Itzá

The Guardians...

MY EYES OPEN and focus on the white walls of our hotel room near Chichén Itzá where we've remained for yet another day, unable to tear ourselves away from the tranquility of rural life and go back to busy Mérida. Overhead, a ceiling fan lazily stirs the air. Beyond the open, screened window at the foot of the bed is a whirring sound that rises and falls like the surf, and still half-asleep, I think I'm beside the sea. But no, it's the sound of bugs. Droning. Rasping. Thankfully outside.

Golden light from the rising Sun shines on the bed. David is beside me, his body pliant in sleep, his breath soft on my hair. In that moment, the bed is a Tall Ship taking us safely across the golden water that is our journey to the thirteen Maya pyramids.

"You awake?" David mumbles.

"Yeah."

"You want to try and find that other cenote this morning?"

One of the hotel's owners has told us about a cenote which apparently was once part of ancient Chichén Itzá, but which lies outside the boundaries of the present-day archaeological zone.

"Sure," I say.

After breakfast, the hotel owner tells us again how to find the cenote. We're to look for a wide path not far from the hotel and then go "*derecho, derecho, izquierda,*" directions he illustrates with a wide gesture for "straight, straight, left." At some point, we'll come to a *milpa*, a cornfield, which we are to take as a sign that the cenote is near.

"But how far should we walk?" David asks.

"A little ways, who knows?" the owner says.

"Well, then, how many minutes of walking should it take?"

"You're Americans, yes?" the man asks.

We nod.

"Then take my advice," he says. "Be calm. Slow down, let your intuition tell you where to go."

It's apparent that he believes we're brimming with the gung-ho fervor common to our countrymen. Americans abroad have a reputation for approaching everything in Attack Mode—from taking a walk to reading a book to eating a delicate little round of Flan. As a people, we're considered Strivers, with our dial set to Accomplishment. And yet, Mexicans also volunteer the opinion that Americans are the most generous of tourists—and the least likely to be class-conscious.

In truth, we aren't exactly laid back as we try to find the path that leads to the corn field. We examine every animal trail and footpath we come across, backtracking several yards at one point to see if we've missed it. We'd prefer to rely on a printed sign rather than intuition, but finally, we find what seems to be a wide path and turn onto it.

Walking shows us a side of this scrubby jungle that we'd miss in a taxi. It's chaos. "It's a jungle out there" means this: deadly competition. Here plants compete for light, space, water, and sex like hockey-players fighting over a puck. Bushes strive to out-do their brothers, stretching themselves on tippy-toes to be the tallest and thus garner the most light. Their motto is "Shade your neighbor, instead of being shaded." Their ability to reproduce themselves through plump, viable seeds depends on it. Beside the road, blue morning glory vines rocket to the top of trees, then stretch tenuous runners even further. Yellow daisies hoist mustard-colored petals to the sky hoping to lure the pollinators to their ripe sex organs. The lushest flowers attract the most bees, which results in fertilizing pollen. And the lushest are those that get the most light and water.

David and I walk silently in the silence broken only by the small-talk of birds as we watch for the old cornfield where we're to find another small path. "Derecho, derecho, izquierda" occupies our minds.

After a mile or so, trees give way to a big field of dry cornstalks, and we look for a way to enter without tramping through the stalks. This is no Kansas cornfield with neat corn rows that stretch to forever. This is a field that does double, even triple duty as both squash and bean vines climb the stalks. Finally, at the far end of the field, we find a trail leading into it, and run smack into two men bent over a bicycle. We stop, surprised, and they jerk their heads up. Maya farmers.

Buen dia, we say, and they return the greeting with reserved, soft smiles beneath veiled eyes. A machete is lashed behind the bicycle seat like a rifle in the window of a Texas pickup truck. The older man is tying a fully packed fiberglass bag onto the bike's handlebar. His fingers fly over a series of knots as he loops and cinches the rope. Little ears of corn push against the inside of the bag—agricultural gold.

"Corn," I say.

"Yes, dry corn," the older man answers.

They'll take the corn home where the women will abrade the kernels from the ears, and soak them in lime and water to soften and loosen the husks and allow the release of essential amino acids that would otherwise remain locked in the kernels, unavailable to the human body. They'll then take the corn to the *molino*, or grinder, where the kernels will be transformed into dough for tortillas and tamales. Many Maya still call themselves "men of corn," both for the amount of tortillas they eat (the average Mexican eats 300 pounds of tortillas a year, with tortillas making up half the daily calories of the poor), and for the creation story wherein the Grandmother of the Hero Twins helps fashion the first four human men from corn of four colors.

We tell the farmers we're looking for the cenote, and the older one gestures widely to the side of the cornfield. *"Derecho, derecho, derecha,"* he says. "Straight, straight, right." His two front teeth are outlined in gold, making the enamel a little white center in a gleaming square.

Then, with the bag of corn securely on the bike, the men step aside, giving us permission to pass by. Permission is important here, for if this milpa is like others, its four corners were marked before planting, blessings for the corn requested, and assurance received that the *dueños*, the spirit guardians, and *Yum Kax*, lord of the forest, would protect it from harm. This is sacred ground—this ground that grows the family food.

FOR THE MAYA, there is no empty space. Each corner and every moment is an intersection of gods and men, plants and animals. It's an alien concept for us who pluck chickens, skinless and deboned, from grocery store coolers, mindless of their lives. Who drive I-80 through Nebraska and Wyoming, and see only emptiness in a land that's home to myriad species of "weeds" and insects, foxes and rodents. Who move often, bringing our stuff into an empty house and then moving on, never dreaming that we're leaving a bit of ourselves behind. The first Europeans to arrive in this hemisphere saw the whole of it as being empty, a commodity to be used at will. Sitting high on their horses, they felt closer to the Sun than those who walked or ran. They won the competition for space. They spread their seed throughout the land.

The path takes us along the edge of the milpa, then into the corn at one point. It's still the dry season, and these are last year's stalks—tall, brown as mahogany, dry as a whisper. In the Maya creation story, First Father rose up from a crack in the shell of the heavenly turtle to become the glorious, lush, benevolent Corn God who would nurture the coming human beings. But here, before the new planting, the stalks are brown bones where dry ears languish in papery husks. Squash and bean vines crawl up the skeletal stalks where squash hang like old breasts, and skinny beans rattle in the breeze.

A short distance beyond the milpa, the path dead-ends at a tumble-down mountain of stone—a pyramid destroyed by generations of opportunistic trees that have sent its stones spinning.

"This *is* still part of Chichén Itzá," David says, his voice excited.

"Look there, do you see something?" I say.

"Where?"

I point to half-a-dozen shimmering lights about half way up the pyramid. They aren't lights exactly, and I don't exactly see them. Especially if I look directly at them. Rather, they're more like a movement, or the sense of movement, about a foot tall. From the corner of my eye, they look like heat rising from a steam-grate or campfire (only there is no heat). Like water falling over rocks (only there is no water).

I glance at David, and it's apparent that he sees something, too. But when I look again, the shimmering has faded to nothing.

"What was that?" I say.

He pokes me. "Leprechauns."

I chuckle without enthusiasm remembering that the Maya believe that *aluxes*, or spirits, can be mischievous and at times even mean, which is why people put out little dishes of food to appease them.

We walk on, picking our steps around the pyramid, and then without warning, we're on the lip of a deep cenote. We stop short, aware that we have almost fallen into it. Scrawny trees and vines veil the steep banks that descend some seventy-five feet to the dark, subterranean waters below. One venerable, old specimen tree has had the strength to rise up from inside the opening, and now stands with its feet in the Underworld, its head in the sky. Decades old, it's thick of trunk, with branches and leaves that plunge its struggling neighbors into deep shade. Slender feeder roots dangle from its trunk into the dark water below like sippy straws.

Peering through the foliage, we see the water below racing like dark blood pushed by a silent, pulsing current. Moist, cool air rises from it like breath. A sudden breeze rustles the tree leaves, and as we watch, one slender finger of sunlight lasers through the foliage and penetrates the water, making a shaft of electric blue light.

In that moment, we notice vertical walls of violet-gray limestone on the far side of the cenote just above the level of the water.

"If the Itzá left any writing here, it's on those walls," David says.

We decide to get down there, and we start down the steep incline of dark, spongy dirt. I weigh less than David, so I descend first. Suddenly my foot dislodges a stone that rolls a few feet, then drops fifty feet into the water. It hits with a splash and plunges into the depths.

"What do you think we should do?" I ask.

"I guess we should stay up here," David says.

We climb back up to the top, but then we see another possibility for descending, and try another way down the spongy soil. We're about twenty-five feet below ground level when the stone I'm standing on shifts. I realize that what we believe to be solid soil is merely compost poised to surrender at any moment to the water. We carefully climb back up to the rim.

But we don't easily give up our desire to descend. In our third attempt, we place our hope in some tree roots. Hanging into the abyss from trees on the rim, they seem supple and strong enough. We tug on them, testing whether they'll bear our weight. They crackle in protest.

"You want to try it?" David asks.

"You go ahead," I say. "I'll hold your cameras for you."

David grabs hold of the root like he's going to rappel into the cenote. He takes a step and the dirt under his foot tumbles down into the water.

"Gulp, gurgle," the water says, "come on in, you'll be fine."

I'm not certain we'd drown if we fell into the water—there seems to be an iota of a ledge just under the water's surface on one side where one of us could hang on while the other went for someone to bring a rope. But then the watery Underworld is treacherous and unfathomable, according to the Maya, with nine levels (like Dante's vision of Hell), so that even if a person does manage to return from it, he doesn't come back unchanged. One Maya king who threw himself into the Cenote of Sacrifice at Chichén Itzá survived the ordeal for three days, and returned with a prophecy. (A mixed blessing to be sure.)

Others aren't so lucky. One day, when we were in the village of Libré Union not far from here, a man told us about the day his father fell into a cenote. "I was just a small boy," he said, "when he fell in."

I began to laugh at the image of the startled man falling into the water, shattering its surface into a million ripples. But the laugh caught in my throat as he continued.

"Of course, I don't remember it," he said, "but my mother has told me many times about the day he drowned."

Now, David and I decide it's enough to sit and watch the water rather than descend into it. Birds flit, breezes blow, butterflies flutter. We open a brand new bottle of Cristál water and spill a little on the good Earth to acknowledge this special place. We've inhaled the cenote's breath, and in turn, it has felt the vibration of our words tickling its surface. That's enough contact. For now.

In leaving, we pass by the pyramid again. If the shimmering guardians were ever really there, they've disguised themselves in the stones.

"I know why the spirits were watching when we came," David says. "They were saying 'I want to see how those two big gringos manage to get back up out of the cenote.'"

WE EAT DINNER beside the hotel's round swimming pool where a concrete Plumed Serpent spits water into the pool. The smiling waiter brings us grilled, tender chicken breasts, which we drench with lime. We finish with desserts of rich, cinnamony Spanish cremé before we go to our room and undress without turning on the light.

The Sun has loosened its grip on the sky, and night has risen. Mist has found new life. Like the fat cells in our bodies, mist in the jungle is always there. Shrinking during the moisture famine of the day. Plumping up in the feast of damp night air.

Jungle trees and flowers fly their fragrances like flags, hoping to seduce the pollinators. Excited by the perfume, bugs begin to sing— Dee-Deet, Whirrrrrrr, and Clickety-click being the most vocal. They're singing *Staying Alive*. They're hot with *Saturday Night Fever*. They're sauntering down the tree trunks like John Travolta in tight pants. They're feeling the rhythm that urges them to be the flowers' gigolos.

After midnight, the night turns cold, and we snuggle in. David sleeps, taking even little breaths that sound like the snuffling of little waves on a sandy shore. I doze and drift. Suddenly, David half-opens his eyes, silver slits reflecting the moonlight beaming in the window.

"The secret is in the water," he mumbles.

"What?"

"The Itzá built their city here because of the water," he says. "The secret is in the water."

"But what is the secret?"

But he just falls into sleep. ▲

9. Mérida

A Little Light...

WE FLAG DOWN a second-class bus heading to Mérida, preferring to take it rather than wait for the first-class bus from Chichén Itzá in the late afternoon. We give the driver our eighty pesos and step up into the narrow aisle already crowded with standing people.

"Move back," the driver orders, and we comply, squeezing past people staying put—stomachs rubbing against backs, backsides rubbing against backsides—as we try to make ourselves skinny.

David and I have stood in the aisle of second-class buses before. We're wise to the signs of people preparing to leave and watch for them so we can claim the soon-to-be vacant seat: Quiet eyes becoming suddenly alert. Sleeping children being awakened. Red plastic shopping bags being gathered up. But no one is getting off the bus on this stretch of highway, and we stand loose, letting our knees become the shock absorbers for the road bumps as though we're skiing moguls.

I feel body heat radiating from the people beside me: Maya women wearing impossibly white *huipiles* with embroidered flowers at the neck, so that in dressing each morning, they emerge into the day through a wreath of flowers. Babies, cherished and held close.

Men with strong noses and bodies thin from field work while the women are wide with life. They smell of hot hair over humid scalps. Sun-warmed skin. Work-warmed armpits. Woodsmoke from the cookfire. This is not the city smell of Aqua Velva or an overpowering drench of Calvin Klein's Obsession. It's just the honest smell of people, and I'm comforted by it, remembering the summer smell on my skin as a little girl bunched into a hot heap on my grandma's lap.

David nods at me as two women and their kids, then three men, get up and push their way up the aisle to get off of the bus. We sit down—widely separated—David farther back than I. Seat-getting on a second-class bus is a game of chess: As people get up, we move into their seats, strategizing our moves so we move closer and closer until we are finally sitting together.

While first-class buses take the most direct highways, the second-class buses give an impromptu tour of the villages en route to the final destination. This bus passes through tiny San Roman, then larger Libré Union, then through Holca and Kantunil and Hoctún. Many (or all) of them have roots in the past as the ancient, tributary settlements that grew food for the Maya metropolises.

At the outskirts of each village, *topes*, or speed bumps, slow the bus to a crawl, giving us a good look into people's yards. Stone fences painted white surround each parcel of land. Inside the fence stands a traditional Maya house—oval in shape, made from vertical poles plastered over with stucco, and having a thatched roof and center doors front and back to let the cooling breeze blow through. Beside it stands the cookhouse covered by a roof of rusty corrugated tin to protect the cook fire. The household well has a make-shift covering of tin, plywood, or plastic to keep out varmints. A mama turkey and her awkward little babies scratch the dirt around the house. An adolescent pig roots among the trees. A fat, proud rooster with a swollen comb struts along the fence. A cream-colored dog lies in the shade, one eye half open. A woman with an infant hanging across her chest in a sling walks toward the corn grinder, balancing a yellow plastic bowl of soft corn on her head.

Farther into the village are the *tendajóns*, or little stores, stocked with cold soft drinks and little bags of Ruffles potato chips and Fritos. Beside the stores are butchers' stands with naked, yellow-skinned chickens hanging long from hooks over wooden poles.

Finally, the bus pulls into the village *zócolo*, the navel of the community with its century-old municipal buildings and Catholic church. The church, with its tall bell towers and broken windows, reminds me of the stark, white grain silos of the American Great Plains that at a distance signal the presence of towns now bypassed by interstate highways. Once a symbol of order and affluence, now they're signs of Times Past.

BACK IN MÉRIDA, we climb the stairs to the second-floor room we've retained as a base during our short sojourn to Chichén Itzá, and re-enter the hotel's biorhythm. The structure once housed a Catholic boys' school where exuberant boys horsed around in the open-air corridors beside the courtyard between classes in the deeply recessed (and therefore cool) rooms. Now travelers occupy the rooms for a night or two, and it's the hotel's employees who patter down the corridor in the steady pace of Getting Things Done.

Stewards show new guests to the rooms. (Bent under the weight of their bags.) Usher out those who are leaving. (Bent under the weight of their bags.) Carry clean sheets up to the second-floor storeroom. (Bent under the weight.) Carry sodden towels down to a truck. (Bent under the weight.) The women who care for the rooms move sheets and towels, mops and buckets from room to room to room, their sandals making a slap, slap, slapping sound on the white-and-black tile like the hotel's pulse.

Two toucans squawking in their courtyard cage contribute their two cents-worth, sounding like new athletic shoes on a polished gym floor. Squeaky Air Jordans.

Our return is met by employees' friendly calls of *hola* and *buenas tardes* and *mucho calor*, for it's very hot.

"*Si, mucho calor,*" I say, knowing from a previous misstatement that *mucho caliente* (which can mean spicy—as in a chile pepper) is also slang for "I'm horny and want sex now." Not always something you want to say to a stranger. I once told a man selling purses that I wanted to buy something to hold my breasts, when what I actually wanted was a small purse for coins. I told another man that I was pregnant, when I meant to say I was embarrassed. There *is* a difference, you know. Oh, well, it adds to the fun.

Men of the Yucatán love to laugh. They love a joke and laugh all around when someone says anything the slightest bit amusing. *Taxistas*, waiters, workmen laying stone on the pyramid, laborers chipping plaster off a building—they all laugh often, their gales escalating to the high-pitched giggles of girls. At the hotel, one of the stewards once came to work in a red-and-yellow plaid jacket, darted so that it hugged his slender frame.

"*Payaso,*" said one of the waiters. Clown.

The other waiters and cashier laughed. The steward laughed, too.

"Payaso, payaso," the waiter repeated, and they all laughed some more. They laughed on and on about the jacket, renewing the joke every time it started to fade, wringing every last laugh from it, every last chuckle and smile, their faces relaxed and happy.

Now, hot from our return trip from Chichén Itzá, we head upstairs to the quiet, little rooftop pool that holds a few cubic yards of water captive for awhile in its cycle. A replica of a Chakmool (like Augustus Le Plongeon's) presides over its west end. David opens a new novel by Nelson DeMille while I sit, notebook in my lap, staring at the rippling reflections thrown up into the courtyard trees by the pool.

Without the day-to-day busyness of making money and a home, I feel I'm slowly reuniting with a creative part of myself I had somehow lost track of—perhaps my "writing" self that got shoved to the back of the bus by more pressing matters during my teenage years. (Like my emerging sexuality.) For a couple of weeks now, I've been remembering myself as an eleven-year-old girl—I'm in a family photo, bright-faced and smiling, sitting up straight and happy on a park bench beside my grandma, with my mom and dad, two brothers, and sister on my grandma's other side. Somehow, I'm beginning to reconnect with the potential of that happy child, although I can't quite fathom how to hurry the process.

My reverie is broken when the steward Mario hurries along the corridor toward the pool, a sheet of white paper in hand.

"Victoria! " he says as he approaches. "Fax!"

He hands me the paper, and David jumps up to read it. It's from our daughters: Apparently the balance in our household checking account has gotten low. Suddenly the issue of money—with all of the emotional charge it carries—seizes the moment.

Financial and family matters are difficult to handle at a distance, and David and I become agitated as we try to recall the bank deposits we made before we left. We pull clothes over our swimsuits and hurry down to the street to telephone the bank from a pay phone (cheaper than calling from our room). Fortunately, we get through to the bank in one phone call and move money into the household account.

Back up at the pool again, the tranquility has evaporated. David picks up his book but lays it down. I open my notebook and close it. We've been reminded that our faith in our decision to change career horses midstream in our lives wasn't a one-time declaration of "I do," but a commitment that must be consistently renewed. We aren't blessed with having a trust fund—just savings and a small loan and the grit not to look so far ahead that we're overwhelmed. Yet, with that, we've given ourselves the opportunity to write and take photos (who else would be willing to back us?). We've provided ourselves with a chance to take charge of our lives, and now we're "riding the jaguar"—the Maya symbol for the power of authority. We're barely holding onto it by the tail sometimes, only by the whiskers at other times. Grabbing a handful of fur once in awhile, but rarely feeling that we have a really good grip. Yet.

But what we do have is faith in the process—however it presents itself—and our ability to see it through.

AFTER A MARVELOUS dinner of cream of cilantro soup followed by a main dish of *cochinita pibl*—succulent pork seasoned with *achiote* (similar to chile powder) and the juice of sour orange, before being steamed in banana leaves—and then a delicate little pyramid of Flan, we retire to our room.

We've never had a room in Mexico with enough light for reading, and this one is no exception. When God created Mexican hotel rooms, the command must have been, "Let there be a little light."

It's just after nine when we give up and turn off the light, and not yet sleepy, lie silent and close together, listening to the whir of the ceiling fan. Light from the corridor drifts in the open slats of the window, and gradually our eyes adjust to the dim light.

Suddenly, movement on the wall catches my eye.

"What's that?" I say, pointing.

David reaches out and turns on the light. We see a cockroach half the size of a banana. It's on the floor now, running toward us.

In a single moment, I come to dwell solely in my animal body. I jump up on my knees on the bed. The bug is heading toward the closet, and I reach out to slam the closet door and keep it from hiding in our shoes or David's camera bag.

"Where'd it go?" David says. He's on his knees on the bed.

"It's hiding in the bedspread," I say.

Large folds of the spread touch the floor.

"Gimme a shoe," he demands, and I reach long and retrieve one of his sandals.

We wait on the bed, poised like hawks—alert, big, fast, able to deduce the beastie's probable path. We—who don't squash spiders at home and avoid treading on ants, who catch a bee trapped against an inside window and release it outside—wait like predators for the chance to kill.

Suddenly, I catch a glimpse of motion above.

"Yeow!" I say, my voice shrill.

The beastie falls from the ceiling to the floor. It's body thumps the tile as it lands hard, but it gets up and runs.

"How'd it get up there?" David asks

"Wouldn't it be gross if it fell on the bed?" I say, shivering at the thought.

"Where is it?" David demands.

I bend low and scan the floor beneath the bed.

"Good heavens," David says, "people are lining up at the window to see this. I could sell tickets."

I look at him quizzically, then remember that we're naked, and that the window slats are open.

"There it is!" I shriek.

David bounds from the head of the bed to the foot in a single movement, striking at the beastie with his shoe. We hear the crunch of its shell.

It's down.

David flattens it.

It's dead.

"Where's the other one?" David says, scanning the room.

"It's alone," I say.

"They always come in twos," he says.

"I didn't see another one."

"You wait."

I declare the removal of the bug carcass "Man's Work," and sit on the bed while David flushes it down the toilet. I need to make it clear here that insects are a natural part of life in the tropics, and that our room in this hotel is exceptionally clean and well-maintained. Our bug experience in no way detracts from our day. In fact, as winners of the bug-tussle, we laugh and replay the action and the beastie's brilliant end-run across the ceiling. We lie down again and discuss how one large insect just plugged two fairly worldly people into their animal selves—an interesting, exhilarating experience.

And David's right: In the morning, we find another cockroach, legs up, dead outside our door.

Perhaps the pair was running from the scourge of insecticide sprayed in the constant battle against bugs in the tropics. As I said, this is a good hotel. ▲

10. Oxkintok

The Door...

OUR PLAN IS to take a day trip to the ancient Maya city of Oxkintok near the Peninsula's northwestern edge, and we're talking about it over dinner at a nice Mérida restaurant where we often eat. It's early—the Sun hasn't yet set—and we have the small, pretty courtyard to ourselves in this land of late diners. I order a grilled fillet of *guachanango al mojo de ajo*, or red snapper with crushed (toasted) garlic, while David wants grilled pork chops accompanied by cinnamony cooked apple slices and a vegetable medley of steamed sweet peppers, cauliflower, carrots, and summer squash with a hint of onion. I also order sangria, and its fruity bouquet wafts up from the glass the waiter sets in front of me. The decision we're mulling is, do we want to visit only Oxkintok or shall we try to combine it with a visit to another ancient city, perhaps Mayapán?

"You know, there's a door to the Otherworld in Oxkintok," says a man standing in the doorway to an interior dining room. He's dark-haired and trim in a white, long-sleeved, linen shirt above gun-metal gray trousers. His eyes are intense behind the lenses of almost frameless glasses. "Forgive me for interrupting—I'm just

here to make a reservation for later this evening—but I overheard your conversation and thought you might like to know."

"Yes, we would," David says, "but what do you mean, a door to the Otherworld?"

"To the realm of the gods," the man says. "Just as a cenote is thought to be an opening into the watery Underworld, there's also portals into the Otherworld of spirit. In Oxkintok, such a door lies deep inside a labyrinth."

"A labyrinth!" I say.

"You haven't heard about it?"

I shake my head.

"Really?" the man says, and sitting in a chair several feet from our table, he leans forward, propping elbows on his knees, putting fingertips together, and begins the story.

Once, more than a millennium ago, a shaman in Chichén Itzá received a message in a dream. A bird came and sat on his finger, and told him: "Go to Oxkintok, and you will know."

Chichén Itzá was the most powerful city in the land at that time, and Oxkintok just an old grandfather city bent with age.

But the shaman nevertheless told the leaders of Chichén Itzá about the bird and the message.

"You should go," the leaders said. "But take a legion of warriors with you and send a runner back to us each day with news."

In a few days, the shaman and his contingent set out toward the old city—a journey of several days to the west. All the way there, the shaman kept wondering: "What will I learn?"

When he arrived in Oxkintok, he was surprised to find an underground labyrinth—already centuries old, it had been built by men long gone. He knew that this was what the bird had wanted him to find, and he knew that the answer to his question lay inside it.

"I and two men will prepare to enter," he said.

The shaman avoided food and water. He suffered in the heat of the *temescal*, the sweat lodge, to purify himself. He pierced his tongue and offered blood from the wound to the gods and ancestors knowing that any other offering he might give—honey, corn, jade—would actually be a gift from Nature. For a man has only his own body to give as a true offering—his blood, labor, and his time on Earth.

Being a shaman, he also knew that his will was the real instrument in being able to give his offering, and he meditated on strengthening his resolve.

On the morning the shaman was to enter the labyrinth, he told the men who would remain outside, "Wait three days. If I don't come out, then come into the labyrinth and find me." He said this because three is the largest number of days that the Moon ever disappears from view between its dying (waning) phase and its (waxing) resurrection. Then the shaman entered the doorway.

The day and night passed, and the shaman didn't come out of the labyrinth. A runner set out for Chichén. The second day and night passed, and the shaman didn't reappear. A runner ran to Chichén. The third day and night passed, and still the shaman didn't return. Another runner left for Chichén.

On the morning of the fourth day, a warrior entered the dark labyrinth as the shaman had instructed. He didn't return with the shaman, and a runner was dispatched to Chichén. The next morning, a second warrior went in, and he didn't reappear either. Fear of darkness and the Unknown gripped the warriors in an almost unbearable terror as each man prepared to enter the labyrinth while none returned. This went on for days, until finally, the last runner took this message to Chichén Itzá: "All the men are lost."

Chichén Itzá's leaders were horrified. They summoned their shamans, demanding an explanation on why the first shaman failed to return. One of the oldest—a blind man—stood up.

"The reason," he said, "is that now our brother knows."

"But what does he know?" the leaders demanded.

The blind man answered, "In the labyrinth, he has found an earthly portal to the Otherworld."

"Then it must be sealed," the leaders declared, "before any more men are lost."

Because the blind man had such great wisdom, it was him whom the leaders sent to Oxkintok, accompanied by Chichén Itzá's best warriors. His mission: forever close Oxkintok's door to the Otherworld.

In Oxkintok, the blind shaman entered the labyrinth without a fuss. He was so old that he no longer took pleasure in women, and he only ate like a bird and drank very little water. He had already given his fair share of blood during his lifetime. He had no fear of darkness—being blind from birth, he had long since made a friend of it. He entered the labyrinth at dawn, telling the warriors that he would return before sunset.

The warriors sat down beside the entrance to wait. Barely a quarter of the day had passed when they jumped up in surprise as a figure emerged from the entrance—it wasn't the blind man, however, but one of the warriors who had earlier been lost. In a little while, another warrior emerged, and then another, until all the lost warriors stumbled out of the labyrinth. They squinted against

This unassuming structure beside an unexcavated pyramid hill is the labyrinth of Oxkintok, one of only two labyrinths known to exist in the Maya realm.

the sunlight and had no memory of where they had been or for how long. Some seemed to almost remember, but as soon as they tried to tell it, it evaporated. Like a dream.

The day passed, and the Sun was just about to slip into the mouth of the west when the blind man himself walked out of the labyrinth's entrance.

"It's done," he said. "This portal to the Otherworld of the gods has been sealed."

But the warriors were puzzled. "What about the first shaman?" they asked. "Where is he?"

"Oh," the blind man said, "he knows the gods now, and one who knows has no desire to return."

Here in the restaurant, the man finishes his story just as the waiter Jorgé bustles in with our food. The man quickly stands, and declining to join us for a glass of wine, makes his reservation for a late dinner and leaves. David and I set about eating. The pork is sweet and moist, the fish fillet exquisite.

"What's interesting to me," I say between bites, "is that some scientists have recently theorized that our universe is made up of layers. Kind of like a club sandwich. So there are six or seven other dimensions stacked up next to ours. The fourth dimension could actually be as close to our own three-dimensional world as mayo on a ham-and-cheese sandwich."

"And remember the Fifth Dimension," David says, smiling.

"What?"

"The group that sang *Age of Aquarius*," he says.

I laugh. But I go on to tell him that the ancient Maya also believed that the universe is multilayered. They saw the watery Underworld as having nine layers and the Otherworld of the gods as having thirteen, with our human world sandwiched between them. To show their dominion over everything, kings sometimes had themselves portrayed in murals as sitting on a cloth or blanket having many folds.

"The question is," I say, "how could the ancient Maya have possibly intuited something so unique as a universe that looks like a sandwich?"

"Or more accurately," David says, "a stack of tortillas." ▲

11. Oxkintok

The labyrinth...

FERNANDO DRIVES THE taxi toward Oxkintok on the old highway that goes on to Campeche in the southwestern part of the Peninsula. Along the way, each successive town is smaller than the last. There's Umán, where Fernando buys a bag of habañero peppers for his father-in-law, then tiny Chochola and Kopoma, and finally minuscule Calcehtok, where the road to Oxkintok narrows to a rut little better than a wagon-track. Even before the tiny road reaches the archaeological zone, it passes between cone-shaped, vine-covered pyramids on either side of the road looking like little green volcanoes that pushed up out of the ground during the night.

At the site's entrance, Fernando noses the taxi up onto the grass beside a split-rail fence. A guard in the *casita,* an open-sided shelter with a thatched roof, stands up to greet us—his only visitors thus far today, he tells us.

"If you're going to the labyrinth, you'll need a *lampara,*" he says as he collects our small admission. A flashlight.

"You can go in?" I say, both surprised at having the chance to enter and dismayed at not having a flashlight.

Fernando volunteers his flashlight and fishes it from the back of the taxi. He shines the beam on his palm, the light is barely visible.

"It might need new batteries," he says.

OXKINTOK'S GREAT PYRAMID stands directly ahead of the entrance, but wanting to save it until later, we turn to the left, where two pyramids have been newly liberated from centuries of rubble. These pyramids look different than those we've seen in other sites. Squarish, not very tall, having two or three deep, stark platforms, they seem like stocky dwarves with big chests and shoulders. Like squatty robots.

During reconstruction in 1999, they yielded rich treasures. The broad-shouldered Palacio Ik gave up seven tombs filled with jade and pottery. One held a royal woman's death mask. Nearly life-size, it's made from flat pieces of lily-green jade arranged in a mosaic. Its eyes are large, shiny, green jade marbles in the center of eye-whites made from shell. Its teeth are white, its lips the delicate blush of coral lipstick. A wedge of jade protrudes from between the teeth reminding me of the "opening of the mouth" ritual performed on the dead in ancient Egypt. The mask has one other remarkable feature—a jade "eye," in the same size and color as the pupils, set in the center of the forehead just above the brow.

Walking on behind the pyramids, we find ourselves in a courtyard where we come upon three larger-than-life stone statues. Carved some fifteen centuries ago, they're taller than we are, and rounder. Their features have been battered by weather and vandals with a rock, perhaps engaging in the ancient tradition of destroying the power of an image by defacing it. One still has a deep circle carved in its belly while a companion has a deep circle carved in its torso just above the waist, and a third statue has a shield on its chest.

The name Oxkintok has been translated as *ox*, meaning three; *kin*, Sun; *tok*, flint, which somehow adds up to *tres pedernales*, or three flints, according to archaeologists. Metaphysicians say the name actually refers to three Suns—ours, a star in the Pleiades, and a third in the constellation Orion.

"Do you think these big guys represent the three Suns?" I ask.

"If they went on television reruns with Fred McMurray, they could be *My Three Sons*," David says, before walking on and disappearing around a corner.

I linger in the courtyard. I like it here. No human sound is audible, not the whine of engines nor even the drone of an airplane. Only the birds and the bees and the wind. If I were dropped here blindfolded, I'd figure from the feeling of the place that I had landed in the foothills of the Colorado Rockies on a hot, dry October day. The Sun is frank without being overbearing. The breeze is fresh, and the wide, open sky feels like a window on the universe. There's also a feeling of stasis, a standing-still kind of calm like in the early autumn when the summer's exhuberance is over yet there's still no hint of winter. The Earth here feels gentle but vital and scoured clean as a schoolgirl, an impression that doesn't come from the presence of rivers—this is *puuc* country, or hill country, which is water-poor—but from wind.

I stand in the doorway of one of the single-file rooms on the edge of the courtyard. The rooms are made of blonde stone that has the sunny quality of the sky just before sunset. "I could live here," I announce, and find myself thinking about what it would take to make the place habitable for us for a few nights. "Playing house" is what my mother would call it while I'd like to think of it as trying on possibilities. I'd sweep the dirt floor clean and build a little cookfire outside the door and pull up a couple of rocks to sit on.

David emerges from around a corner. "For a minute there, I thought I was going to have to tell you I'm not going back to Mérida," he says.

I look at him, not understanding.

"I had the sudden thought that I'd like to spend two or three nights here," he explains.

I tell him about my plan to build a cookfire, and we laugh. Have we been having the same impulse independently, or is one of us picking up on the other's thoughts? Or have the buildings themselves been longing for companionship and planted the idea?

"This place feels alive," David says. "It has a different feel than the other sites, a different purpose."

"But what?"

"I wouldn't be surprised if there was once a mystery school here," he says.

I look at him, mildly surprised.

"Initiation," he finishes.

There's that word again.

WE FOLLOW A path leading to the site's great pyramid, the kingpin in a large, central complex known as Ah May. The ancient city of Oxkintok (the "x" is pronounced as "sh") was inhabited from 300 BCE to 1050 CE. Its carved monuments—showing people in frenzied dancing—indicate that it was a major player in the northwestern Yucatán from 300 to 500 CE.

At Oxkintok, work on the city continues as men reconstruct a small temple alongside a newly rebuilt pyramid.

Its once grand pyramid appears to have been built and rebuilt several times between 300 to 750 CE. Now, it's a vagabond in raggedy pants. Its steps are missing their facing stones, making them weathered and uneven and hard to climb. Its underpinnings—a nine-room substructure—stands exposed, doors into its interior bricked up like doors in an inner-city warehouse. Up top, its two-room temple is a tumbledown affair having only half walls. We sit down on one of the walls and take in the scene, saying little, simply looking.

At the summit, Time seems to loop back and return the pyramid to its glory. This man-made mountain sits high atop a magnificent terrace, where it's the hub of a dozen good-sized pyramids radiating off of its corners like spokes. The feeling here is one of peacefulness, as though the pyramid is an indulgent grandfather sitting and watching the antics of the world with no desire to join in the rough-and-tumble play. It's the center of a circle inscribed by the distant sapphire-blue horizon where the trees below and sky above seem to divide Time into halves—our earthly lifetime and the eternal.

Even the clouds are calm. At Chichén Itzá, the clouds race across the sky, the higher ones flying in one direction while the lower ones go the other way like cross-town traffic in New York at rush hour. But here in Oxkintok, the clouds are stationery—pillows pinned to a clothesline.

"You know what Oxkintok really means?" David says, warming up to a joke. "Place where the clouds stand still."

Instead of pushing the clouds around, the wind rushes by at the height of the pyramid's summit. Playful and darting, it's the little-boy aspect of the Maya wind god *Ik*, cute and capricious.

"You know why the Maya invented pyramids?" I say, setting up a joke of my own. "Ancient air conditioning."

The wind plays the irregular surfaces of the stone, making them sing, coaxing high notes from the cracks and crevices. Stones sing, the wind sings, birds sing. The wind makes us sing, too, as it blows across our nostrils and open mouths, eliciting low notes, like breathe blown over the lip of a Coke bottle. The wind is beating, pulsing, playing us like an oompah band.

As we sit on the pyramid, the childish wind grows into an adolescent, rough and rowdy. It shoves us hard in one direction, then changes direction and pulls us the other way. Spinning on a dime and giving nine-cents change.

Then it becomes a powerful man. It drives across the pyramid carrying a storm of pebbles and pelting us with the projectiles.

Then some force—perhaps the mass of the pyramid itself—disrupts the gale, and the wind moves a little distance away. It twists and turns and builds on itself until it becomes a brown specter of swirling dust. It twirls over the plaza, furiously drawing up more and more grit until it stands as tall as the pyramid, a brown spiral of energy. A whirling devil in brown robes.

Suddenly, it's on the move. Jumping low walls. Picking up speed. Swollen by its own motion, it lifts a handful of blue fifty-five gallon steel barrels high into the air, juggling them ever higher and higher, elevating them toward its top, embracing them in a spiral dance, and then dropping them flat. The barrels bounce across the stones, clanging their joyful noise.

One black plastic barrel, bigger than the others, crazily ascends the spiral until it's as high as we are on the pyramid.

The brown column dances on, a ghost come to life. It careers toward a tangle of trees—wallflowers on the edge of the dance floor—inviting them to dance. They sway to the rhythm, but lack imagination, and their stolid grip sucks the energy out of the brown spiral, which shrinks to a shadow of itself.

The stooped-old-man wind still wants to make merry, and shuffles down a dirt path between the bushes. But it can't get going. It shudders and dies. The fun is over.

IT'S MID-AFTERNOON when we descend the pyramid—three

hours having passed without our knowing—and walk toward the small, rather nondescript structure that houses the labyrinth. As we approach, a small blue pickup truck drives across the grass. It stops and two middle-aged men get out—the older one distinguished and portly, the younger man having a neat, graying beard and skin as brown as wood from years of sun exposure. From their conversation, we gather that they're archaeologists checking on the site's reconstruction, and we ask them about the labyrinth. The bearded man points to the little building ahead of us.

"That's it," he says. "The *tzat tun tzat*, the labyrinth."

The words roll across the tongue, turning into rap as they go: *Tzat tun tzat. Sat chit sat. Dis and dat. She said this, and he said that. His big dog chased the cat.*

The labyrinth's structure is built into the side of a hill—much like a suburban house with a walkout basement—giving its far side three distinct levels. Dating to between 300 to 500 CE, it's one of the oldest structures in the Yucatán Peninsula, with its two upper (now roofless) rooms added between 500 to 750.

It's the substructure, however, with its sixteen subterranean rooms, that has surprised and delighted archaeologists. For fifteen hundred years, the substructure survived in almost its original condition. When archaeologists began to evaluate it, they found that it didn't need reconstruction so much as liberation from the tons of bat dung that had piled up in its dark interior.

"When we first went in—before we knew the layout— it was really tedious," the bearded man says. "Bats, and their evil smell."

"But what was it used for?" I ask.

The men shrug in the noncommittal way of scientists. There are theories, and then there are theories—none of them documented.

"As long as there's no written evidence, it's hard to say," says the older man.

But can they make a guess?

"Initiation," the bearded man says.

One of three carved figures in Oxkintok.

"Or it could have been a substitute for a cave," says the older man.

The Maya revered caves as being dark, mysterious openings into *Santo Mundo*, the sacred Earth entity.

"Or it might have had an astronomical purpose," the bearded man says. "There are tiny rectangular openings in each of the four sides of the substructure that allow shafts of light to penetrate into the interior. Maybe they were used to track the Moon or Venus."

During the structure's excavation, a tomb was discovered, although the men agree that the burial was probably an afterthought rather than the building's original purpose. According to locals, it was once used as a jail. And also a storehouse.

"It was probably all of these things and more over the centuries," says the older man.

It's funny how most theories about ancient structures hold fragments of truth, and yet none of them alone is the whole of it. It's as though ancient structures must be understood as a collage of overlaying pictures, each complete during its time and yet obscured and enhanced by the other pictures. Just as we ourselves are a composite of all the things we've done over the course of our lives.

"You'll need a strong light if you're going inside," the bearded man advises. "The layout is deliberately disorienting."

I switch on Fernando's flashlight and shake the sluggish batteries into making a connection.

DAVID AND I walk around to the west side of the labyrinth with its three levels. A gaping black doorway at ground level seems to be the place to start.

"You ready?" I ask David.

"Sure," he says.

It's his best I'm-here-for-you voice—supportive, but without enthusiasm. I know he's torn between not wanting me to have to go into the structure alone, and needing to protect his cameras from the humidity underground. And, he doesn't really like tight, hot places. But I'm determined to go.

Entering the labyrinth, we find ourselves going down a slight incline that leads us a few feet below ground level, then taking a hard right into a passageway running parallel to the structure's outer wall. At first, the blast of daylight shining through the doorway illuminates the passageway, and the narrow stone tunnel is navigable without the flashlight. Overhead, the ceiling is a typical, Maya corbelled vault. Underfoot, the soil is spongy and organic. The smell is like fetid breath after eating old cheddar.

We slowly make our way twelve or fifteen feet into the diminishing light. But then the passageway dead ends at a wall, forcing us

to turn left. As we enter another narrow passageway, darkness engulfs us, and I switch on the flashlight.

I gingerly lead the way, swinging the flashlight's weak beam from side to side and up and down, trying to reconnoiter any hazards. We walk slowly, going forward step by careful step, our eyes wide open and straining to see.

But Dark has made this place its home, and the flashlight's dim light is no match for it. I don't see a sudden bump. I stumble and reach out to the wall to steady myself. My fingers find soft padding over the rough stone. I shine the light on it and see webs as thick as gauze. Something dark retreats into a crevice.

"Spiders," I mutter. "Which means there must be bugs for them to munch on."

This second passageway also terminates in a dead end, forcing us to take another left turn into another stone tunnel. As we step into it, the flashlight suddenly blinks off. Dark surrounds us, making us, in effect, blind. I shake the flashlight, the beam flickers uncertainly. I sense David's growing desire to leave this dank, skin-tight dungeon.

"I'll just see where this one passage goes," I say, "okay?"

He grunts, and I walk a few feet ahead, leaving him without light.

"It's a blind alley," I say.

But Dark catches my voice and hides it in its pocket.

Determined to examine the labyrinth more fully, I play the dying light on the oily soil of the floor, on the rough walls, on the corbelled vault above. Movement flickers in the light as a little brown shape stirs. I stare at it, shining the light on it, trying to figure out what it could be. Wings open, and the furry brown creature emits a screech of protest at being disturbed.

It's a bat.

I struggle to find the flashlight's off switch, but my fingers fail to locate it. I press the beam into my leg with one hand, and duck and cover my head with the other. I hope not to feel the little creature's feet becoming tangled in my hair.

Oxkintok's great pyramid is one of the city's eight large and three small pyramids, indicating that it was an early, major site.

"What is it?" David says, his voice sounding as though he's a long way off.

"A bat," I say.

"Great!" he says.

I don't think he means that in a good way.

I hurry back to him, shaking the flashlight batteries again, hoping to squeeze out the few last ohms of energy. But the batteries die on the spot.

David leads as we retrace our steps. Outside again, we suck the fresh air and blink in the strong light. We laugh.

"I think we need a stronger flashlight," I say.

"You've heard the expression, 'he ran like a bat out of hell?'" David says. "Well, that's how fast you came out of that tunnel."

Dark House—I remember it was one of the hazards the mythic Hero Twins faced in the Underworld kingdom of the Death lords.

And in the Dark, it was a bat that cut off Hunabk'u's head. ▲

12. Oxkintok

The Light...

WE ATTEMPT THE labyrinth at Oxkintok again one afternoon when we're returning to Mérida from Edzná, an ancient Itzá city to the south. Again, Fernando approaches Oxkintok on a tiny road, albeit this time from the opposite direction. Even on this side of the park, green pyramids-in-the-rough line the road—Oxkintok has at least eight large and three small pyramids, with another one located on a distant ridge, an orange microwave tower for a companion. Again, Fernando parks the taxi beside the split-rail fence where the guard in the *casita* awaits us, his only visitors at the moment. Again, Fernando and the guard settle down to visit.

"You'll need a *lampara*," the guard says, "if you're going into the labyrinth."

Unlike the last time, I pull from my pocket the long, slender, red-handled, high-tech flashlight that lit our way through the tombs at the crumbling pyramid of Meidum, Egypt's oldest pyramid. It's small in size, and the guard looks doubtful, but then he lets his expression drift into a polite look of "oh-well-no-harm-done."

Harried from the long drive from Edzná, David and I hurry toward the labyrinth, barely noticing the trees turned to gold by the low-hanging Sun. Or the perfectly still air. Or the silence broken only by the soft trill of birds. Reaching the labyrinth, we head directly to the doorway. David has his hands full with his cameras, so I lead the way in. As we walk down the sloping entrance, I turn my right ankle on a stone and fall against the wall. I groan.

"Are you okay?" David asked.

"No, it hurts," I say, but I limp on, making a mental note to mull the symbolism in turning my ankle on the first step into a labyrinth.

Inside, we move quickly down the first narrow passageway where we're on familiar ground. But as we turn the corner into the second passageway and leave the sunlight behind, we pause to get our bearings. I switch on the flashlight. Dark gobbles the beam, and yet a bit of light withstands the onslaught.

A traditional labyrinth is a tool of transformation that has been used for millennia in ceremonies by ancient Cretans, Egyptians, Celts, and Norse, as well as modern Native Americans, Aborigines, and Maori. For traditional peoples, who revere the spirit of the Earth as co-creator of Time-Place, the labyrinth can serve as a metaphor for a cave, a sacred space that becomes a place of communication between human

Fernando stands with his taxi in front of the pyramid of Acancéh.

and the Mother Earth entity through ritual. One of the most ancient examples of a labyrinth is the half-circle, or seven-circuit, labyrinth of Crete. One of the most well-known is the full-circle labyrinth in Chartres Cathedral near Paris, France, a design that has been reproduced in Grace Cathedral in San Francisco. Typically, a labyrinth is characterized by a single, winding, unobstructed path from the outside to the center. You walk its curves knowing that it will deliver you to its center, which variously symbolizes the womb, the heart, a rose, or the Underworld. To go out, you follow the path you came in on. Many labyrinth walkers equate the journey with rebirth and renewal.

The configuration in the Oxkintok structure makes it technically a maze—a rectangular course with dead ends from which you must backtrack in order to proceed. Examples of a maze are the old

hedge mazes of England where people have reportedly become lost and perished from fright or hunger. It's the nature of the maze to disorient—you follow its twists and turns not knowing whether you'll ever reach its conclusion (or be able to return to the world). Being underground, Oxkintok's maze has the added element of sensory deprivation. In that way, it's like a meditation tank.

We move more slowly and deliberately through the second passageway, our eyes open wide and straining to see in the dim light. We walk without speaking, staying close together and alert. I hear David's breathing deepen, and feel myself expel a long, tremulous sigh.

As the second passageway ends, we turn into another stone tunnel even darker and deeper inside the structure. I suddenly switch off the flashlight—I don't know why I turn it off or why David doesn't protest—and we're plunged into a darkness so absolute that our eyes are useless. As we creep slowly forward, the closeness of the walls muffles the sound of our breathing, leaving us in silence. Even the acrid smell of bat dung fades from perception.

David and I surrender to the darkness. We carefully make our way through the passageway, using not our vision but depending on a different kind of knowing, of letting our feet feel the way.

Toes touch something solid, it's a dead end—we go back and try a different passageway.

Moving slowly forward. Steadily.

Toes touch something else solid. Feet find a step, and then another. The "deliberately difficult orientation" that the bearded archaeologist described includes varying levels. Steps go up at the same time the ceiling closes down, and we hunch over as though passing through a keyhole.

Gliding slowly forward. Certainly.

Our breath becomes our guide, an invisible little extension of ourselves. When it comes back quickly, it warns: Too close, too close. And we encounter a wall. When it rings hollow, we face a turn or step ahead.

Walking slowly forward. Surely.

In this man-made cave, nothing happens to distract us from ourselves. There's nothing to see. Nothing to hear. (Is this a definition of Hell—spending eons with no focus except oneself?) We begin to sense our bodies in a new way. I hear the beating of my heart inside my chest, and feel the flow of blood in my arteries and veins. In the busy, bright, human world on the Earth's surface, I see myself as a body having a spirit. Here in the quiet darkness underground, I am a spirit that happens to have a body.

We turn a corner and a tiny rectangle of light in the distance of an outer wall presents itself to our eyes. It's one of the little windows built into the maze for sighting planets and stars, and beyond it lies the shine of day. I lift my face to its hint of fresh air like a dog lifts its muzzle to the wind. I suck it into my lungs. Reading its scent. Cherishing its promise.

Then we turn another corner, and the light and air are gone.

Stairs force us to climb, corners make us turn, dead ends cause us to backtrack as we navigate the stone tunnels. Then stairs take us up and up, and suddenly we're tossed headfirst into the day. The crowns of our heads are the first to enter the golden light. Then our torsos, then our legs, and finally our feet as we ascend the stairs and find ourselves standing on top of the structure—roofless in its decrepit state—blinking against the light of the Sun hanging low in the west.

We laugh with exhilaration and a sense of accomplishment.

"Wow, did you think we'd make it all the way?" I ask David.

"Sure," he says.

I peer down the shaft into the darkness from which we emerged, and it occurs to me that if we were to re-enter the maze from here, we'd exit it at the lower door, coming out feet first into the world. Running. Instead of standing here, contemplating.

I don't know the original purpose for this maze, but the thought comes to mind of rebirth. I can imagine a warrior living inside it for days or weeks, gradually letting go of his reliance on sight, hearing, touch, smell, and taste, as he learned to depend on his body's wisdom

The road to Oxkintok runs by a green hill, a pyramid that hasn't yet been restored.

in a new way. Perhaps a shaman would enter the maze in accordance with a heavenly cycle such as the appearance of Venus as the evening star. Deprived of other sensation, he would anticipate the joy of catching sight of the planet's heavenly light through a small rectangular opening on the west side of the structure, and track its starry brilliance night after night. Venus would become his guiding light in the stifling atmosphere of nothingness. He would learn to call it friend. And when the cycle turned and he emerged from the maze, he would have been reborn a New Man.

Free from the maze, David and I climb down from the structure and hurry to climb the great pyramid again, wanting to emerge from the man-made cave and immediately ascend the Maya's sacred mountain. Within minutes, we're standing at the pyramid's summit, overlooking the green land rolling expansively to the edge of the azure horizon. In this final hour of daylight, shadows have grown long and are merging in gleeful anticipation of the moment when night will escape the Underworld to cover the sky. A breeze is coming to life. In the east, a pale Full Moon is rising.

In the last light of the day, something shiny in one of the pyramid's stones catches my eye. Lit by the golden sunlight, it's a fiery spark in the plain rock matrix, and I climb up over the wall of the temple and out onto a ledge to get a better look at it. I find myself staring at a smooth, shiny crystal about the length of my thumb embedded in one of the stones. This crystal came into being in the heart of a dark cave as dripping water deposited its shiny minerals drop by drop for ages. And from the depths of a cave, it's now part of the summit of this ancient mountain.

I open my notebook and write:

Fear is born in the absence of faith
from a belief in the dual nature of things,
rather than the oneness of the Divine.
Which is the better teacher—Dark or Light?
The wise heart heeds both and neither.

BY THE TIME Fernando gets onto the highway to Mérida, the Sun has quit the day shift and gone on while the night hasn't yet punched the clock. In the power vacuum, the sky bleeds color until there's only gray. Down the road a ways, a sign advertises a cenote swimming pool. There's a wire gate across its access road, locked now because of the lateness of the hour, but the water beyond it gleams in the rising Moon like an opal. I suddenly recall the dark-haired woman with the lime-green collar during her initiation in Dzibilchaltun's cenote. I can see her emerging from beneath the water, gasping for air as she rises, droplets of water jumping from her face and hair in their return to the cenote. I can't help but wonder, what is initiation, really, but the moment when one chooses to move beyond the comfort zone into the Unknown? Of course, we fear risks to ourselves and our belongings, and fight tooth and nail against changes that might bring them. Yet Life is change—moment to moment and day to day—and in trying to prevent change and maintain our status quo at all costs, we put ourselves at risk in ways we can't possibly foresee. Perhaps initiation is deliberately choosing change before change chooses us.

But like entering a maze, it can be disorienting. ▲

13. Uxmal

Chaak...

THE SWIMMING POOL at my feet is the tender blue of baby's eyes. David has gone back to the room for a moment, and I'm waiting for him beside the pool of our hotel, which sits just outside the entrance of the ancient Maya city of Uxmal.

Like Oxkintok, Uxmal is located in the northwestern part of the Peninsula, in *puuc* country, or hill country, which has no natural surface water. This is where ancient royalty once shed blood and tears to coax the rain god Chaak into bringing life-giving moisture to the young corn plants. Where every drop of good water was once conserved in underground *chultunes*, or cisterns. Where the thirsty Sun now wants to slurp every drop of water from this hotel pool and lick it dry.

Now electric pumps bring water. Without prayers, without sacrifice. With only the turn of a knob. Water pumped up from a vast underground river fills this big pool and another equally large pool a few feet away—as well as bathtubs the size of small pools in each of the hotel's rooms.

Now we who have the money to travel are the royal ones, but without the Obligations of Office. We climb the ancient pyramids that were once the sacred domain of shaman-kings. We eat the best of food, served with a smile. We cool ourselves in the jewel-blue pools. And we make very few real sacrifices in order to do it.

I took a bath this morning, but ever the conservative queen, I stopped short of filling the huge tub completely, thinking that even six inches of water in it would fill the whole tub at home to overflowing.

And anyway, the bathtub leaks. While I bathed, it made a puddle on the white tile, which I then had to mop up with a towel.

DAVID AND I enter Uxmal as it opens at eight in the morning. The broad, stone path into the park leads directly to the Pyramid of the Magician with its voluptuous curves like the soft shoulders of a fat woman. But we turn to the left before we reach it, our immediate destination being the site's great pyramid.

Dew—the kiss of night—still lingers on the grass. Walking across the grass, we hear a buzzing like an electric current surging through high wires. We look up into the trees, thinking that bees are mining nectar from the blossoms. But instead the insects are at our feet. Thou-

sands of them. A carpet of bees is working the fruiting heads of grass, and we walk slowly, careful not to squash them or present our nearly bare (sandaled) feet as the enemy. But they don't attack us while they work—just as the ancient Maya abruptly stopped fighting their wars when the time came for them to go home and plant corn.

For it's peace that feeds the children—war feeds only history.

Reaching the great pyramid, we pause to look up its stairway of seventy steps made from sharp-edged, uniform, gray stones that fracture the slanted, morning sunlight. I feel a hint of fear rising in my stomach at the thought of climbing them, but then David offers his hand, and I follow his zigzag course up the pyramid.

Built in about 850 CE, this pyramid is roughly contemporary with Chichén Itzá's K'uk'ulkan pyramid. Its north face, the only side so far restored, measures two-hundred-forty feet while its summit is nearly eighty feet high. Here the sacred motif is not the feathered serpent, as in Chichén Itzá, but the macaw parrot, which symbolizes the creator god Itzamná in the form of his holy bird. The ancient Maya of the Yucatán variously saw Itzamná as the father-creator, the son-creator, or the holy spirit. Dozens of carvings of this celestial bird adorn this temple, half of them diving to Earth to receive the offerings of the faithful with the others soaring skyward, taking petitions to heaven.

But at the summit, it's not the carved macaw parrots we notice first, but the huge stone face of a creature with bulging eyes and an elephant-trunk nose peering out at us from inside a ruined temple. Otherworldly faces such as this one have long been called *Chaak* faces and identified with the rain god. But some linguists now theorize that the name Chaak is a slurred pronunciation of *Cauac*, the Maya storm god and hurler of lightning who was present at creation, and that the Maya didn't intend Chaak to portray the rain god so much as to identify a pyramid or temple as a Place of Conjuring or Making. Chaak faces often adorned the four sides and corners of Maya pyramids and temples, so that when a shaman came there to conjure or image (imagine) rain or victory in war, he had Chaak as his spiritual guide. In this way, Chaak is the face of magic. Of invocation. Of the human desire to enlist the power of God in creating favorable conditions.

Now the stone Chaak-Conjuring face peering out at us from the ruined temple gives us a lop-sided grin. While its trunk curls up perfectly, many of its components—flowers, squares, Xs, and Os—are missing, leaving gaping holes in its cheeks and forehead. It's like Mr. Potato Head midway through the game and still missing an ear and eye, and I wonder if someone once dismantled it in an attempt to negate the power of the pyramid.

David and I sit down with our backs to it to watch workmen restoring an enormous terrace at the foot of the pyramid. The dirt of ages here conceals the rock of ages, and one man is brushing organic dust from the long-buried stones. He pries out the loose stones with a short, stout stick and carefully sets them near their original position in the wall. A second man sorts lesser stones, keeping those large enough to be reset into the terrace. A third man tosses the dime-a-dozen, fist-sized stones used for fill into a pile. A fourth man throws the smallest of them into a wheelbarrow and carts them away. (The wheel is a convenience the ancient Maya never used for work.)

In ancient times, labor such as this was a form of tribute—like the taxes we now pay. Instead of handing a check to the Maya Internal Revenue Service, the men gave their labor. Each family was responsible for gathering certain-sized stones. Some collected the small fill stones used to form the center of walls or a terrace, while others looked for good-quality stones to serve as veneer over the fill and still others gleaned fine, large stones that could be carved into the upraised, trunk-like noses of the Chaak-Conjuring faces.

Perhaps thinking of taxes, David turns and says, "Maybe an ancient Maya saying was, 'Nothing is certain except death and stones.'"

BY MID-MORNING, the Sun is high and hot, and we paw through

A climber ascends the great pyramid of Uxmal, which bears carved images of the macaw parrot, symbolic of the holy bird of the god Itzamná.

my backpack for a Clif bar brought from home and a bottle of Cristál water. People in tour groups have begun to arrive, although fewer tourists visit Uxmal than Chichén Itzá or Tulum on the Caribbean coast, and even fewer manage to get over to this pyramid.

A group of Germans huff up to the top, then turn around and go right back down—Blitzkrieg tourism.

Italians seem to have more fun. They laugh and talk and call loudly to friends to take their photo. "Pizza, pizza," they say, presenting their teeth to the camera.

Mexicans arrive in family groups, helping old grandmas over the rocks and hoisting bright-eyed tots up the steps. At the top of the pyramid, they talk history and discuss whether their ancestry might include some Maya blood.

Asians arrive in unison on top of the pyramid as though tuned to each other like birds in a flock.

Americans seem to be preoccupied with gore. "So is this where they performed human sacrifice?" a man demands of his guide.

"Yes, in a minute we'll see it," the guide says.

But the man won't let it go.

"But they ripped the hearts out here, right?" he persists, demanding blood.

"Probably, yes," the guide says wearily.

A man of about forty climbs the steps alone. While he could sit anywhere on the ample summit, he sits down beside me on the edge of the platform, folds his legs into a yoga position, and closes his eyes. I look at him, slightly annoyed by his proximity to me. He has dark-blonde hair receding at the temples and a sharp nose. He's rail thin and naked to the waist. He sits with his hands on his thighs, palms up, thumbs touching index fingers to make a circle. I'm reminded of a stone image of the shaman-king of Uxmal, sitting in the doorway to the Otherworld, arms out straight in front of him, hands held vertically, palms forward, fingers slightly bent in an awkward pose.

Suddenly the man opens piercing blue eyes and looks at me.

We stare at each other, blue on blue eyes. He looks like a Teutonic Ralph Fiennes, intense and moody.

"Excuse me if I stink a little," he says, bending to sniff his right armpit. "I've been climbing a lot today, and it's hot."

I say nothing—what is there to say?

"What's your experience of the energy here?" he asks.

It's a question I've longed to ask strangers on the pyramid, and now I know why I haven't: I'm speechless as I consider what the word "energy" might mean to him.

"It's intense," David says, leaning forward to look around me at the man.

"Yes, very," the man says. "You can certainly feel it."

"But not like at Chichén Itzá," David says.

"Oh, no," the man says, "I feel very uncomfortable there."

The men talk, making the connections that ease them into conversation, like computers connecting to the Internet: "Zeeeeeet, zwaaaaaa. You've got mail." The man is from Germany and like us, he's finding his tour of the Maya pyramids something of a vision quest. He has spent four months touring the Peninsula, he says, sometimes sneaking into a site to spend the night on a pyramid.

"Chichén Itzá can be very harsh," David is saying.

"Yes," the man says, "the energy there is like a huge billboard that says 'power.'"

"It's demanding," I say. "I usually get some little scrape or cut there that bleeds a little. A friend of ours who's psychic told us that she sees bits of what she calls 'spider energy' at Chichén Itzá— little pockets of pain like spider bites."

The man nods. "A woman—she's a psychic and a sensitive— did a study of energy at various places around the world. At Chichén Itzá, she tested the energy beside the open-mouthed serpents beside the north stairs—you've seen them, yes?—and she found it so disruptive that she fainted."

"Which stands to reason if blood was offered there," David says.

"But Uxmal is different," the man says.

"They're all different," I volunteer, thinking of the deliciously peaceful feeling of Oxkintok. And it suddenly occurs to me that David and I are developing a sense of discernment about the pyramids that runs deeper than just what we see.

"What did you feel inside the temple at Chichén Itzá?" the man asks me.

"To me, it feels like a void," I say. "Like an elevator shaft. Neither negative nor positive."

"I have the same feeling," he says. "I think it's because the Maya knew how to manipulate the Earth's energy grid. Have you heard of ley lines?"

Ley lines supposedly form an invisible grid of energy or spirit that covers the Earth's surface like a huge fishing net. They are described as "energetic" longitudinal and latitudinal lines but with their intersections on a much, much smaller grid. Some people believe that they are the Earth's "nerves."

"As humans we're affected by their energy even if we don't consciously notice it," the man says. Especially at the points where the lines intersect. "It helps to explain why we sleep well in some places, and not in others. If the energy is too much, or too little, we feel out of sorts."

Sensitives say that the ancient Maya positioned their pyramids in such a way as to make use of the Earth's energy field, he tells us, by disrupting or rechanneling the energy around their temples. In this way, they "set" the energy of a temple to be optimal for ritual dreams, contact with the ancestors and gods, and conjuring.

"They placed the stairs of the pyramid to funnel energy around it," the man says. "I think this is one purpose of the serpent heads at Chichén Itzá. To control the energy."

He suddenly opens his rucksack and rummages in it till he pulls out a photocopied page of a book.

"Here, take this," he says, handing me a photocopied page from a book showing a graph of peaks and valleys of energy in various parts of the world. "When I was making a copy of this book, this page printed twice. I didn't know why, but I carried it all the way here from Germany. I guess it was for you."

AFTER THE MAN bounds down the steps of the great pyramid, I slowly descend and stand on the ground beside the first step to see if I can feel anything. I don't think of myself as being particularly sensitive, but I stand with an open mind. There's a distinct sensation of the movement of air, as well as the feeling of something huge beside me. Of course, this is hardly a mystery, and nothing more than I would expect.

I'm reminded of Feng Shui, the ancient Chinese system of design and placement that can be used to increase or improve the energy in a temple, house, or garden. For example, it warns against living in a house on the side of a steep hill because energy is always rushing past, possibly thwarting the ability to hang on to good fortune.

But standing here I see another purpose for the pyramid's stairs: They isolate the temple by controlling access to it. They also enclose it in a series of diminishing squares. Many Maya pyramids are square, and with their several platforms, they form (when viewed from the top) a square within a square within a square with the temple in the center. Could the Maya's energy management be this subtle?

I look up the seventy steps that seem as sharp and even as teeth. Warmed by our conversation with the German man, I descended them easily, but now the fear of having to climb back up flutters in my stomach like a moth. I put my foot on the first stair, and the Moth of Fear tries its wings. As I climb the next few steps, it shakes its little feet and slicks its antennae, preparing to fly. I hurry straight up the steps, pushing myself hard to out-run my growing fear. But as I leave the ground behind, the Moth throbs in the hollow of my stomach.

A few steps higher, and the Moth thinks itself bigger and unfurls huge wings colored with dark, iridescent circles like hollow eyes.

A view of the Dovecote from on top of the great pyramid.

This giant Moth rises up into my chest and beats wings that constrict my breathing, leaving me gasping.

I push myself higher, and the Moth ascends into my throat where its great wings block my air-way, and I wheeze as my throat tightens.

But drawing on the power of will, I climb higher, putting hands and feet, hands and feet on the steps. I'm desperate to make it to the top before the Moth rises up into my head and places the hollow eyes on its wings over my eye sockets, blocking my vision, blotting out consciousness so I fall down the stairs.

My lungs burn and my leg muscles scream as I race up the steps daring not to look down or up, but keeping my eyes on the step beneath my hands. Then suddenly, there are no more steps. The toe of my sandal catches on the edge of the last step, and I stumble forward

onto the pyramid's summit, gasping for breath, then sitting down hard. The Chaak-Conjuring face gives me a crooked smile.

"Oh, stop it!" I say.

David is leaning over the far edge of the pyramid, looking through the camera, no doubt taking photos of the Dovecote structure below, with its fancy, high roofcomb. The men who were working below have gone to lunch and in their place, gray iguanas lounge like little dinosaurs. Overhead, ghost birds spiral white in the pale sky.

Finally calm, I pull from my backpack the German man's xeroxed page showing mountains and valleys in the Earth's energy. It occurs to me that maybe the pyramids are power plants and the Chaak-Conjuring faces their transformers. Maybe the shaman-kings once climbed the pyramids to plug into a consciousness beyond the "world mind" of senses and substance, and envision what could—and will—be.

And maybe when the last shaman came here to switch off the pyramids' power before he left the city, he ripped the eyes and ear-flares off of the Chaak-Conjuring face and scattered them to the four directions. To be reunited at the Right Time.

I pull out my notebook and write:

We're beginning to see what we haven't seen before,
a subtle language of symbolism
—of intuition.
The pyramids are speaking,
Books of Stone
relating ancient wisdom.

David comes and sits beside me.

"Maybe the Aztec pyramids in Mexico City were never capped," he says. "You know—decommissioned. The *conquistadores* came in and took them so suddenly that maybe there wasn't time for the Aztec shamans to shut them down. Which would definitely help to explain the intensity of that city."

IT'S NOON WHEN we walk across Uxmal to the Pyramid of the Magician that we earlier passed by. Now directly overhead, the Sun is a blow torch, and when I place my palms on the pyramid's stone shoulder, it's hot enough to fry eggs.

According to legend, the pyramid was built in a single night by a dwarf, but the story actually begins with a childless old woman who finds an egg in the forest. Being a witch, she recognized the egg as something very special, and she cared for it until the time came for whatever was inside to hatch. One night, the egg cracked open and a dwarf emerged. The witch was delighted with her new son and taught him how to make magic. But while he quickly became a man with a man's beard and a man's desire for power, he never grew taller than a young corn plant.

One day when the witch was away, the dwarf was poking around beside the hearth and found the source of the witch's magic—a *tunkul*, or drum, made from a hollow log. He thumped the drum, and the note thundered through the land.

Hearing the drum, the king of Uxmal was terror-stricken for he knew it signaled the end of his reign. He summoned his shamans.

"What shall I do?" he asked.

"You can do only one thing," they said. "Follow your destiny."

The king summoned the one who had sounded the drum, and he was even more terrorized to see that his adversary was a dwarf. For ages, the Maya had believed that a dwarf was a traveler between the worlds. A soul having a child's body but all the wisdom of a man. An enigma. A riddle inside a puzzle inside a conundrum.

The dwarf saw that he had the power of terror on his side and suggested a competition to see who should be king. He suggested that both he and the king place a nut on their head, and whoever could withstand it being cracked opened would rule Uxmal.

"You go first," the king said.

The dwarf shook his long, luxuriant, black hair and placed the nut on his head, which the witch had cleverly fortified with stone. The executioner (who favored the king) raised his stone mallet and with all of his force brought it down hard on the nut. The nut cracked open. The dwarf smiled.

The king placed the nut on his head. The executioner used only half of his strength to hit the nut, and yet the king's skull cracked open, and he fell down dead.

In this way, the dwarf became the king of Uxmal and ruled for many years. On the night the old witch died, legend says he built the magnificent, oval Pyramid of the Magician to the great height of one-hundred-twenty feet. To this day, locals call it simply *Adivino*, which translates as soothsayer.

Despite the centuries-old fable, the pyramid was constructed over an older structure during a period of many years. Uxmal means "thrice built" or "three times occupied," and the Adivino pyramid shows signs of seven reconstructions, each one grander that the last, like a woman reinvents herself to suit the times.

The city was occupied from 800 BCE to 1200 CE, and was a powerful force in the Peninsula from 800 to 1000 CE. The Tutul Xiu (pronounced "shoe") who led Uxmal to greatness are thought to be related to the Itzá. While the Itzá who built Chichén Itzá possibly migrated up the coast of the Caribbean, those who settled in Uxmal might have migrated from Guatemala through the Usumacinta river basin in Chiapas and up coast of the Gulf of Mexico into the Peninsula in a journey that lasted eighty years. According to Maya chroniclers, the Tutul Xiu participated in the Itzá alliance held in Dzibilchaltún in 790 CE, and reigned in Uxmal from 751 to 928. It was during this period that king Chan-Chak K'ak'nal-Ahau created the House of Governors, the four buildings in the Nunnery Quadrangle, and the Pyramid of the Magician in their present form.

One side of the Adivino has dainty, but extremely steep stairs. In modern times, they felt the footfalls of royalty when Elizabeth, Queen of

England, climbed them in 1974, during a rainstorm while her footman held an umbrella over her.

Its other side also has stairs—these as sharp as a serrated knife blade. Flanking them are twenty-four Chaak-Conjuring faces, with a twenty-fifth face in the center of the stairway, designating the pyramid as a Place of Conjuring. A thousand years old, most of the faces still have their carved components—bulging eyes, a downspout nose, eyebrows made of Xs and Os like kisses and hugs in a love letter.

King Chan-Chak K'ak'nal-Ahau's building frenzy required a million stones. Even ten million stones. Little stones for fill come easy here—Uxmal's hills are alive with rocks. But fine, large stones suitable for being carved into Chaak noses were harder to come by. The endeavor required a king who could gain the favor of the gods and ancestors. It required ample rain to grow food, healthy men to respond to the unifying power of the king's vision, and healthy women to make corn tortillas.

Finally, the building came to an end. The last date found on an Uxmal monument is 911CE. After that, no new Chaak noses were carved here, and the pyramids began to fall into disrepair. No one knows why. Maybe the king could no longer summon the gods.

Maybe the Chaak-Conjuring faces fell mute.

Maybe the storm god turned a deaf ear on the people's pleas for rainfall and Uxmal dwindled in the drought.

THE ADIVINO IS now getting a facelift, as is one of the structures behind it in the Nunnery Quadrangle, a group of four magnificient buildings surrounding a plaza. A tripod made from poles stands on the roof of one of the buildings and supports a pulley strung with nylon rope. On the ground, three strong, young men pile rocks in a white, five-gallon plastic bucket. These containers made to hold mayonnaise and pickles are among the most useful building tools of the last fifty years. Stones and mortar go up to the top of the pyramid in them. Rubble comes down in them. They bring water and remove trash.

We watch as the three young men thread themselves into loops of yellow nylon rope connected to the pulley on top of the building. They hook a white, five-gallon bucket full of stone to the rope, then pit their weight against its mass. Straining and bent nearly double, they slowly walk forward, slowly lifting the bucket off the ground to the top of the pyramid.

Several tourists stand by, chuckling at this method of work.

"If the pyramid was in the States," a man says, "there'd be a conveyor feeder to take the rocks up, a cherry picker, dump trucks, a cement mixer, a back hoe, gasoline engines, and walkie-talkies between the ground and the roof. All the men would have hard hats."

A woman shrugs. "But would it work any better?"

What I'm wondering is, how will the Adivino look twelve hundred years, in the year 3200 CE. Who will be rebuilding it then?

IT'S JUST BEFORE eight in the evening when the Uxmal Light and Sound Show begins. Metal folding chairs have been set up on a platform of the Nunnery Quadrangle, and people jockey for the best place to sit, although all the seats are good since this is where the king of Uxmal once sat on his Jaguar Throne. The air is cool, and I hug my shawl around my shoulders. Overhead, the night sky is frigid space burning with the fires of stars.

The "light" portion of the show begins. Red, blue, yellow, and green lights splash color on the nearby Adivino, and then on the House of Turtles, House of Governors, and the great pyramid on the far side of the city. The spotlights blink slowly and at random like torpid Christmas bulbs. Then the "sound" portion begins, and tinny voices cry out in Spanish.

People descend the Pyramid of the Magician as one of the resident dogs soaks up the Sun on the base platform.

"*Ayudenos*, Chaak," the voices cry in piteous wails. "Help us, Chaak. We need rain. The crops are drying up. Chaak, Chaak."

Two elderly American men come late to the presentation. They have tape players and cassettes of the program in English, but they can't get their tape players going.

"Can you hear your tape?" one of the men yells over the disembodied voices crying out to Chaak.

"No," shouts the other man. "What part are they on?"

Meanwhile the canned voices cry out: "Chaak, Chaak, help us. Our children are dying."

I lean back and look at the stars, feeling blessed to be seeing these otherworldly Suns from this royal plaza. I pick out the triangle of stars sacred to the ancient Maya—Alnitak, Rigel, and Saiph—in the area of the sky that we call Orion's belt. To the Maya, these stars form a heavenly Turtle. At the moment of creation, the storm god Cauac hurled the lightning bolt that cracked the shell of the cosmic turtle. Through this crack, the *Maize*, or Corn, Lord emerged from the Great Nebula M42 and grew tall. As he grew, he lifted the sky off the face of the water and made a place for the coming humans.

"Chaak, Chaak," the whiny voices say. "Have mercy on us."

Canned thunder from the sound track splashes off of the stones of the ancient pyramids as Chaak answers their pleas. The wailing voices get their rain.

THE SHOW ENDS, and we walk back to our hotel just beyond the park's entrance. We skirt the hotel's swimming pool, which is as quiet as a dark turtle without the pumps going. Starshine makes a connect-the-dots puzzle on its inky surface.

We go to bed and sleep until I awaken in the middle of the night to a strange noise. I can't remember what I was dreaming, but suddenly the dream channel switches and plunks me down in a coin-operated laundromat where I hear washing machines filling. Slowly I become aware that the sound is real, and I get out of bed and go into the bathroom and turn on the light. I step into a shallow lake.

"David, come here!" I say.

The pipe under the washbasin in this fancy hotel has burst and is spraying water all over the bathroom. The floor is flooded, and the water is threatening to run into the bedroom.

"Call someone," David says, and warm from the bed, he throws himself into the spray of cold water to try to stop the flood.

I dial the operator—at three in the morning it takes several minutes before a sleepy male voice answers. I blurt something about there being water in the bathroom, an emergency. He says, "In Spanish please." I babble on about water in confused, sleep-tinged Spanish, almost able to recall—but not quite—the word for pipe, which I later remember is spelled as pipe but pronounced *pee-peh*.

The bathroom is now a swimming pool with lots of wet footsteps into the bedroom. I throw on some clothes, while David masters the shutoff. He gets dressed just before two men arrive at the door—without tools. They scratch their sleepy heads, then go get the key to the room next door, and at three-forty in the morning, we haul our stuff to another room.

We lie down to sleep away what's left of the night in a strange bed. We turn on our sides, and I feel David's comforting warmth.

"It's a good thing you got the water turned off," I say. "If you'd have waited for them, the whole bedroom would've been flooded."

His voice is sleepy in answer, "Next time someone starts wailing to Chaak, let's leave." ▲

14. Edzná

Time...

WE'RE DRIVING TOWARD Edzná, an ancient Maya city on the western side of the Yucatán Peninsula about thirty miles inland from the Gulf of Mexico. The map shows its closest modern city as Campeche, located in the state of Campeche, and upon leaving Mérida early one morning, we head west on Highway 180, a newly rebuilt, two-lane, heavily traveled road connecting the Peninsula to the whole of Mexico. Semi-trucks carrying gasoline and freight, interstate buses, smaller trucks, cars, and a caravan of seventeen campers from the United States share the pavement. A few men on bicycles brave the traffic, peddling on without a backward glance at the tons of steel breathing down their necks. Ahead of us a truck hauling two tankers of petroleum whooshes by a man riding a bike. The force of the wind created by the truck blows the man off his bicycle, and by the time we pass him, he's picking himself up from the shoulder of the road, his bike still on the ground.

A little farther on, three tiny, white, concrete houses stand beside the pavement, each adorned with a cross and dusty plastic flowers, memorials to the road warriors—men, women, or children—who have gone on to that great white road in the sky, the Milky Way.

I'm reminded of a riddle: What do you call a man walking down a dusty road?

The answer: Time.

On our odyssey to thirteen Maya pyramids of the Yucatán Peninsula, Time is a trickster. Some days are so intense that by evening the morning seems in the far distant past, and discussing it, David and I ask each other, "Was that only today!" Other days seem compressed into minutes, and Time becomes one of those collapsible drinking cups you take camping—flattened it fits into a shirt pocket, and yet when you pull it open, it holds a full cup of water. We see Time's passage in the rapidly filling pages of my notebooks and David's rolls of exposed film. But then, it isn't Time that's flying—it's we who are racing, moving, dashing through the moments of our lives.

Then there are the tricks of déja vu and synchronicity—glitches in the sequence of reality when Time seems to spool backward to replay a scene or lurch forward and bring two separate threads together in a single moment. One such moment occurred when Christopher Columbus, sailing in the Caribbean in 1504, happened to catch sight of Maya traders paddling long canoes laden with goods. In that instant, he

realized that land must lay beyond the known "Indies," and upon returning to shore, he suggested to Francisco Hernández de Córdoba that he should go have a look.

AT HIGHWAY 24, we take the turn toward Campeche. On the inland side of the road are great chalky cliffs, now high and dry, that once bore the pounding of waves, while the other side is flat, sandy land covered with scrubby bushes and short grass—a once-and-future beach according to the changing levels of the world's seas.

Mile after mile, we sense the waters of the Gulf of Mexico before we're able to see them, not so much from the smell of moisture or salt as from the openness of the sky. Then the road curves and we're suddenly beside the Gulf. Its surface is the deep blue of cold water. The color is ceramic blue—Wedgwood blue, Delft blue, Ming-vase blue. Caught in the semi-circle of land that is Mexico on the west and Louisiana and Texas to the north, it doesn't seem like open water so much as captive water. It gives no feeling of romance or glamour—nor even of recreation—but seems more like the utilitarian water of shipping and oil production. In the past, it was the fast-track for *conquistadores* and pirates.

The highway takes us into Campeche, past a concrete boardwalk that's deserted at mid-morning on a weekday, past office buildings and two boxy 1970s style hotels. It funnels us toward a great stone wall twenty feet high and seven feet thick, and plunks us beside an old, fortified rampart with gun turrets on top. Just as the Maya of Ek Balám once fortified their city against attack, the people of Campeche, once isolated on this stretch of beach, built a protective wall against interlopers. Against the terror of the seas. Against pirates.

We park the car near the rampart at the city's *zócolo*, feeling like we've entered Times Past. With little traffic at mid-morning, the city has a charming slowness of pace that seems reminiscent of another century. Under the spreading shade trees, an ornate, round, Victorian-style bandstand serves ice cream at dainty, white, wire soda-parlor tables nestled under a wooden ceiling painted the shiny brown of dark chocolate. Its rococo charm seems straight out of the old romantic musicals my mother used to watch as television reruns on the afternoons when she ironed, and I expect to hear the Music Man singing about "trouble right here in River City."

Across the street, quaint shops are fronted by a wide, covered corridor that protects window-browsers from the weather. Beyond the shops, narrow side streets have elevated sidewalks left from the days when people arriving in horse-drawn carriages stepped directly from the carriage to the sidewalk, avoiding the soil in the street. The streets themselves are cobblestone, fake now and made from patterned concrete, but nonetheless charming.

But it's Campeche's houses that enchant: block after block, street after street of narrow houses wearing a painter's palette of colors. Flat-fronted and hard against the sidewalk, they're joined wall-to-wall and painted in dusky hues that create an earth-bound rainbow—yellow beside green next to red, then chartreuse, lapiz, gold, and purple. Door jambs and window frames painted bright-white accent the hues so the houses seem a Crayola-box of color. Only the massive stone ramparts remind of the city's previous peril.

Campeche, unlike Mérida and other cities of the Peninsula, wasn't built over an ancient Maya ruin. At most, the previous settlement was a prosperous stop on the Maya sea-trade route around the Peninsula. Called *Kin Pech*, or Sun Tick (like the ticks on deer), it flourished under the leadership of the plucky Moch-Cuouh.

Moch-Cuouh and the Maya of Kin Pech caught their first glimpse of the *conquistadores* when the ships of Hernández de Córdoba appeared on the first day of spring in March, 1517. Having sailed around the Peninsula from Isla de Mujeres near present-day Cancún, the Spaniards desperately needed water. Moch-Cuouh gave them some, but refused to let them stay. Seeing the lushness of the land, de Córdoba decided he wanted more than water. He took his ships a little ways west and put in at the mouth of the river near the present-day city of Champoton. But Moch-Cuouh's forces put an end to the incursion when they attacked the expedition, killing and wounding many men, and even Córdoba himself, who soon died of his wounds.

But the wave of *conquistadores* couldn't be stopped. A year later, Juan de Grijavala landed his ships in Champoton. Again Moch-Cuouh sent the Spaniards on their way. In 1531, Francisco de Montejo the Elder tried for Champoton. He held it for a while, and even managed to take Kin Pech, but when disease and thirst claimed so many of his men that the rest started looking for jobs with better working conditions, Montejo was forced to abandon the settlement.

It wasn't until 1540, when Moch-Cuouh had succumed to disease, that Montejo's son El Mozo was able to retake Kin Pech. He established the first Spanish city on the Peninsula here, naming it San Francisco de Campeche. In 1545, Franciscan friars arrived and built the Peninsula's first permanent church, which they named for their patron saint. It was in this San Francisco church that the grandson of Hernán Cortés, conqueror of the Aztecs and founder of modern Mexico City, was later baptized. Even now, the church is open for Mass.

The city of Campeche was the rising star of the Peninsula. Politically separate from Mexico, the Peninsula was governed directly from Spain, and Campeche became a direct link in those communications. As the Peninsula prospered, Campeche became a major port with shipbuilding and other industries, sending fine tropical dyewoods to Europe and receiving goods for its residents.

But the city's wealth soon attracted the unwelcome attention of pirates. It was scarcely twenty years old when French roughnecks overtook it, causing its citizens to huddle in San Francisco church, fearing for their lives.

For a century, the pirates continued to attack. The rogues changed, but not their motives. In 1598, the Englishman William Parker pillaged the town. In 1635, the Dutch pirate called *Pie de Palo*,

Campeche's San Francisco church was the Peninsula's first permanent church.

or Peg Leg, seized the town and made off with everything his men could carry. In 1661, the pirate Henry Morgan ordered his booty "to go" when he heisted two newly arrived Spanish ships before they could be unloaded. When the Flemish pirate Laurent Graff made off in 1684 with a grand haul of booty, the Spanish governors decided to do something to stop the robbers. They levied a special tax and began building a ring of ramparts around the city. Later, during the 18th Century, the wall was further improved against possible attacks by the British Navy.

The city's fortune declined after Mexico won its independence from Spain. Campeche lost its trading status with Europe and its commerce collapsed. Not wanting Mexico to step into the place vacated by Spain, the Peninsula existed as an independent entity for two years, with some hope of coming under the wing of the United States. When it finally entered the Mexican fold, Mexico divided it in 1863 into the states Yucatán and Campeche and the territory of Quintana Roo to deconsolidate its power. Since then, the state of Campeche has prided itself on enjoying a moderate portion of prosperity enhanced by a jumbo serving of tranquility. New finds of oil along its shores are now adding some gravy.

Today, the city's wall against pirates is an intriguing curiosity. While it was once nearly two miles around, great chunks of it were torn down over the years, leaving the longest remaining section at about fifteen hundred feet. Still, it's an impressive feat of engineering and labor, especially with its seven *baluartes*, or fighting stations.

David and I walk to the wall and climb a ramp to the top of it to stand on the San Carlos baluarte. This fort, elevated some twenty feet above the ground, offers a clear view of the city and the blue waters of the nearby Gulf. Cannons still populate this fighting station, their barrels pointing out narrow slits in the wall. Once at the cutting edge of killing technology, the old iron weapons are now pockmarked with age. Various sized cannon balls lay beside them looking like rusty eggs. Yet even the smallest of these iron balls—spheres barely larger than ostrich eggs—are too heavy for me to lift.

Down the ramp, the ground level rooms of the San Carlos baluarte house a museum of pirate paraphenalia.

We descend even further down steep stairs into its underground dungeon. With its curved stone walls and arched ceiling, it could be the interior of a hollow loaf of bread. It's humid, despite an electric fan, but if men ever died here, no dank feeling of misery lingers.

Despite their dungeons, the people of Campeche were famous among pirates for not being able to hold their prisoners. In 1667, the Frenchman Jean-David Nau, caught in a skirmish with Spanish troops, played dead when his men were taken prisoner, then later made his way to the city, freed his men, stole a ship and escaped. Two years later, the Dutch pirate "Rock Brasilano" was thrown into the dungeon but won his freedom when he had a letter sent to city officials threatening an attack by a fictitious pirate if he wasn't set free.

Now the dungeon houses a small gift shop and, for only 18 pesos, we liberate a jar of honey produced by the bees of Campeche.

WE TRAVEL EVEN farther back into Times Past when we set out on the road to ancient Edzná. After leaving Campeche, the narrow road curves like a drunken snake between outcroppings of cliffs once pounded by the sea. Immediately, it shows signs of people being in the wrong place at the wrong moment: Hills of glass are heaped on both sides of one curve as though a truck carrying window panes has lost its entire load. A little way further, a large truck is stopped dead in the middle of a curve, its driver out and examining damage done by low branches that have struck the windshield.

The farther the road penetrates the jungle, the fewer the vehicles. There are no taxis. No tourist buses or vans. No villagers on bicycles, old rifles slung over their shoulders. No men peddling tricycles loaded with firewood. When the road finally straightens out, it's bordered for a few miles by neat orchards with orange trees heavy with ripe fruit and nurseries with little trees and bushes all in a row. But we see almost no small towns along the way.

Instead, the forest deepens. Trees here are taller and denser than in the state of Yucatán, indicating a deeper, more fertile soil than the thin covering of dirt farther north. Trees push up against the pavement on both sides of the road and overhang it like a dense, green awning. The only signs of civilization are poles marching across the countryside carrying electric wires and an occasional blue road sign with a picture of a pyramid that keeps us going.

In fact, we almost miss the turn to Edzná when the road suddenly forks, but at the last moment, we veer right and within a hundred yards or so drive into the site's car park. A guard hurrying out of a nearby house is still chewing, probably lunch, and after we give him a small admission, we're walking into the site over leaves that turn to dust under our feet.

The name Edzná is translated as Itzá House—*Edz* for Itzá, *ná* for house. Like the cities of Chichén Itzá and Uxmal, which were built by branches of the Itzá family, Edzná has a remarkable presence. Once a wealthy crossroads of trade and culture, it still retains a grand sense of Self, Drama, and Image. Perhaps that talent for image-making is a hallmark of the Itzá.

Strolling through its spacious, manicured grounds, we come upon an enormous stairway made from stones so large that we push ourselves up the knee-high risers of each step with a little "oomph." Reaching the top, we find ourselves looking into the site's grand ceremonial center where two large temples flank a majestic great pyramid having five levels. Facing west and warmed by the afternoon sunlight, the regal pyramid is the light-golden yellow of amber. A large square altar lies at its feet. As in Oxkintok, we are completely alone.

"It's like we've stumbled into a Maya Shangri-la," I say.

"It feels more like 'pyramid-gate,'" David says. "If you know the code, you can open a doorway to the cosmos."

We're not the first to feel this awe in Edzná. Metaphysicians claim that each of the ancient Maya cities has a different vibration and purpose, and that the purpose of Edzná is communication with the universe. It's a place of contact, they say, a place for sending and receiving information—the ancient equivalent of Carl Sagan's SETI. A few believers have been working to reawaken its energetic function with ritual and meditation, but they've not commented on how it's going.

Edzná's first focus was agriculture, its founders probably farmers from northern Guatemala who settled here around 400 BCE. (In an ironic twist, Guatemalan refugees fleeing persecution in their country have been the site's primary caretakers since 1986.) From the years 100 BCE to 250 CE, the city experienced phenomenal prosperity

These hieroglyphs are set into the risers on the four lowest steps of Edzná's great pyramid.

and growth, during which time its residents constructed the massive terrace that lifts the great pyramid and its sister temples some twenty-six feet above the general level of the forest floor. Then in the odd way the Maya had of leaving their cities dormant for centuries, construction at Edzná abruptly stopped.

People returned in 600 CE, and began a new flurry of building. The pyramids and temples of the grand ceremnial center were constructed over older structures in the period from 750 to 950 CE.

Edzná's great pyramid reaches one-hundred-twenty-six feet, counting the height of the terrace. Its lower four levels are punctuated by doors opening into ritual and residential spaces, while the fifth level holds its temple. On top is a remnant of a high roofcomb once as dainty and complex as a woman's lace mantilla.

David and I walk across the ceremonial plaza to the great pyramid, where we come upon an astonishing series of hieroglyphs on the risers of its first four, wide stairs. These intricate glyphs show the faces of gods carved into the stone some thirteen centuries ago when Europe was still in the Dark Ages. It's amazing to be in contact with something so ancient on our own hemisphere, and I kneel and let my fingers trace the gods' faces, outlining their noses and chins, helmets and headdresses, and wondering what they represent.

According to a diagram archaeologists made of the carvings, there are sixty-eight hieroglyphs on the stairs, with another fifteen on the side of the staircase. Linguists have devoted a great deal of attention to trying to read them, and while they've deciphered the date 731 CE, they haven't been able to read the glyphs. It almost seems that rather than being made for the stairway, the glyphs were chipped out of existing monuments in other parts of the city and incorporated into the stairway by men who couldn't read.

Above the hieroglyphic stairs, a central, narrow stairway ascends the pyramid. Little more than a dozen feet wide, it has a length of stout rope for climbers' peace of mind. David begins to climb and I follow. The Moth of Fear flutters in my stomach, but before it can fly, I've already reached a landing at the top of only fifteen stairs. There's a second landing after only seventeen more stairs, and a third after another sixteen stairs. I climb the remaining fourteen steps to the top, making the summit before the Moth can fully awaken.

We stand looking out over tangle of trees that seems to stretch to the end of the Earth, broken only by the green hill that is the Pyramid of the Old Witch, still unrestored. Beyond it are the miles and miles of water channels once dug by the city's residents to funnel rainfall onto the fields or into reservoirs as needed.

Finally, in about 1000 CE, Edzná was mostly abandoned. A few people stayed on until 1300, but then the city was completely forgotten until being rediscovered in 1907. The last date carved on any of its monuments is 810 CE.

Oddly, the final dates on monuments in cities throughout the Maya realm spanned only a little more than a hundred years. The last date recorded in Palenque is 799 CE, in Copan 820, in Tikal 879. The latest date found so far is 919. It was as though the Maya clock had run down, and no one knew how to wind it up again.

The question is: What crisis caused this collapse? The Maya realm wasn't a single empire with an overarching government, but was instead a collection of powerful city-states with tribute cities supplying food and goods, making it hard to fathom what crisis could bring them all to an abrupt halt within little more than a century. One factor might have been a long drought that drastically cut the food supply. A study of lake-beds in the Yucatán Peninsula shows that the area undergoes a drought every 208 years, due to a cyclical brightening of the Sun, and that the crisis around the year 900 came in the midst of the driest period in the area in more than a thousand years. An examination of the bones of nobles has shown that while the elite were larger and better fed than the average commoner, even the nobles suffered from malnutrition in later years.

Then there's the factor of depleted resources as the Maya kings constantly quarrelled and even undertook wars to capture slaves and victims for sacrifice. Warfare, combined with drought, may have brought about a slide from which the cities couldn't recover.

Plagued by drought lasting more than a century and dwindling wealth, kings and nobles were hard-pressed to bring a unifying vision to the people. The failure resulted in the erosion of their power and influence, and people moved away.

Chaos ensued. The Maya culture was based on a healthy community, and when the old order ruptured, citizens no longer had the organization or man-power to maintain ditches and fields, which further contributed to the food shortage. Public literacy—the tradition of carving names and dates on monuments—ceased, and large building projects died. Finally, even public buildings were stripped of their stones, which went into the foundations for individual homes.

Edzná's great pyramid has five levels and reaches a height of one-hundred-twenty-six feet.

As people succumed to the diseases of malnutrition, the survivors struggled to maintain. They retained their culture—the *multepal* style of governance by a council of men is still in place in villages today—and their *h'men* or shamans continued to communicate with the divine as they conducted rituals for planting cornfields and accepting babies into the community—as they do now.

But during the six hundred years between 919 CE—the final public date so far discovered—and the coming of the *conquistadores* in the 1500s, the Maya never fully recovered from the crisis.

THE ANCIENT MAYA had no word for Time per se, according to linguists, and instead focused on the importance of cycles. They observed the Sun rolling across the heavens each day, and moving back and forth across the horizon during the year from its extremes in the north and south. They observed the Moon growing fat, then wasting away during its phases. They noticed Venus disappearing as the morning star in the east, then reappearing in the west as the first star of evening. They watched the constellations sweeping across the sky and the planets appearing on cue as though directed by a grand hand weaving the brilliant threads on the celestial loom.

In the ideal, the cycles demonstrated the harmonic movement and measure of the Divine, and the Maya timed their rituals to coincide with the cycles and thereby link themselves to the gods.

In practice, the kings and shamans often used their knowledge of the cycles to exert control over the political environment.

While Edzná may be (or not) a telephone booth for cosmic communication, it does reflect the Maya view of cosmic order. The square of its great plaza manifests the concept of a universe having four corners and four sides with the altar in the center its ninth point. But it's the great pyramid that demonstrates a knowledge of complex astronomy. The astronomers positioned this pyramid to exactly face the point where the Sun sets on August 13, which the ancient Maya believed was the first day of the current cycle of creation that began in 3114 BCE and will end December 21, 2012 CE. Positioned in this way, the pyramid also divides the year into 260 and 104 days, which reflects the 260 days in the most important of Maya calendars, the ritual calendar known as the *Tzolk'in*.

The Maya were keen observors of the heavenly lights. One of their almanacs, which is thought to date from around 850 CE, shows that they calculated the tropical solar year at 365.2420 days (modern science puts it at 365.2422), and even knew the cycle of sunspots. They figured the Moon's cycle at 29.5 days, and were able to predict lunar eclipses 33 years ahead. They forecast the dates of future New Moons so accurately that in 405 lunar cycles, the error was never greater than a day. They calculated the visible cycle of Venus at 584 days (science puts it at 583.92), and made periodic corrections so that their predictions were accurate to 0.08 of a day in 481 years. They also knew that the actual orbit of Venus takes 254 days.

To these cycles, they integrated the cycles of Saturn, Jupiter, Mars, Mercury, some meteors and comets, the Pleiades, and at least thirteen constellations.

But the most enigmatic of all Maya cycles is the 260-day Tzolk'in. This ancient ritual calendar has twenty day-gods that combine with thirteen number-gods to form a different combination of influences every day for 260 days. Known to have been in use by 1500 BCE, the Tzolk'in has been kept unbroken for centuries by the Highland Maya of Guatemala, and it has now been resurrected in the Yucatán. But the significance of the 260-day cycle isn't clear to researchers. It's known to be roughly the number of days a human spends in the womb before birth. It's also roughly the cycle of Venus. But since neither of these is exactly 260 days, it seems more likely that the Tzolk'in is a "hub" cycle that integrates many other cycles including that of those of the Sun and Venus.

The Tzolk'in, together with the cycles of the planets and stars, is seen by the Maya still keeping the sacred count as presenting a picture of the influence on any given day. In this way of thinking, each moment comes to life in the presence of gods and number entities and the cycles of the Sun and Moon, planets and stars. Add humans into the mix, and each moment becomes a snapshot of the Divine and humans in relationship.

"OH, EXCUSE ME," says a woman climbing the stairs of Edzná's great pyramid. She stops short of where David is looking at the distant Pyramid of the Old Witch through the long lens of his camera.

David lowers the camera. "It's okay, I'm not shooting."

The woman is about sixty with frank blue eyes and gray hair pulled back into two short braids held with barrets. Her shirt is blue denim, her trousers khaki Dockers. Two cameras hang from her shoulders. Stepping onto the summit of the pyramid, she tells David that she was part of a photographic safari to the Peninsula's ancient sites, but upon returning home, she found her photos disappointing. She has come back to see if she can improve them.

"I find it particularly hard to take good photos of the pyramids, she says. "They're so stark."

David laughs. "It's one reason I shoot a lot of black-and-white. If they were still their original red color instead of bleached limestone with black mold, I might shoot more color."

Sitting behind David and the woman in the doorway of the pyramid's temple, I watch David in profile—the bill of his cap pulled low over his sunglasses; his well-shaped nose; the angle of his jaw outlined by his graying, close-cropped beard. I look at the mass of his broad shoulders and his legs tan and muscular from years of skiing and biking. He and the woman are talking shop about David's Nikon cameras and her Canons and the speed of the film they use.

"What do you go for in your shots?" the woman asks.

"I want to capture how the pyramids look now," David says, "so I shoot them with people climbing them, workmen restoring them, dogs sleeping in front of them. I'm not into isolating them. Unless that's the way I find them."

I smile—the woman is the first person we've seen in Edzná except for two caretakers of the grounds.

"I wish I could find a style for my photos," the woman says.

David tells her that he developed his style after learning the parameters of his cameras and film and shooting enough film to feel comfortable with the equipment. Then he deliberately shot enough different types of subjects to discover his interests and strengths.

"I try to look beyond the obvious," he says. "I watch for that exquisite moment when two or three or four elements come together for the briefest 1/125th of a second. I'll be focused on a pyramid, and then maybe a tourist will enter the picture in an unusual pose, and then a large bird will circle overhead, and maybe a little kid will jump into the scene. This allows me to give several layers of information in one photo. For a split second, everything comes together perfectly, and then it's gone. The perfect moment rarely happens, but when it does it's magic. And you'd better be ready."

I hadn't realized how fragile a moment is until David went back to a hacienda to try to retake a photo, and we realized the impossibility of trying to recapture the moment. Aware that his original shot was the strongest, he left without taking even one photo. For 1/250th or 1/125th of a second, the camera opens its mechanical eye, and that's the shot. The moment passes. People move, clouds move, the mood changes. Even different photos of an object so seemingly unchanging as a pyramid are subtly unique as the quality of light changes. A moment flickers to life only to be covered by another moment, then another, and then they all dissolve into nothing. No moment is remembered for itself, but only for what we experience during its brief life. A birth, a death, a kiss, a photograph.

I open my notebook and write:

Each moment in Time
fractures into a zillion possible paths
leading to a zillion different futures.
Of which we choose one.

I like hearing the things David tells the woman—it reminds me that we approach things differently. Over these months spent climbing the Peninsula's pyramid-temples, I've come to believe that the purpose of my existence is to experience my life. I'm driven to know, and I can really only know that which I experience. Writing is my way of processing my experiences, and sometimes I don't really know how I feel about an experience until I write about it.

I don't know what David believes is his purpose, but in his photos, he's the observer who puts us in relationship with his view of the world. He's the witness. What he sees is etched in silver on the film.

Light and shadow. Textures. Geometrics. Shapes and their juxtaposition to other shapes. Men, women, children, animals and objects captured in their intersection with the moment, heavenly cycles, and divine influences.

"Some days you're a complete outsider," David is telling the woman, "and you can't get into the flow at all, so your response is a fraction of a second off and you miss the shot. Other times, you can get into a zone where you become part of the ebb and flow of a moment and you can tune in and press the shutter time and time again at precisely the right instant."

"But what I want to know is, does what you see affect you?" the woman asks.

David shrugs. "Sometimes I'm so concentrated, I don't even know exactly what I've shot. I have to wait until I see the film." ▲

15. Mayapán

Becoming...

WE FLY DOWN the highway in Fernando's white taxi, heading toward Mayapán, the last ancient Maya city to be built in the Yucatán. Miles upon miles of whitewashed stone fence parallels the road—big and little stones showing the way (with Dorothy and the Tin Man singing "Follow the white-stone fence"). Near the village of Telchaquillo, we slow for men on bicycles. Rifles on their shoulders, they are hunters in search of game—pheasant and rabbit—to feed the family. Before deer became scarce, it was the prized meat.

Venado, or deer, is good meat, Fernando tells us. Especially when it's cooked tender, shredded, then grilled for a few moments over an open flame before going into a tortilla. "Yummmm," he says, his smile reaching chocolate eyes visible in the rear-view mirror. The only son of a mother who died young, he was raised by doting sisters who fed him rich foods such as spicy meatballs with a boiled egg yolk inside. He loves food, and at forty has the start of a tummy that defies being conquered by his belt. Much of our conversation over the miles is about cheese and seafood.

Just outside of Mayapán, Fernando pulls up beside a massive wall of black stone. It's a black giant snaking across the land—millions of stones piled high and wide to slow attackers once intent on invading the city. Mayapán was a latter-day city. By the time of its heyday from 1200 to 1400 CE, the Classic Maya cities had slid down the slippery slopes of Time, and even the late Classic cities of Chichén Itzá and Uxmal had faded. Mayapán was born into a period of great upheaval for the Maya, and was the last great hope for establishing order in the chaos. But, then, Mayapán, too, went tumbling into Time.

Its pyramid, as we see upon entering the plaza, isn't a powerhouse like that of Chichén Itzá, but a weak son born late to old parents. Its resemblance to its big brother in Chichén Itzá is obvious: Nine platforms. Four stairways. A north-facing temple. But it's smaller—with just over sixty steps, far fewer than Chichén Itzá's ninety-one steps. Instead of dominating a grand plaza, it's squeezed by other structures—a reflection of the diminishing world of its residents as their Department of Defense poured resources into building a wall.

The pyramid seems cramped by tall trees that lean in like eavesdroppers. The city's observatory and civic buildings stand at its elbow. A cenote lies at its feet, and we peer into this *Ch'en Mul*, or well beside the pyramid. All but dry now, its nooks and crannies, ledges and recesses

are a toothless mouth providing endless places for the Maya to hide a treasured manuscript or precious statue from the Spaniards' prying eyes. Only four Maya almanacs are thought to have survived the Spaniard's destruction of the culture, and they're now called the Dresden, Madrid, and Paris for the cities where they are housed, and the Grolier in Mexico City. Legends tell of a manuscript that will appear at the Right Time and reveal the prophecy for a Maya king-coming. Who knows?—perhaps it's already known to these people who know this land as well as their own face.

A TRAIL LEADS away from the ceremonial plaza, and we follow it, passing remnants of tumbledown structures and scrambling over a wall like the one in Ek Balám. Vines pull at our feet and lasso the buckles of our sandals. Fat gray tubers like the torsos of ashen voodoo dolls roll under our feet and throw us off balance. Still the path goes on, taking us up on top of stone dunes that are really hidden temples. Suddenly, the path ends at a steep drop-off.

"We're on a pyramid," David says, pointing to a crevice at our feet, and we kneel down and peer into the inner sanctum of a pyramid. From another opening somewhere on the other side, a shaft of sunlight lasers through the dark interior.

I hear movement off to the side and nudge David to look. A little deer is standing on the slope of the pyramid. Her dark eyes are luminous, her coat the soft tan of an old chamois. She's small—scarcely larger than an antelope or a Great Dane dog—and frozen with fear.

According to the Maya creation story told in the *Popul Vuh*, we're now living in the fourth creation of the world, the age of the True Humans. Earlier, in the third creation, the creators made a race of men from wood and women from the inner pith of reeds. But these mannequins neither thanked the creators nor praised them, and so they were destroyed in a rain of fiery resin. Before them, the beings

of the second creation were even less perfect. They were men of mud, who spoke nonsense and couldn't remember the creators, so they too were destroyed when flood waters melted them away to nothing. The creatures of the first creation were simply animals—the deer and birds and jaguars—who were unable to speak and thus bless the creators.

"So be it," the creators told the animals. "This must be your service then, let your flesh be eaten."

This is the fate of the deer whom some Maya call "Our Mother" because she gives of herself so that her human children might survive, just as the great buffalo of the northern Plains once fed her people.

"We won't hurt you," David whispers to the little deer.

But she bounds off. While the Spirit of the deer might have agreed to serve the human race, this little doe wants to live. No matter how respectfully she might be shot and gutted. No matter how good her flank might taste inside a tortilla. It's her nature to survive, and she evaporates into the woods as though she had never stood before us at all.

"She's gone," I say.

"Too bad," a voice says.

It's not David's voice, but I look at him to see if he's teasing me.

"Did you hear that?" I ask in a whisper.

A cowbell tinkles in the distance.

"Probably farm cows," David says, and standing, he walks to the far edge of the pyramid and steps off onto the slope. "I'm going to see if I can find the other opening into the vault."

I get my notebook and pen out of the backpack and set about describing the mood in Mayapán. But a glimmer of orange at the edge of my vision distracts me. I turn to look, but see nothing.

"How're you doing?" says a voice.

I stare into the shade below. I'm beginning to feel like a deer caught in the headlights. But then I see the recognizable orange glow of a smoldering cigarette, and the movement of an arm. A man is smoking, sitting against an upright stone. The dappled light camouflages him as well as anything the U.S. Army could devise.

On Winter solstice, December 21, 1998, triangles of light and shadow descend the north steps of the great pyramid in Mayapán for the first time in more than five hundred years.

"Oh, I thought . . . , " I say, but stop mid-sentence, unwilling to admit that I believed I was seeing magic here where anything seems possible. Instead I say, "I guess I wasn't expecting to see anyone."

"No, me neither," the man says.

I see him clearly now. Short hair blond at the ends, dark near the scalp, fashionably spiked up with gel so it looks like an agitated hedgehog. Dark eyes, steady on me. Brownish skin. Well-built arms muscular below the sleeves of a sage-green T-shirt. Black jeans. The man looks to be about thirty.

"Would you like a cigarette?" he says in a voice that is perfectly American although he appears to be Mexican.

"Sure," I say, although I don't smoke. Never have.

The man gets up easily and crosses the thirty or so feet to me, pulling a red-and-white pack of cigarettes from the little pocket on his T-shirt. Marlboros. I've never actually seen anyone carry cigarettes in a T-shirt pocket. He flips the box open and expertly shakes it so that just one slender, filtered cigarette presents itself for my taking. I put it to my lips, and he flicks open the top on an old, metal Zippo lighter and touches the flame to the end. I suck the cigarette, letting the smoke come into my mouth, holding it a reasonable amount of time, and then blowing it out, ever so casually, aware that if I were to actually try to take it into my lungs I'd cough like crazy. His eyes never leave my face, but if he notices the fake smoking, it doesn't register.

"Thanks," I say.

"Sure," he says. "That your husband?" He looks to where David has disappeared.

"Yeah," I say. "He's a great guy."

I take another drag on the cigarette and blow out the smoke, feeling like a teenager, awkward and playing at being myself, and wondering what's gotten into me to make me act this way.

"Is that a stele you were leaning against?" I say, looking at the rectangular, upright stone where he'd been sitting.

He nods.

"Any good?" I ask. "Most of them are so worn."

"Better than most," he says. "Want to see?"

He turns, and I get up and follow him down the slope of the pyramid to where the weathered monument stands like a tombstone for Times Past, its eulogy erased by age. It's about four feet tall and two feet wide. The top is jagged, mutilated. A flat round of stone underneath it serves as its base. A square of odd-shaped stones surrounds it.

Born late in the game, Mayapán nevertheless revived the Classic tradition of raising carved monuments to commemorate special occasions, and thirteen good examples have been found here. This isn't one of them—if it were, it would have been carted off to a museum. It's badly worn. Some carving is still visible—the hint of hieroglyphs, the outline of a person, the suggestion of a face—but not much.

"What do you think?" the man says.

"It would take some imagination to see anything in it," I say.

"Look here," he says, urgently stepping up next to the monument and dropping to his knees. "Here's the figure of a man, okay? Here's his headdress, here's his belt, all decorated up. This date here—shown by these here glyphs—is the k'atun 2 Ahau, 11.1.0.0.0., or about 1244 according to our calendar."

"Really? But how do you know?" I say. "About the date, I mean. Are you an archaeologist?"

He gives a short laugh and stands up.

"No way!" he says. "You can know things in other ways."

"Yes, you can read a lot," I say.

"I don't read anything," he says, "except the breakfast orders the waitresses bring me, and the black ink on my paycheck. I'm a cook."

I become aware that I'm forgetting to smoke. I take a drag.

"Look, you'll think I'm crazy when I tell you this, okay?" he says, "but I was the guy that carved this stone."

I look at the monument, not getting what he's saying, wondering if he's telling me that he found it in the forest and placed it here. Which would explain the new square of rocks around it.

"No, look," he says, seeing my confusion. "I found it out through past-life regression, okay? I lived here once. I was a scribbler."

"Scribbler?" I repeat. It sounds like a character in Batman.

"That's what the Maya called it," he says. "A scribbler was a scribe, a writer, an artist, a creator—the guy that carved stones like this one, okay? I talked about it once under hypnosis, and then I listened to myself on the tape, and I couldn't believe it either—that I had a pastlife, my God! So I came here to Mayapán and walked straight out here to this carved stone. And I recognized it! I could see it in my mind—what it looked like new! When it was first carved."

He stubs out his cigarette, gets out another, and offers me one. I refuse—mine is burning low, and I don't know what to do with the remains so it won't light the dry forest on fire. I smother it against a rock and put the filter in my pocket.

"So I went back home, and I made a drawing of the way I saw it new," he continues. "I took it to a museum, and this guy there could actually decipher what I'd drawn. The date and all. It blew me away. This is not normal, is what I was thinking."

"Are your parents Maya?" I ask, looking for an explanation.

He shakes his head. "Not in this lifetime anyway—they're migrant workers. Up from a tiny pueblo in the state of Michoacan, on the west side of Mexico. They used to work each year around Watsonville, California, picking strawberries. They managed to stay in California and raise us kids. But you know what?—it doesn't matter what your race is in this lifetime, people're connected to so much more. Like you. Your skin's white as snow—you're what? Scandinavian?—but you're probably here because of some pastlife here in these parts."

I'm doubtful.

"Why not? You see any other tourists busting their butts to come out here? There's got to be something here for you, okay?" he says. "Or for your husband."

"But the pastlife regression," I say, "what made you do it?"

"I was drinking myself to death," he says.

In 1997, the central ceremonial complex of Mayapán is being rebuilt brick by brick.

I lean against a round stone—part of a column or the base of a stele—and look up to the top of the pyramid, making sure David will be able to see me when he comes back. The man squats on his heels a couple of feet away. He picks up a twig and breaks it into smaller and smaller pieces as he speaks.

"For years I was a drunk in Watsonville. Manuel Humberto de Léon Jaramillo, that's me, okay? Never married, but I've got a son somewhere. I drank myself senseless each afternoon and night. I was laying cement then—every Mexican man knows how to lay cement—and I drank to numb the pain in my back and knees. It finally got to where I couldn't even get up and go to work in the morning. When I lost my job, I was out on the street. I spent eleven months homeless, sleeping in missions, lying and stealing for money for booze.

"Well, I started hearing a voice in my head when I was drunk, okay?, which was all the time. I knew it wasn't me talking. It was violent—it kept wanting me to do stuff—punch someone, or push the guy ahead of me down the steps. Sure, I get mad sometimes, but I'm not violent, okay? It scared me to death. I was afraid I'd do something I couldn't fix. All this time, my mother was praying for me—she was lighting a candle for me each morning to Our Lady of Guadalupe. Finally she convinced me to go to AA."

I nod. Alcoholics Anonymous.

"Around the same time, my grandpa died in Michoacan, okay?, and my mom went down for the funeral. She brought his stuff back in a cigar box—that was all he had after eighty-five years—and there was this little stone figure. I took it out, and I got a little charge from it. A little zing in the palm of my hand, okay? Like putting your tongue on a little battery."

I remember a light switch in the basement of our house when I was a kid that gave me a little shock each time I touched it.

"My mom didn't know where he got it—we sure didn't know what it was. But I took it to the library and found some pictures of little figures like it. It seems the Maya used them on their altars, especially here in Mayapán. "

He reaches into his pocket and holds the figure out to me. It's a carved face, about three inches tall, of an old man with a prominent nose and toothless mouth, except for two teeth protruding from the corners. A god, I suppose, maybe Itzamná. It's warm from his pocket, which seems to me to be too personal. I hand it back.

"It took me a year to sober up, and another three to understand who I was without that damn voice in my head," he says. "I was working at the mission then, okay?, helping other drunks, and this psychologist offered me free counseling. He arranged for the hypnosis. When I started talking about my past life, my brothers thought I was crazier sober than drunk. That's when I became obsessed with knowing how this little statue of my grandpa's connects to me."

I nod although I've never had that experience.

"When I listened to myself on the tape, I had no idea where the Yucalpeten was—that's what I kept calling this area under hypnosis, which is what the old Maya called the Yucatán. Then I came here and walked right up to this stone, and a whole new dimension of myself opened up," he says, stubbing out the cigarette.

"But to be drawn here after so many centuries," I say. "How could that happen?"

"All I know is emotions are powerful. Love, hate, fear—they connect you to the time when you had them. Even if it's centuries ago."

"Well, we must be able to resolve them," I say, "or we'd all be condemned to living the past."

"Oh, yeah, you can resolve them," he says. "With some conscious effort. Otherwise, it takes lifetimes."

"So you actually remember events from your past life here?" I ask, somewhat increduously.

He shrugs, probably thinking I don't believe him, but I smile, and he continues.

"Only a few old memories are real clear—like when my kid died. Most are just an idea of something that's too faded to see. Like an old photo that's gotten wet, okay? But people have told me a lot of stuff, so I put two and two together, and I know a lot of details from the past."

"Like what?" I say. "For example."

Manuel of Watsonville stands and lights another Marlboro before he begins to talk about a pastlife in the late 1200s as a Scribbler in Mayapán.

"PEOPLE LIVED AROUND these parts," he says, "for centuries before Mayapán was built, okay? We found pieces of their pottery in the dirt, and we used the stones from old foundations for our houses.

They probably settled here for the same reason we did—twenty-six good cenotes. The bad part is the soil—it's as thin as frog skin. Won't grow corn. Won't grow beans. So we got most of our food from farmers in the villages.

"By my time here, no one was keeping the traditional Maya Long Count anymore—which they kept as a running count from what they figured was the zero date on August 13, 3114 before Christ. But anyways, I have a very distinct impression—if not a memory—that my grandfather carved the first *te tun*, or tree stone, which is what the Maya called a stele, which I read was carved here in Mayapán in about 1185. There was a big ceremony, which is probably the reason I can get an impression of it, okay?

"There's a legend that the ruler Hunac Keel of Mayapán used a charm to trick Chak Xib Chak, the ruler of Chichén Itzá. Old Hunac Keel gave him a love potion made from a plumeria flower, which caused Chak Xib Chak to lust after the bride of the ruler of Izamal. This made the ruler of Izamal really mad—especially since his people had given so many sons in sacrifice for the sucking snake of Chichén Itzá. Hunac Keel used this problem as an excuse to attack Chichén and drive the Itzá out, and then he attacked Izamal. Later, the Itzá and the men of Izamal ganged up against Mayapán, but we beat them again, and they retreated. Again they attacked us—I tell you, revenge is like an open sore in a person's heart—and this time they won.

"There was chaos, okay? People turned against the leaders like pet dogs attacking their master. No man, woman, or child could find peace. Drought killed the corn, and people scavenged for food like vultures picking at rotting flesh. There was no order. Just corruption and fighting within families. Men practiced sorcery. They became thieves. They were sexually perverse. Evil walked the land.

"But finally, the wheel turned, and order restored itself. The Itzá established themselves here in 1263. They built houses for their nobles, and gave them towns according to their lineage and wealth so they could collect food and goods. But after twenty years, the Itzá leaders became corrupt too, and so other lords rose up against them and gained power. The city wall was reinforced.

"I have a vague memory of being a boy here. I was happy. I had five brothers, and my father, like his father, was a scribbler, an artisan who carved stone, so we had good standing and a good home.

"Twelve thousand people lived within Mayapán's walls. There were high priests and lords, rulers and officials, mercenary soldiers and servants, merchants and traders, and artisans who did masonry, stone cutting, wood carving, weaving, and tool making. The richest people got to build their houses on little hills, which kept them up out of the wet when it rained. The poorest lived at the edges of the city, and they had to walk the farthest to get water from the cenotes. My father was a scribbler so we lived right next to a cenote. Our house had two rooms and stuccoed walls and a thatch roof. There was a low stone fence around our property—and beyond it were streets and alleys.

"When I was a boy, kindness was the law. Food was abundant, and the farmers in outlying towns sent in birds, maize, honey, salt, fish, game, cloth. It was the time of the *halach uinic*, the true man.

"As a man with children of my own, I made four pilgrimages to the great Cenote of Sacrifice in Chichén Itzá. I can still remember one offering I made—I threw a necklace of thirteen jade beads into the cenote in the hope that my oldest son would live. He was sick with an infestation. The shamans couldn't cure him, and the jade beads I offered didn't do any good either. I can imagine the beads still laying there silent in the mud just like my son's body lays in the Earth.

"Some people made human sacrifices. As a special petition to the gods, they'd throw a slave into the Cenote of Sacrifice. One of my younger sons wanted to offer himself for the sake of his brother. But I wouldn't allow it. I didn't want to lose two sons.

"After awhile, the good times ended. Maya fought Maya. My grandsons defended our land, but Mayapán was overrun. Our people were captured and enslaved, and our nobles joined the Tutul Xiu from Uxmal.

"By 1400, most everyone had left Mayapán—this is what the

history books say—I was long dead by then and don't remember that part. People burned the city as they left and robbed treasures from the caches and burials. By 1520, the Europeans brought the Maya the deadly gift of smallpox, and the people fell like flies. In 1542, the Spaniards conquered the Yucatán, and Christianity became the religion.

"But that was long, long after my lifetime. By then I had died of pneumonia, leaving dozens of grandchildren and great-grandchildren. Some of my descendants still live in Telchaquillo.

"And that's my story," he finishes.

"But what good does it do you to know all of this?" I ask.

The man smiles. "I know now I'm part of something bigger than just me, okay? Maybe it happened so I'd sober up and stop wasting my life. Maybe so I'd see that what I choose to do each day will affect me in some way forever. Maybe you're part—aw, hell, who knows?"

IT'S LATE AFTERNOON when David and I walk back to Mayapán's ceremonial pyramid. The wind has come up and it tosses the trees, making their stiff joints creak and complain. Parrots flap across the sky, squawking as they fly. The Sun hangs low in the west.

We climb the pyramid's sixty steps. Up top, the temple is roofless, but its floor wears a nice, thick coat of stucco, and I take off my shoes and feel it underfoot. It's strangely comforting. Restored in 1998, this pyramid brought a surprise with it into the 21st Century. When its reconstruction was complete, it revealed a pattern of nine triangles of sunlight descending from its temple to the ground on the winter and summer solstices. While Chichén Itzá's pyramid marks the spring and fall equinoxes on March 21 and September 22 with seven triangles of light, Mayapán's pyramid marks the solstices on December 21 and June 21.

David and I sit in the pyramid's temple watching the Sun drop. The trees that border the plaza seem to catch the yellow bulb and

shatter it into a billion fragments of light. I get my notebook and write:

Mayapán—a bridge between the old order of the ancients and the New Order that is Our Time.
The past becoming the future.

I remember the cigarette filter in my pocket and touch it and smile about the inanity of pretending to smoke. Where is Manuel of Watsonville as the Sun dies to the day? Does he see it differently because of the ancient scribbler that watches through his eyes? Whether or not I buy the idea of any of us having a pastlife, certainly the altar figure from his grandpa changed the course of his life. As humans, we're always becoming our new experiences. We're always becoming.

I glance at David and wonder if there's something in his long-past that whispers the word "Maya" to him.

FERNANDO TURNS THE taxi onto the road to Mérida, and we ride through a canyon of dark foliage. The air blowing in the open window smells of damp leaves and chicken feathers and manure. The Sun has passed on, and the sky bleeds red from smog and dust. Venus twinkles as the evening star. "Twinkle, twinkle, little star . . ."

I remember being a little girl and wishing on the first star of the evening, probably brilliant Venus, whose appearance in the west at sunset signaled to the ancient Maya the time for blood sacrifice. When I was ten years old, I got my little brother Rob from star-wishing (my mother's sacrifice) and also a piano (my father's work). I make a wish now as the shadows lengthen over the Yucatán, although I'm bound by the Law of Star-Wishing not to talk about it until it comes true.

The crack of rifle fire sounds in the distance, the shot cleaving the silence like an axe striking the slaughtering block. I think of the little deer we saw in the forest, and I wonder if deer will be becoming human. ▲

16. Mérida

On the Road...

WE'RE SICK. WE'VE eaten in a once-popular restaurant (closed now, or I'd name it for everyone's protection), ordering spaghetti bolognese for David and alfredo for me, and now we're both as sick to our stomachs as we've ever been. Within a couple of hours of eating, we're taking turns in the bathroom, hurling the curdled contents of our stomachs, time after time, until there's nothing left, and the cruel act of retching yields nothing but pain and indignity.

I vomit so violently that if I were wearing shoes, I'd check to see if they still had their laces. I retch so deeply that my body tightens like a slingshot. The sound is so loud (echoing through the open-air corridor) that when I later order room service just before the restaurant closes—Diet Coke and lemonade—the waiter José also brings chamomile tea with honey and lemon.

"For *dolor de estomago*," he says. For a bellyache.

"How did you know?" I ask.

He just smiles.

I sip the delicate warm liquid, which stays awhile before presenting itself again going the other direction from my mouth. But at least it's easier to vomit than the diseased pasta.

David and I lie in bed like sad turtles on a sterile beach as the hours of the night glide by, and then the next day, without much participation from us. In the afternoon, Rita wants to know if she can tidy the room. David hauls himself up to the pool for an hour, and I sit in a rocker in the corridor, hunched over and patted with sympathy in my run-down state by passing hotel employees.

Normally, it's easy to stay well in Mérida. The municipal water supply is treated to be potable, so dishes and utensils are safe, even when damp. Visitors can rinse their toothbrush in tap water without fear of getting something horrible. But because the water is generally considered to have too many minerals to be good-tasting, the restaurants all serve filtered water. So there's double protection.

Visitors to Mérida aren't exposed to the assault of exotic respiratory viruses that often grip beach resorts where the influx of people from all over the world swamps the waiters (who then serve microorganisms with orders of pasta and guacamole). Most colds here occur when an El Norte cold front whistles down from Canada (blame Canada!) bringing cold rain and wind. Nighttime temperatures of 60

José brings an order of food from the restaurant.

degrees Fahrenheit or below are difficult for people when their homes have no heating system.

When Rita is done with the room, I slip back in between the soft, comforting sheets, becoming nothing more than an S-shape under the apricot-colored cotton. My body is, by turns, cold and hot. It's miserable. Bed-bound. It's a clunky no go, like a car on a sub-zero morning—you turn the key and there's the er-er-er-er-er of the ignition, but no spark. Today there's just the call of the bathroom again, and that awful retching with no result. In passing, I catch sight of myself in the mirror and see in my sunken eyes a look like a young mother-dog giving birth to puppies for the first time. Pained. Confused. Trapped, with no choice but to submit. Reflecting the suffering of the incarnate since Time Immemorial.

Back from the pool, David crawls into bed, and soon sleep envelops him. I close my eyes and let the soft up-down of his breathing relax me. But even as I doze, the idea for a book begins to feverishly write itself in my head. The mind flows like a cascade of water. It shimmers. It's brilliant and intriguing. It's like a seductive river—I have to stand back and marvel at its complexity.

I consider getting up to write what I see, but I'm feeling sick again, and anyway, when the mind (spirit?) is rolling, it races almost too fast for the fingers (with pen or keyboard) to catch. It leaps from exploring earthly caves to imagining cosmic beaches and returns from its odyssey with plans and memories too densely compacted to be easily set down. The body can barely keep up with the layer upon layer of visuals swirling in the mind's eye. Mostly a faithful companion, the body cannot do what it cannot do. Especially when it's sick.

With the door to thought now open, I begin to fret over experiences not yet recorded and missed days on the road. I sneak out of bed to get my notebook and decide to break my own rule about not reading my journal entries and subjecting them to the harsh light of judgment. In the dim light from the shuttered window, I read handwriting that goes from neat and meticulous for historical details (and especially dates) to scrawling loops for breathy descriptions to words meandering all over the page for dreams recorded by moonlight.

But suddenly, my descriptions seem trite to me. They have skips in the logic. The accounts of the sites seem either barren—like a skull without fat and flesh—or as over-the-top with emotion as if they'd been written by a hormonal adolescent. The notes seem like part of a jigsaw puzzle composed of two hundred days' worth of experiences with no overriding picture (from the lid of the box) to follow in putting them together. I have the dreadful feeling that I'll never be able to pull them into a cohesive whole.

And for what?

I'm suddenly so tired (and my stomach hurts again), and I wonder what in the hell we're doing here in Mérida. Whether we should just go home. Whether I'm capable of finding my way on this new path. Whether there is a path! There's a hole in my middle that isn't related to the diseased food as I think of all the things at home that need me—family, house, bank account—and I wonder if we're deluding ourselves. I shut the notebook and let it drop to the tile floor beside the bed.

These are not thoughts I want to share with David. It would be like handing him a stinky, dead fish, and since he's in the same canoe as I am—sick and fatigued—I keep quiet. In the seventies, I thought that people had to get to the bottom of every last feeling about everything. Now, I can let a few things pass without comment. My general guideline is that if something bothers me for four days running—and doesn't seem to be related to mood—then I'll bring it up.

But David has caught wind of my misgivings on the PNN, the Psychic News Network. He sits up. He stands up. He turns on the light and goes over to pull open the big drawer of the floor chest we've designated as his while my stuff is in the dresser. He gets out the perfectly organized plastic pouches of fresh film awaiting his artistry among his folded shorts and T-shirts and socks. He puts them on the bed (in the curve of my knees) and begins to count them. I keep my eyes shut, keeping myself on the margin of this page.

Then he gets up and opens the wall-safe. While the fresh film resides among his clothes, the exposed film is kept in the wall-safe with our passports and plane tickets and money. Like an auditor reconciling an account, he counts the canisters of film. There are thirty-four rolls of exposed film for this segment of the trip, and thirty-one rolls of fresh. He's disturbed. Things don't add up. One roll of exposed film is missing.

"How can that be!" he says.

"Did you check the pockets of your photo vest?" I say, turning over. I know what good care he takes of his film.

"Yes," he says, and begins a recount.

Exposed film is infinitely more valuable to him than fresh. It's not just the cost of the roll, nor even the investment of time and money it takes to shoot it. It represents Potential. It might hold the one unique shot that would pull a series together. It's irreplaceable. And it's impossible to know which photos are on the missing roll.

David counts again. My stomach hurts and I drift. I hear him putting the film away, feel him coming to bed.

"Did you find it?" I ask.

But he's already asleep again. I touch his face, it's feverish.

A few more hours and we feel duty-bound to feed our bodies something. Although the thought of eating seems repugnant, we've gone almost twenty-four hours without food. A phone call to the restaurant brings the waiter Julio with *sopa de lima*, chicken soup with lime, for David and lentil soup for me.

After we eat, David attempts a recount of the film. Again the fresh rolls come out of the shorts drawer. Again the exposed film comes from the safe. Again the count is off by one roll. (I can't understand how he knows it's exposed film instead of fresh if it's missing.) I cluck sympathetically.

"Did you check your photo vest?" I ask again, remembering that it has twenty-two (patented) pockets.

"I did," he says, irritated.

"Well, maybe you should check again."

More counting. More trying to recall where things stood at the last accurate count (like a bed check in prison). More frustration over where the missing roll might have gone.

"Have you tried all the pockets of your shorts?" I ask.

He gets up and checks the pockets of his photo vest. He pulls out the missing roll of film—which has indeed been exposed.

"I swear I checked it," he says.

"You're sick," I say, and wish my doubts over my journal entries could so easily be explained away.

The tally complete, the film goes back into the safe and drawer.

We sleep until morning without seeing the *sopa de lima* and lentil soup again during the night. Breakfast goes well, and from that point on, we quickly regain our strength.

My body is beginning to feel strong again. It's ready to go. I sometimes think it's the weak link when I want to do something and can't manage it physically. And yet, it's the body that takes the gossamer threads gathered by mind (spirit?) and begins to weave them together, asking, "Now what can we make from this?"

That's what I like about the body. It finds a patch of sunlight, and wants to sit in it. It finds cool water, and wants to put its feet in it. And when the mind comes upon a seed of an idea, it's the body that sits behind the keyboard of the computer hour after hour after hour quietly making the idea manifest.

A COUPLE OF days later, David and I are walking over to the newsstand for a copy of the daily *Mexico City News*. In the corridor near the Governor's Palace, a man is pushing a big, gray string mop back and forth across the cement.

"You know that spaghetti we ate?" David asks.

"Yeah."

"Well, it was actually the strings from the mop the restaurant had been using on the floor," he says.

I don't laugh. I don't smile. In fact, it makes me shudder—it's probably way too close to the truth. Now, whenever I see a string mop with its industrial, metal bucket (and milky, pine-scented water), I think of that horrid pasta—vomited, but not forgotten. ▲

17. Izamal

Pilgrims and Miracles...

MANUEL'S TAXI PURRS like a lap cat as we wait for a traffic cop to clear the knot of buses from the narrow Mérida street. Manuel is our *taxista* today, and our destination is the quaint little city of Izamal, where ancient pilgrims once asked for favors from the Maya god Itzamná—and where pilgrims still ask for miracles from the Virgin of Izamal.

As we wait in the snarl, a bit of poetic graffiti on a wall catches my eye. On the broad expanse of a yellow building, a street philosopher has spray-painted in red, foot-tall letters a sentence which I copy into my notebook:

Morning flutters on angel wings,
and sighing, gives herself over to the day.

The image is bitter sweet—pristine beauty sacrificing her joy of flight to harness herself into the day. The old Maya saw each day as being the work and responsibility of the day-god (there are twenty) whose duty it is to carry the day from dawn to dusk. (Just as we work our jobs from nine to five.) As such, each day is a creation never-to-be-repeated in all of Time. In each day, there is magic, which we can act upon as we see fit. I write in my notebook:

Do I see this day as being sacred,
and everyone I meet?

Manuel gets a wave from the traffic cop, and the taxi glides forward, warming to the hour-long drive ahead. Today David and I are in the backseat of Manuel's '89 Dodge Dart on our way to climb the largest pyramid in all of the Maya realm. We've ridden with Manuel several times, splitting our day-trips between him and Fernando. He's originally from a small town not far from Chichén Itzá where most of the people have Maya ancestors. In his late thirties, he's stocky, muscular, shorter by a head than we are, and has an easy laugh that bubbles often to the surface. He reads The New Testament or the AA way of twelve steps while he's waiting at a site for us. Or sleeps with a newspaper over his face. He's as right as rain.

He also drives with no hurry, finding the perfect speed to baby his taxi while serving his clients. At this speed, tree trunks beside the

road have a distinct shape, as do many of the flower stems. The Pepsi truck passes with ease, and the taxi calls after it, hey, what's your hurry?

As he drives, Manuel provides a commentary on the scenery. If Fernando's into food, Manuel's into context. Passing a clothing factory where Lee jeans are assembled, he points to a tangle of a hundred bikes parked in front.

"The factory's a good thing," he says, "people can find work here in their village without having to go to Cancún."

At a pile of trash dumped beside the road—"A bad thing, it doesn't look good for the tourists."

At a village where women embroider and cross-stitch the finest *huipiles*—"A wonderful thing. Only a few women in the Yucatán still keep that art alive."

And as we approach Izamal—"City of three cultures. Maya, colonial, and modern," he says.

"Now four cultures," David says.

Manuel looks in the rearview mirror, his lips curving, ready to open for a laugh.

"Tourists," David says.

Manuel's laugh begins in his belly. "Yes, tourists. City of four cultures."

IZAMAL: CITY OF huge pyramids made from huge stones. Named for either the Itzá who once conquered it or the Maya god Itzamná, seen as the father-creator, the Sun, and the macaw parrot symbolizing the celestial bird. While the city was once called Itzamal, the "t" fell from its name at some point, perhaps dropped by the Spaniards who wanted to let the whole Itzamná/Itzá thing drop into ancient history. But now the "t" is starting to reappear on maps and in publications.

Izamal is also known as the Yellow City. For years, the buildings in its city center had worn yellow paint. Then, in 1993, in preparation

for a visit by Pope John Paul II, who was coming to present the Virgin of Izamal with a gold crown, every government office, house, storefront, wall, and fence was repainted in the rich yellow of old gold. The yellow-green of duck egg yolks. Daffodilly, buttery, mustardy yellow. The traditional Maya color for the direction south.

"Now everyone wanting a miracle comes to the Yellow City," Manuel says.

On our last trip to Izamal we climbed its pyramids, so this time we decide to start at its intriguing old Catholic mission, the ex-Convent of San Antonio de Padua, which occupies the base of an ancient pyramid. Manuel drives to the center of town and carefully parks the taxi in the *zócolo* under a shade tree.

"It'll be awhile," David tells him.

"*Si, claro,*" Manuel says. Yes, of course, and he picks up a thick red cloth with which to shine the little taxi.

We walk across the street to a long, stone ramp leading up to the mission. Beside the ramp, a man is setting votive candles on a little wooden stand. A boy is unloading plastic flutes from a backpack, placing them on a cloth on the stone. A woman is placing on a rack little medal *milagros*, or miracles, cast in the shape of a heart, an arm, a leg, a man, a baby. They swing from brightly colored embroidery thread.

"Do you want to buy a milagro?" she asks as we approach. "Just three pesos."

It's a small price for a miracle. I take two.

The ramp is wide, its worn stones slick and shiny from so many shoe soles. (And souls?) At its top is the large atrium, or courtyard, that fronts the church, and we stand at the edge of a broad expanse of clipped lawn enclosed by deep, graceful arches delicately posed on square columns. Elevated sixteen feet above street level, the atrium measures some four-hundred feet long by two-hundred feet wide, which makes it the second largest enclosed atrium in the world (only smaller than that of the Vatican). And yet it takes up only the front portion of the ancient Maya terrace, which also supports the large mission and its cloister.

"Look through that arch," David says.

He points to the distant Kinich Kak Mo pyramid perfectly framed in the semi-circle of the arch, and then takes shot after shot of the pyramid, the arches, and the arches' shadow phantoms on the ground. With each shot, the whir of the camera's motor drive advances the film, as though making a small exclamation.

I sit on a concrete banquette beside the atrium's back wall, enjoying the bright morning. The courtyard is as pristine as a Zen meditation room. Green grass (floor). Blue sky (ceiling). White arches (pattern and order). The stone walkway that divides it (humanity).

After several minutes, David comes to sit down beside me. "I've been thinking," he says, "that we should do a book."

"A book?"

"Of what we've been seeing—notes and photos. You know, travel to the Maya pyramids."

I look at my notebook in my lap, the third I've filled so far. But before I can answer, a man approaches. Purposefully. Another human in this Zen Eden.

"Do you know that on special feast days people crawl to the church on their knees until they bleed?" the man says. He extends his hand to David and introduces himself as Humberto, of the Tourist Police. He's trim in a brown uniform. In his forties, with graying hair and large, soft, brown eyes. "Do you also know that the old Maya pyramid Ppap-Hol-Chaak once stood here? The House of Heads and Rays."

"Heads and rays?" I say.

"Chaak faces and lightning bolts," Humberto says. "For the storm god who once brought rain."

Chaak, always Chaak, in this land where people depended on rain for their corn and honey.

"Yes, we met him in Uxmal," David says with a smile.

The mission's enclosed atrium is the world's second largest, smaller only than that of the Vatican.

IT'S IMPOSSIBLE TO talk about Izamal without mentioning Friar Diego de Landa, the Franciscan monk whose mission it was to convert the natives of the Yucatán to Catholicism. The Christianization of this part of the New World was an extraordinary campaign carried out with great fervor. Governmental regulations of the Yucatán written in 1553 called for each village to have a church, and so after soldiers had secured an area, the first order of business was the construction of a monastery to serve as a base for the Spanish *frailes*, or friars. (Humberto pronounces this as "fri-lays.") With their priest-architects drawing up the plans, the Franciscans turned out missions almost like a production line, giving towns an austere chapel with none of the Gothic frills

A Maya couple stands in the atrium under the protective gaze of the statue of Pope John Paul II. The top of one of the four large pyramids that surrounded the plaza is visible over the wall.

found in European cathedrals, a plain cloister to house the monks, a wellhead built over a cenote, and an open-air chapel for the natives, or *indios*, as the Maya were called. But while Izamal's mission conformed to the Franciscan style, it was—and clearly is—extraordinary, made grand by de Landa's interest in it.

De Landa arrived in the Yucatán in 1549 as assistant to Friar Lorenzo de Bienvenida, guardian of the northern Yucatán. In touring the area, de Landa one day climbed to the top of one of Izamal's pyramids, and it so impressed him that he later wrote: "There is here in Izamal one building among the others of such height and beauty that it is frightening."

When de Landa himself became guardian of the Yucatán in 1552, he ordered an army of Maya men to dismantle the "Heads and Rays" pyramid down to the level of the terrace and build a mission in its place. A later Franciscan wrote that de Landa chose the site for the mission so that a "place that had been one of abomination and idolatry could become one of sanctity."

The mission became one of the grandest undertakings in the Yucatán fueled by the number of available stones and de Landa's desire to sanctify a pagan place. With the Maya giving their labor as a form of tribute to the Church as they had once given tribute to the Maya lords, they laid course after course of stone. The mission took nine years to complete, and was finished in 1561. Later, one bishop, remarking on its size, said, "It is a fine thing to see and a scandal to permit it, for surely Saint Francis condemns it in his Rule."

"But it wasn't de Landa who dictated its size," Humberto says, "but the base of the pyramid."

David and I nod, ready to return to our pre-Humberto reverie, not immediately aware of the synchronicity in meeting him.

"Come now and see the window of the Virgin," Humberto urges, and we somewhat reluctantly get up and follow him into the center of the atrium where he points up to a large window in the mission's front wall. Shaped like a keyhole, it frames a stained (or painted) glass image of the young Virgin of Izamal looking out over the courtyard. Two keys hang from cords around her waist—the keys to heaven and the Church, Humberto tells us. At her feet is a thin, silver crescent of the New Moon, upturned and with a star on each of its points.

"The Moon was a device to draw the indios into the Catholic church," Humberto says. "The Maya greatly loved their goddess Ixchel—and when the fry-lays explained the similarities between her and the Virgin Mary, little by little the indios accepted the new religion. You see?"

Yes, we see.

"And see beside her on the wall—the two frogs?" he says. "People still say that when it's going to rain, those little frogs still sing."

Humberto walks us toward the church door, passing a statue of Pope John Paul II keeping watch with the Virgin over the atrium. Inside, the church is cool and silent and shadowy in this early morning hour with a dozen or so people praying in pews toward the front. The nave is long at one-hundred-seventy feet and narrow with a high, medieval, vaulted ceiling. On the altar is a small, gold crucifix. In the center aisle, a gap two fingers wide runs the length of the church. I turn to ask Humberto why.

"Because of the cenote underneath," he says. "Its humidity would ruin the floor if not for the gap."

"There's a cenote?" I say. "Can we see it?"

"It's sealed," he says, "But look up and you'll see our Virgin of Izamal, our lady of miracles."

The statue of a petite young woman surveys the sanctuary from a niche high above the altar. She's dressed in white and wears a gold crown on top of a veil that covers her long, dark hair. But the finer details are hard to see.

According to chroniclers, Friar de Landa brought this statue of the Virgin from Antigua, Guatemala, in 1558, and saved it until the mission was completed in 1561. Even on the long journey to Izamal, miracles began to happen: Strapped to a donkey, the Virgin stayed dry during several rainstorms.

Once installed in the mission, the Virgin became the first official Catholic focus of pilgrimage in the Yucatán, which already had a strong tradition of pilgrimages to Cenotes of Sacrifice such as the one in Chichén Itzá. The Maya had long traveled to Izamal to petition Itzamná for favors, but they especially venerated Ixchel, the great Mother goddess. In her, they saw the virginal New Moon—the pure mother who bore the Hero Twins who defeated Death and prepared the way for humanity. Ixchel was also seen as the celestial midwife, defeater of disease, weaver, female counterpart of Itzamná, and Lady of the Rainbow. She was attendant at every new birth and the salve for every sorrow. People loved Ixchel, and under the instruction of the friars, they came to transfer their love for her to the Virgin of Izamal, the woman of purity and mercy standing with the upturned slice of Moon with two stars at her feet.

During the 1600s, love for her bloomed in the hearts of Maya and Spaniards alike. People loved her so much that parishioners in the city of Valladolid, near Chichén Itzá, became jealous that the Virgin resided in Izamal, and asked the bishop for permission to move her to Valladolid.

"They wondered why she should remain in Izamal—which had mostly indios—when Valladolid had more Spaniards," Humberto says.

Their request granted, twenty Spaniards on horses came to Izamal on the appointed day, and ordered forty Maya men to carry the Virgin to Valladolid on a great palanquin. The troupe had gone scarcely more than a hundred yards from the mission door when the Maya men set the palanquin down, saying that the Virgin had become too heavy to carry. Believing this to be a ruse, the Spaniards dismounted from their horses and prepared to lift the palanquin themselves. But they couldn't budge it, even when they ordered the Maya men to help. The Spaniards wondered how one small statue carved from acacia wood could be so heavy, but seeing that they could do nothing more at the time,

they ordered the Maya men to carry her back into the mission. This was easily accomplished, and the Spaniards declared the incident as a miracle while the Maya took it as a sign that the Catholic Virgin Mother was as responsive to them as Ixchel had always been.

The Virgin of Izamal continued to develop a reputation for miracles: She was taken three times to Mérida to stop a famine, an epidemic, and a plague of locusts.

Then in 1829, a terrible fire in the church burned the statue of the Virgin. And yet, miraculously, it was revealed that de Landa had actually carted two identical statues of the Virgin from Guatemala—the one that was destroyed by fire and her twin, which had been safely harbored in a home in Mérida. The twin statue of the Virgin was taken to Izamal, and the miracles continued.

When the Maya rose up against their "white" oppressors in the War of the Castes in 1847, they rampaged through Izamal but spared the mission and the Virgin, even stopping to pay their respects to her.

Then, in 1949, Our Lady of Izamal was declared Queen and Patroness of the Yucatán by papal decree. In 1993, Pope John Paul II came to town to present her with a precious, bejeweled, (real) gold crown. Now on the feast day of the Immaculate Conception on December 8, men and women (many of them Maya, with the women wearing the traditional *huipil*) come from throughout the Yucatán to pray at the feet of this beloved image of the Virgin, whom they believe can help them better their lives. After Mass, many then take a walk up the Kinich Kak Mo pyramid.

HUMBERTO POINTS US to a side door of the church, and we step out into a small, sunny courtyard where an almost life-size picture of the Virgin of Izamal is sheltered inside a stone grotto. Dozens of candles are burning at her feet.

"Candles are forbidden in the church since the fire," he says. "But you can light one out here if you want."

"But, we . . . " I begin, stopping when he produces a small candle from his pocket. Like the ancient altar figure that I held in my palm in Mayapán, it's warm from body heat.

"I noticed you didn't buy one on your way in," he says, and turns and goes inside the church.

David and I survey the tall, iron, spiked fence across the front of the niche. I think I can squeeze through the opening at the end.

"Shall we light it?" I ask.

"We've lit them everywhere else," David says, probably thinking of all of the Greek Orthodox, Christian, Coptic, and Catholic churches in which we've lit candles, and the shrines, grottos, and caves.

"Well, what's our intention for it?" I ask.

"To be able to turn these photos and notes into a book," he says without hesitation.

"Really?" I ask, turning to look at him. "Is that what we want to do?"

"Yes, do you agree?"

"Yes," I say, and we shake hands on it before I squeeze past the last iron spike at the end.

Inside the fence, I light the short wick of our candle from one that's burning. I hold my hand up against the draft that threatens to extinguish it. The flame is small, flickers uncertainly, and comes dangerously close to dying, and I wonder what it would mean to our request if it were to go out. But slowly, slowly, the little fire burns through the wax on the wick, and the slim taper grows fat and strong. I set it among the other candles. Flames lit by the faithful flicker in tall and tiny glasses: Old-fashioned ice-tea tumblers with happy borders of blue, yellow and red flowers stand alongside souvenir shot glasses with "Yucatán" on them in gold letters. Wicks near the bottom of the tall glasses get little oxygen and produce oily smoke that blackens the glass. Glasses that have gotten too hot have shattered, sending shards flying over the altar like black seeds.

The Virgin stands serenely above it all. Around her, thumbnail photos of smiling and serious people have been pushed between the frame and the glass to make a wreath of faces around her like a cartouche. The people pose in front of the heavy curtains of discount-store photo booths and the sky-blue backdrops of school photographers. Men and women, grandmas and grandpas, babies and little girls and boys stare out from their place in the Virgin's garland, souls pleading for a miracle. Some of the photos are curled and faded with age, and I wonder if they've outlived the people they show.

"She truly does grant miracles," a woman says.

I turn and look at the woman on the other side of the iron fence. She's dark-haired, in her twenties, with a plump, round face. On her hip is a little girl of about four wearing a frilly pink-and-white dress, her hair caught up in two high ponytails.

"See that picture," the woman says, pointing to a little girl smiling from a photo pushed into the frame. "That's her, my little daughter here."

She tells me that when she was six months pregnant, she began to bleed heavily. She knew she was about to miscarry—she had lost three babies when she reached six months.

"They were too young to survive," she says. "And so I was desperate. I didn't think I could live through another dead baby. So I told my husband to bring me here. He couldn't borrow a car, so we took the bus. I thought I'd lose the baby on the way."

Inside the church, she threw herself down at the feet of the Virgin of Izamal.

"I prayed for my baby with all of my heart," she says, tears welling in her eyes and running down her cheeks. "I called upon her compassion as a mother."

Within hours, the bleeding stopped, and she carried the baby full term.

"This is my miracle," the woman says, squeezing the little girl. "Now, each year we come here on her birthday to visit the Virgin and put up a new picture. Tomorrow we'll have a party."

I start toward the opening in the fence, saying, "Here, I'll move so you can get in here."

"No, wait," the woman says. "Can you put this photo for us? I can't get through the fence." She pats her belly, which is just beginning to swell with pregnancy.

She passes a little photo of the girl through the iron spikes, and I retrieve last year's birthday photo and put the new one in its place.

"Next year, I'll have two pictures to put up," the woman says.

AS DAVID AND I walk back into the church, Humberto jumps up from a pew. He motions to us, and we follow him out a door on the opposite side of the church into an open-air corridor beside a court-yard. He leads us up a flight of stairs (made from pyramid stones), then another, then final steps that form a curved apron of stone at the entrance to a single, high room.

"You're in luck today," Humberto says in a whisper. "The camarín is open."

The *camarín* is the chapel behind the sanctuary where the Virgin of Izamal is dressed and cared for and resides when there's no Mass in session. The room is large and high-ceilinged with walls the deep coral-orange of Tibetan monasteries, the sky at dawn, ancient Maya pyramids, and the Sherwin-Williams paint Valencia 1616. (What *is* there about that color?) Its only furnishing is a single, old pew facing a glass door. The pew has three stark wooden chairs and a kneeler of purple crushed velvet where a priest is hunched in devotion. Opposite the priest, a middle-aged man and woman stand at the glass door, pressing their palms against it. Only then do I realize that behind the glass stands the statue of the Virgin.

She is petite—perhaps the size of a delicate young woman of the 1500s. Her hands are raised to the level of her heart, fingertips lightly touching in an attitude of prayer. Her face—beautiful with its perfect,

even features—is tilted down and a little to one side. Her skin color is the delicate tan of milky coffee with the slightest blush in the cheeks. Her lips curve in a soft pink smile. Her rich, walnut-colored hair tumbles long, and on her head is a stunning gold crown studded with sapphires (a replica, Humberto says, with the Pope's precious gift locked away for safe-keeping).

"More luck!" Humberto says in an urgent whisper. "You can see the Virgin's wardrobe."

The door to a walk-in closet stands open a few inches, and we press our faces between the jamb and the door and look in. The Virgin's clothes hang from a rod on the right side of the closet—size zero dresses of fine, brilliant, white lace with linen petticoats and velvet side-panels the color of sea foam. Rich brocade dresses beaded with tiny pearls. White dresses embroidered with gold. Blue velvet cloaks with gold trim. Garments fit for a queen.

Cupboard drawers on the left are closed, and I can imagine the little undergarments and slippers in them, the wigs and lace veils. A feeling of intimacy—of knowingness—rises in me as I stand among the trappings of this revered, miracle-granting queen as though I were in my sister's or mother's bedroom.

A flock of noisy middle-aged American women flies into the camarín, and the women squawk about the high cost of their hotel accommodations. The priest rises from the kneeler and hurries to pad-lock the closet door. Only the middle-aged couple at the glass door seems oblivious to the women, their faces lifted to the Virgin of Miracles, their eyes pleading as their mouths form silent words, in-voking, I imagine, the Law of Grace to grant their request. Was it this spirit of mercy the ancient Maya called upon for the miracle of rain?

As we wait for the middle-aged couple to finish their prayers and move on so we can see the Virgin more closely, we examine the many oil paintings hanging on the red walls. Several show scenes from Jesus's life, while in others once-famous bishops and priests of the Yucatán gaze across the centuries from their place in history. In one,

A priest watches a ceremony from the top of the church wall.

A tiny, old "Mamita" patiently waits outside the mission door for pesos.

Friar de Landa, thin faced and with ashen skin, looks not outward, but at the floor, his eyes downcast and veiled beneath their lids. In his zeal to replace the Maya religion with Christianity, it was he who ordered the destruction of all of the Maya almanacs and history books. Who denounced Maya altar figures as idols and ordered them to be smashed. Who tortured the Maya men in an *auto de fe,* a brutal New World Inquisition, until they were broken and looked at him with blood in their eyes.

Turning from his portrait, I suddenly realize that on either side of the glass doors is a simple wooden grill with nothing between the Virgin and the viewer. I think of Manuel, waiting in the *zócolo* with the taxi, and I hurry down to get him.

Manuel is burnishing the taxi's white paint with a damp cloth. The decade-old Dart was never an expensive car—even new—and

yet it's the venerable workhorse that helps him support his family. It's his team of Clydesdales. His wealth. And yet, he immediately stows the polish cloth and comes with me to climb the steps and see the Virgin in her private chamber.

In the camarín, the middle-aged couple has gone, leaving sweaty palm prints on the glass. The loud American women have flown, and the priest has left. I take the velvet kneeler on the left, placing my knees on fabric crushed by thousands of bony patellas, and look up at the Virgin. With her sweet face tilted slightly down, she appears to be looking at me, her gentle brown eyes holding mine, inviting my request. My only impulse is to give thanks for the hope she gives all the people who stand before her in prayer. Hope brings its own blessing.

As we prepare to leave the camarín, the middle-aged couple who had earlier been praying approaches us. Dark trails of ruined mascara stain the woman's cheeks.

"Excuse me," she says, "we don't mean to interrupt, but are you from the United States?"

"Yes, we are," David says. "Can we help you?"

"Do you know the name of a good children's hospital in Houston?" she asks. "Our little grandson—he's only a year old—needs a liver transplant. We're praying for a miracle."

We tell them what little we know about hospitals and transplants, and they thank us and leave. I glance again at the Virgin, where their prayers—as hand prints—are still visible in front of her on the glass.

"What happens to people's faith when their prayers aren't answered?" I ask.

"Maybe it just grows stronger," David says. "People usually know why things happen. Even when it isn't what they want, they gradually come to know the good in it. You know that line in the song?—'You get what you need.'"

He's quoting the Rolling Stones.

"Really," Humberto says confidentially, "I think it's better to adore Jesus. People should turn their prayers to him now instead of

Confetti and balloons rain down on the Virgin of Izamal and the men who carry her through the streets on the feast of the Immaculate Conception on December 8.

the Virgin. Jesus can do more because he's God's son."

I take a final look at Our Lady of Izamal standing with the Earth at her feet and an upturned slice of the Moon studded with two stars. Holding the keys to heaven and the Church. And, not so obviously, the key to people's hearts. As the Mother, she is the carrier of life. Comforter of the sorrowful. Inspiration to the hopeless. Bestower of tender mercies.

"Humberto," I say, "which do you think were more important in the Maya culture—men or women?"

"Oh, men, of course," he says. "Even now, women have so many obligations. The old people, their husband, the children, the house and cooking. Where can they go? What can they possibly do?"

OUTSIDE, THE ATRIUM is still a (mostly) deserted Zen meditation room. Grass-green floor (growing). Water-blue ceiling (changing). White-washed arches (opening). Stone walkway playing tag with the shadows (amusing).

Beside the ramp going down to the street, a tiny old woman, as thin and dry as a corn husk, holds out her hand for a peso.

"Oh, *Mamita*," Manuel says warmly, addressing her with respect and affection as "little mama." He gives her a coin.

David gives her a coin, too.

"Gracias, *Papito*," she says, calling him "little papa."

"She called me Papito!" David whispers. "How old does she think I am?"

"Old enough to have a peso to give her," I say. "Come on, Papito, let's go get some lunch."

As we leave, the boy who had earlier been laying out the plastic flutes is playing a tune, and the piercing notes of Mary Had a Little Lamb rise in the air. ▲

18. Izamal

Eye in the Sky...

WE STROLL IZAMAL'S *zócolo* with its manicured trees and bushes and dozens of concrete benches (that withstand rain and termites) looking for somewhere to eat. Izamal has a few recommended restaurants with linens and menus, but we want to eat simply. Across the street, we see Mesón de Landa, the "table of de Landa," in a plain, little inn occupying one of the city's centuries-old buildings. I balk at going in—still vexed with the man who (according to one account of his zeal) destroyed "five thousand Maya idols of distinct formation and dimension, thirteen great rocks that seemed to be altars, twenty-three smaller rocks, twenty-seven columns with hieroglyphs, and one-hundred-ninety-two pieces of pottery." (Not to mention the men he ruined by torture during the *auto de fe* inquisition.) But we peek into the restaurant and find a pleasant courtyard where two tables of locals are eating lunch and decide to enter.

Manuel, David, and I sit at a long, plastic-covered table on a wide *portico,* or lobby, beside the courtyard. A boy of about fifteen emerges from the dark kitchen behind an old screen door and sets knives and forks on the table before he recites the three midday offer-

ings: *pollo pibil,* a traditional chicken dish; pork *empanizada,* a style of preparation I don't recognize; and a mixed meat dish. David and Manuel order the chicken, and I order the pork, and after the boy delivers our Diet Cokes and coffee, we settle back to enjoy our surroundings.

The building is wonderfully old. Like an elderly gentleman, it's beyond the stage where the focus is on its decline, and well into the stage where its survival makes it especially charming. The ceiling is twenty-five-feet high and made from *vigas,* or stout poles, with plaster filling the gaps between them. The smooth walls are the rich ivory of farm-cream (Ralph Lauren would love them)—from choice or age (I can't tell which)—accented with wooden molding painted a deep coconut brown. There's a bay for a horse-drawn carriage, now separated from the portico by brown, lathe-turned spindles. The floor is ceramic tile.

Near the kitchen door, a large, rectangular sink hangs on a wall, and I get up to wash my hands. The sink is high enough for Michael Jordan to use without stooping, and I step up onto a foot-tall block of stone in front of it to reach the faucet handles, feeling like Alice in Wonderland when things have gotten very, very big.

I've barely finished my coffee when the boy brings our food. The appointed meat choice takes center stage on large oval plates having generous helpings of rice and black beans. David begins to remove the banana leaves from around his *pollo pibil*—*pibil* referring to the traditional Maya style of cooking meat in a *pib*, or pit, in the ground. The meat is rubbed with achiote seasoning and the juice of a sour orange before being wrapped in banana leaves and steamed until tender. While Yucatecans still cook in a pit for special occasions, a conventional oven can turn out chicken that tastes almost as good.

My pork is delicious—it's pounded or cut to be very thin, then breaded. (So that's what empanizada means—"chicken fried.") The coating is thick and flavorful with just the right degree of flakiness, so that it's neither a coat of armor nor a sprinkling of crumbs. There's just enough grease for it to be supremely satisfying. The rice is plain, but the black beans are perfection—slow-cooked with onions, black pepper, and *epazote* (a mint-like leaf) until soft, then smashed into a rough paste. For accent, there's a mound of crisp pickled red onions.

The meal comes with a stack of warm tortillas, and David and Manuel dig into them, Manuel tearing each one into pieces and then holding the piece between his thumb and forefinger to neatly pinch bits of chicken, rice, or beans, eliminating the need for a fork.

As we eat, the waiter runs out of the kitchen with a platter of sliced tomatoes—meaty, deeply red, and more flavorful than any we can get at home except from the garden—dotted with slivers of white onion. There's no charge for them when the bill arrives.

Seeing us, an American couple come in, following the great Commandment of Tourism that says, "If a fellow tourist already has his food and still looks happy, then maybe the restaurant will work for you, too." But they just have Cokes and leave.

I ASK THE location of the restroom and am given a key attached to a large wooden paddle and pointed toward the back of the courtyard with the direction of *"derecho, derecho, izquierda,"* which seems to be the way to everything in the Yucatán. The traditional courtyard of the Yucatán is the family's own little *zócolo*: It provides the household with a center and order. It's here that the household well is located, along with the wooden sinks and washtubs necessary to clean babies, dishes, and clothes. Its trees provide shade and greenery, and perhaps there are some vegetables or herbs. Located at its front is the room that opens onto the street—the equivalent of a family room in the suburban United States—where the family chats with visitors, watches television, and sits down to a meal at a big dining table. Bordering the courtyard on one side (or both if there's enough land) are the bedrooms that shelter two, three, or even four generations of the family.

This particular courtyard has been enlarged toward the back, growing elongated with Time, like earlobes. In my search for the restroom, I follow a maze of walkways into the warren of small rooms that comprise the inn. Some doors are closed with padlocks while others stand open, revealing small, bare rooms lit by a single bulb where men sit on wooden chairs, smoking. Other people sit outside their rooms, leaning their chairs back against the wall, smoking. They watch my progress toward the rear of the compound like I'm a lab rat.

I turn down avenues that have neither an outlet nor the restroom I seek, but which reveal more of the building. Added onto room by room by room, it's a jumble—like the old miners' houses of the Rocky Mountains where rooms were added onto one side and then the other, like growths, as children and money came along. Towards the back, the amount of clutter increases—there's a cracked plastic mop bucket, an old Coke bottle, a broken, rusty bedspring. And then the rooms and walkway end. At the foot of a pyramid.

The inn's cubbyhole rooms abut the foot of an ancient pyramid like it's the house next door, albeit of a much older style. It's a startling juxtaposition, as though a big, gray, stone mushroom unexpectedly pushed up out of the ground beside the Mesón de Landa inn during a midnight rain storm and being too big to destroy (and of course, now protected), it has held its ground. With the cracked bucket and the rusty bedspring.

I suddenly get the picture of how and why the pyramid stones have gotten reused over the centuries. Quite simply it's because they're there. Like lemons on a tree planted by an ancestor, they've become ripe for the picking without much work from those who need nice, rectangular stones for a wall—the work of the long-dead making the work of the living much easier.

The roomers in the inn quite simply live with the pyramid. They move into and out of rooms. And in and out of Time.

VISITORS TO IZAMAL'S ex-Convent of San Antonio de Padua usually don't climb the Kinich Kak Mo pyramid, one of the city's twelve large pyramids, except at the feast of the Immaculate Conception. Even though Manuel has driven clients to Izamal many times, he hasn't been to the pyramid and drives right by its entrance—a narrow walkway in a row of shops and houses. Ironically, its lack of popularity is probably due to its enormity.

"You never see this pyramid on a postcard," I remark.

"Because it's too big to show up in a photo," David says. "Which is why it's hard to find. You don't even notice it from the street."

From the street to its summit, Kinich Kak Mo is as tall as a ten-story building, but its height is dwarfed by the dimensions of its enormous base—it's more than two football fields long and nearly as wide. This behemoth was built to honor Itzamná in his form of the celestial bird. *Kinich* refers to the spirit or entity that is the Sun—basically Itzamná as the Eye in the Sky keeping watch over humankind. *Kak Mo* translates as fire macaw, the big, red-feathered, bow-legged, talking guacamaya parrot of the tropics. *Kinich Kak Mo,* then, designates the pyramid as the "Place Where the Solar Entity Appears as the

Manuel, with his taxi, comes to collect us before sunrise one cool morning in Mérida.

Celestial Bird," and it was to this Maya pyramid that the holy bird came daily to collect the offerings of the faithful.

Manuel has turned the corner of the pyramid, going around it for another try at its entrance. Workmen are rebuilding this side, and as we pass we hear them speaking Yucatek Maya, one of the twenty-five dialects of Maya still spoken today. David wants to take photos of the newly worked stone, and Manuel stops the taxi and we all get out. The *jefe*, or boss, of the crew stops working to greet us.

"Big pyramid," I say. "It must have taken a lot of work to build it."

The jefe smiles, revealing gleaming gold teeth. He's probably about seventy, his face sun-worn and dissected with deep wrinkles that hold the memories of a lifetime. His brown eyes are bright and piercing, his proud back is ramrod straight. He wears a white guayabera shirt and a well-used Panama hat stained with rain and sweat, its brim roguishly curled. I can see it on Harrison Ford, or Clint Eastwood.

"It's going to take us fifteen years to restore this pyramid," he says. "And then there are the other ones."

Kinich Kak Mo's massive stones, the largest ever used in the realm of the Maya, have been its saving grace: Over the centuries, they've been simply too huge and too heavy to plunder. The smallest stones we see are the size of a microwave oven, while its cornice stones are the size of a dorm refrigerator. Its foundation stones are bigger still—as high and wide as the fancy double-wide refrigerators found in million-dollar homes, and weighing more.

I ask the jefe the Maya word for stone.

"*Tun,*" he says, adding that there are many words for something so vital to the Maya. He asks, "Do you want to learn to speak Maya?"

"Many people are coming here to study the language," I say. "They want to know a little Maya so they can understand the place names."

Like towns in the States are named "Sandy Point" and "Pine Bluffs" for a physical feature of the land, Maya place names incorporate such words as *sas* for white, *cab* for soil, and *ch'en* for a cenote.

"But the pronunciation is very difficult unless you're born to it," the jefe says. He utters several words having harsh glottal stops not normally used by English-speakers unless they're clearing a fish bone from their throats. "With the wrong accent, they can mean something else—something terribly offensive."

I nod my understanding. But as with most conversations undertaken in the Yucatán, there's a tacit commitment to seeing a topic through innumerable permutations. The old man goes over the subject of pronunciation three or four times as though working fertile ground—spading it, raking it, smoothing it, preparing it for whatever comes next.

"Of course, some Maya words sound like English," the jefe continues. "But they mean something different."

"Like what?" I ask.

"Like *miss,*" he says, "the word for a young woman—it means cat in Maya."

Manuel nods. "My family all spoke Maya when I was growing up," he says, "but it wasn't allowed in school. Only Spanish."

He tells us about an incident in his childhood just after his family moved to Mérida. His mother apparently had a problem with the gas bill—she was either applying to get cooking gas delivered to the house or was questioning the cost. (I don't know which, I can't quite get this nuance.) Manuel stands with his feet apart, holding the imaginary paper in his hand and bending his head as though to look at it. He's replaying the scene for us, acting out the role of his mother asking a question about the bill.

Then he becomes the man in charge and says, "Of course, you don't understand. You're only a *mestiza.*"

Contempt drips from the word *mestiza* and stains the ground.

Mestizo, masculine, or *mestiza*, feminine: A person of mixed blood, having Maya and Spanish ancestry. According to the standard for judging blood in the young colony, pure Spanish was best—the more recently imported from Spain, the better. Even now, *Ladino* describes someone of mixed blood who identifies more with his/her Hispanic heritage or who has been in the city for awhile, while *mestizo* is used to describe a person from an outlying village or someone who has come to the city to do manual labor.

Manuel still holds the imaginary gas bill. "You're only a *mestiza,*" he repeats, and here beside the Kinich Kak Mo pyramid, some thirty years after the incident, with the Sun shining on us all, the invalidation of that moment weighs heavy on his shoulders.

Then his stance changes, bringing the scene into the present. He straightens his shoulders and lifts his head. He prepares to say what he would tell that man now—what the family has no doubt repeated a thousand times over the years as they've discussed it.

"We're ALL *mestizos,*" he says in a voice that rings with authority.

The jefe nods, and they rake the subject back and forth, working it, tilling it, lapsing into Maya.

Unable to contribute even a word to the conversation, I float my own thoughts. It was 1511 when a Spanish ship wrecked on the coast of Yucatán near Tulum, and thirteen sea-sick sailors made it to shore. All but two died—Gonzalo Guerrero and the priest Jeronimo de Aguilar, who survived and became slaves. When the men fell as war booty into the hands of the Maya lord Nacanchan, Aguilar was given fieldwork, but Guerrero gained favor by advising Nacanchan on strategies that allowed him to get the upper hand in battles with other Maya. Becoming a trusted friend, Guerrero married into Nacanchan's family.

In 1519, when the Maya saw the eleven ships of the *conquistador* Hernán Cortés, the priest Aguilar ran forward shouting "*Dios, Santa Maria, Seville,*" or God, Mary, Seville, words the Spanish would recognize and not shoot him dead on the spot. He became an advisor to Cortés against the indigenous, helping him to conquer the Aztecs. But Guerrero refused to go with Cortés, instead choosing to stay with his adopted people and fight the Spaniards. Cortés branded him a traitor, but the Maya still revere him as a hero. His children were the first *mestizos* born of a Spanish father and Maya mother.

A DNA test would reveal that most of us have "mixed blood" from ancestors who hailed from all parts of the world. Even the Spanish colonists who arrived in the Yucatán in the 1500s had "mixed blood" running in their veins from ancestors who were, in turn, the conquered and the conquerors, statesmen and slaves, merchants and marauders. As the world has grown smaller, most of us have ancestry we could no doubt trace to the immigrants and indigenous of Northern Europe, North America, Asia, Southern Europe, South America, the South Pacific, Africa and the Middle East.

"We're ALL *mestizos*," Manuel repeats.

"Yes," the jefe says.

"Yes, we are," I say, and the men give me an odd, little look but say nothing.

After Mass on the feast day of the Immaculate Conception, people traditionally climb Kinich Kak Mo.

ADMISSION TO THE Kinich Kak Mo pyramid is free. David and Manuel and I follow the narrow walkway alongside the house with the biggest pyramid in the Yucatán in its backyard to the first set of stairs. From here, the pyramid itself isn't visible—just rows of steel-gray rocks the size of lawn tractors and weighing several tons each, set in courses as even as bleachers.

"Isn't it odd," David says, "that the older the construction, the bigger the stones?"

Izamal once had considerable muscle in the Yucatán. The city was settled in about 300 BCE, and has mostly been inhabited ever since. The Kinich Kak Mo pyramid dates to the Classic period of

Maya development from 400 to 600 CE, and entombs even older structures and perhaps a cave or limestone pit. It reaches a height of one-hundred-ten feet, including the terrace, and in its glory days was stuccoed and painted red and adorned with huge masks of Itzamná.

According to legend, the head of Itzamná is buried in the pyramid. His right hand is buried under Izamal's pyramid Kabul ("working hand"), with his heart under the pyramid Itzamatul, which was renovated as late as 1150 CE. And of course, there was once the fabulous pyramid of Ppap-Hol-Chaak, whose base now wears a church like a hat.

Izamal was still a powerful city-state having tribute cities under its control when the Itzá took root in the Yucatán. Its leaders were called upon to help forge an alliance with the Itzá in Dzibilchaltún in 790 CE. But the pact soon dissolved into a power-grab, and within eighty years, the Itzá warrior Hun-Pik-Tok, leader of eight-thousand warriors, conquered Izamal and made it his capital. In the changing fortunes of the Maya, the balance of power shifted several times—Mayapán attacked Izamal and drove its people into exile, and then in 1244, Izamal allied with the Itzá to attack Mayapán.

But even during the 1500s, when the Maya had scattered like seeds, Maya pilgrims still made the journey to Kinich Kak Mo to seek favors from Itzamná as the fire macaw. Seeing the people's devotion to and faith in their god, the Spanish friars put an end to it by twisting the benevolence into treachery. They spread rumors of a terrible bird that swooped down and carried people away to be sacrificed, and after awhile, frightened women and children covered their heads when they passed by the pyramid Kinich Kak Mo.

WE CLIMB STAIRS nearly two-feet tall to the top of a terrace the size of a city park, where Kinich Kak Mo sits on the north edge. It has nine platforms with rounded corners and rises up some forty feet higher than the level of the terrace. But as we approach, we see that the pyramid is very badly weathered. The fire macaw probably doesn't come here anymore. (And anyway, who climbs up to leave an offering of corn or honey?)

The stairs up to the summit are little more than jagged rocks set in cement, and their sharp edges tear at our feet, forcing us to bend and steady ourselves with our hands. At the top, the grassy summit the size of a double-wide trailer is strewn with trash. There's no visible trace of the temple that once graced the pyramid, just one weathered pole of about six feet standing in a patch of concrete.

Yet somehow, the majesty that Friar de Landa saw on this man-made mountain is still evident. This monument to the Divine is a tour de force of human intention and labor. (And the engineering to cut and move such heavy blocks of stone.) From where we stand more than a hundred feet above street level, the horizon is visible in all directions with absolutely nothing to block the view. Not even the steeples on de Landa's church are higher, even with the sixteen-foot boost given by the Ppap-Hol-Chaak pyramid base. For all we can see, we could be on the top of Mount Everest.

Now at mid-afternoon, the Sun is a zillion-watt light bulb. Manuel has taken sunglasses out of a carrying case at his waist. He carefully cleans them with a small chamois and adjusts them across his round face. The black frames are wrap-around, the lenses pink. He looks like a bug in the wind.

"Do you like those?" I ask, thinking that I have a good pair of Carrera driving glasses I could give him.

"Yes, they are very good," he says.

I nod and turn to look out at the horizon. "That direction must be south," I say, raising my right hand to eye level, pointing to a spot on the far-distant horizon.

"No," Manuel says.

From the position of the Sun, I'm pretty sure it is.

"No," he says. "No."

He turns and faces me, placing his back to the church and the horizon behind it. He raises his arms to shoulder height and opens them wide until they form a straight line across his chest. Then he bends the tips of his fingers inward to make corners.

"This is south," he says. "South, south, south." He takes a step backward each time he says south. "South, south, south. From Belize to Guatemala to Chiapas."

He takes a step to his right, still facing me, still holding his arms out, his fingers bent inward. "This is east," he says. "East, east, east." He takes a backward step each time he says the word. "From Cancún to Playa del Carmen to Chetumal."

He takes another step to his right, still holding out his arms. "This is north, from Rio Lagartos to Progreso. North, north, north, where the waters of the Gulf of Mexico meet the Caribbean."

He steps again to the right. "This is west. For Uxmal and Campeche," he says. "West, west, west."

A bulb lights above my head. Manuel is describing a square. For the ancient Maya (and perhaps their descendants), a direction isn't a single point on the horizon or a compass, but one side or face of a square. It's an expanding phenomenon that gets wider and wider as it projects out from where we stand on the Kinich Kak Mo pyramid to the edges of the Yucatán Peninsula and beyond. It's a square that telescopes outward (conceivably) to the edges of the universe.

I pull my notebook out of my backpack and flip through it until I find the words I've copied from the *Popul Vuh* describing the emergence of the sky-earth from the waters at creation:

> *"The fourfold siding, fourfold cornering,*
> *measuring,*
> *fourfold staking,*
> *halving the cord, stretching the cord,*
> *in the sky, on the earth,*
> *the four sides, the four corners.*

> *By the Maker, Modeler,*
> *mother-father of life, of humankind,*
> *giver of breath, giver of heart,*
> *bearer, upbringer in the light that lasts*
> *of those born in the light, begotten in the light.*
> *Worrier, knower of everything,*
> *sky-earth, lake-sea."*

In the *Popul Vuh*, the Maya account of the beginning, the Maker constructs the cosmos by a method well-known to builders laying out a courtyard, farmers staking out a cornfield, and architects planning a structure: It begins with marking off the four corners and sides of a square. The fifth point is the center, which defines the radius from which a circle can be drawn. In the Maya tradition, the center is the place where the World Tree grows tall and "lifts the sky," transforming the two-dimensional square into the three-dimensional cube that is the world we live in. Perching in the highest branches of the World Tree is the celestial bird.

"Then, given the square you've described—and the circle of the horizon—this place where we're standing is the center of the world," I say to Manuel. "In fact, it's the center of the universe."

"No," Manuel corrects. "No, this is the center of the Yucatán."

I'm not accustomed to the Maya way of tilling a topic, working it back and forth like soil. I'm used to pushing and pulling, to Making Things Happen and Arriving at a Conclusion. So I let the matter drop and write my unspoken thoughts in my notebook:

> *Wherever we stand is the center.*
> *We are always at the center of our world.*
> *We are the center of our universe.*
> *How can we be anywhere else?*

David, Manuel, and I sit on the top of the pyramid with our

thoughts as the Sun rolls onward. Here on Kinich Kak Mo, the current World Tree is a weathered pole. I spot some little white daisies growing at the edge of the summit like a fringe of hair around a bald pate. I stand and go pick a flower and stick it in a crack at the top of the old pole. Its little yellow-and-white face bobs above our heads. And maybe above the spires of the church.

MANUEL DRIVES BY the church again as we leave Izamal. People approaching the ramp are buying milagros and candles to offer to the Virgin. The Maya accepted the friars' Christianity partly because some of it seemed very similar to their own ancient beliefs. The World Tree became the Cross, and the old gods seemed to be a lot like the many Catholic saints. The fire macaw parrot became the dove and the Holy Spirit. The Maya's love for the goddess Ixchel found expression in the Virgin of Izamal and then, equally strongly in the Virgin of Guadalupe. Itzamná morphed into Jesus.

I wonder if Izamal's ancient shamans ever floated a vision that gave them the premonition that this city would still be a place of pilgrimage after more than fifteen centuries. Pilgrims who once came here seeking the heavenly gift of life-giving rain for corn to feed their children have been followed by those praying for God's Mercy for their children and grandchildren and themselves. In a way, Friar de Landa preserved the sacredness of the ground once occupied by the Ppap-Hol-Chaak pyramid, but even more, he preserved Izamal as a place of pilgrimage long, long after it would have otherwise dropped into ancient history. Surely that wasn't his intention. But as Herman Needleman MD, guide to Mérida's Cathedral, told us: One doesn't always know when he or she is acting on behalf of a future that wants to be born. ▲

19. Ak'e

Great White Way...

WE HEAD TO Ak'e from Izamal on the asphalt highway. If this were the Seventh Century, we could go more directly. Across the highway from the Lee clothing factory with its tangle of bikes is the ancient *sacbé*, or white road, that once linked Izamal to Ak'e, some twenty-four miles away. Farmers clearing their fields have removed great portions of it, but a millennium ago, when it was maintained by the Maya Department of Highways, it ran straight-arrow through the forest from one city to the other.

The surface of this *sacbé* was as smooth as skin from dozens of coats of light-colored stucco. If it was like other ancient roads, it had guard houses at intervals to control access and a "tollbooth" at the end. It rose four to eight feet above ground level, and measured more than thirty feet wide. It was used for commerce and perhaps for the rapid mobilization of troops (as the United States' interstate highway system is designed to do), as well as ceremonial processions, and it made for safe travel at night when the heat of the day had dissipated. It was the great white way that brought order to the tangled forest, just as its namesake, the Milky Way, that great Broadway in the sky, seems to bring order to the heavens.

But instead of taking the *sacbé*, Manuel must drive from Izamal to the town of Tixkokob, where weavers knot cords into hammocks, then on to tiny Ek'mul, and finally to Ruinas de Ak'e, a tiny settlement in the remains of a hacienda. Gone to ruin. Like Ak'e's once-great pyramids.

It's Manuel's first time in Ak'e, and David directs him to turn in front of a row of elevated houses, then follow a dirt rut past the hacienda's factory with its tall smoke stack. The hacienda once processed large quantities of *henequen*, or sisal fibers, and it still does some manufacturing—albeit on a much smaller scale. Behind it, an open door to the factory reveals an interior as dark as a cave where the shadowy figures of workmen tend white fibers racing around spools like thin, bristly serpents.

"Rope," I say.

"String," David says.

A little boy of five or six—shirtless, wearing shorts and red, knee-high, plastic boots—comes to stand in the door, and I suddenly remember a dream from last night. (Odd how a tiny event during the day can trigger the memory of a dream.) In the dream, I'm standing

Outside Izamal, part of the sacbé connecting it to Ak'e has been reconstructed.

on the grass in front of a pyramid I don't recognize. Two little boys are sitting on a low wall. One of them looks like an ordinary boy, but the other has a mature, man-sized face atop his chubby, little-boy body. His face is as round as a saucer. His nose is remarkably long and wide. He watches me with solemn dark eyes, and I check my pocket for some candy to give him, but I have none.

"I can answer your question," the man-faced boy says.

"What *is* my question?" I say.

As we enter the archaeological site of Ak'e, David signs the guest book, its first entry in five days, and we walk through the gate onto the park-like lawn where an old man is cutting the grass by hand. He's taller than most men in the area—nearly six feet—and must bend very low to catch the blades of grass in the crook of a forked stick

before he lops them off with a curved knife. The grass covers more than an acre, and I wonder if he's going to cut the whole of it in this way. His clothes seem too good for the job—a crisp, white, long-sleeved shirt; pressed blue trousers; and a clean, well-shaped straw hat. "Sunday-go-to-meeting clothes," my grandma would have called them.

"Good day," he says as we approach.

We stop to ask him about the *sacbé* that once linked Ak'e to Izamal. "Is it still visible here?" David asks.

"Oh, yes," the old man tells us. "The Spanish came in and took most everything, but the *sacbé* remains."

ON OTHER VISITS to Ak'e, we've searched the jungle for the *sacbé* to Izamal, climbed pyramids at the edge of the site, and explored fallen palaces, one of which, according to a guard, gave up a human skeleton with very long leg bones "indicating a person of over eight feet." The site has nearly one hundred structures, all unrestored so far and shrouded in tangled vines and vining cactus. We've climbed its tallest pyramid, which bears a deep gash in its crown—perhaps from the collapse of a vault—where charred trash and branches now lay in a heap of ashes. Pyramids closer to the hacienda have been partially eaten—their stones gone into the building of a church and the hacienda's houses and factory—and now stand as lopsided and irregular as old apple cores.

Today we head toward the structure known as the House of Columns, which is not so much a pyramid as a temple that resembles nothing more than a grand stage. If the gods ever danced in the Yucatán, they danced here. It's a magnificent structure some twenty feet high by one-hundred feet long and nearly forty feet wide. Its entire front is a majestic staircase running its whole length and constructed from colossal stones—six feet by four feet, at least—adorned by fossil seashells that reflect the sunlight like daytime stars.

An elderly man cuts the grass with a sharp machete and a stick in the plaza in front of the House of Columns in Ak'e.

We climb to the top of the giant steps to the stage where thirty-five regal columns still stand, the roof they once held now gone. We are child-sized beside them—kindergartners at most beside these stout, gray, grandfather pillars made from stone rounds piled high. Beneath our feet the stage floor has a downy coat of soft grass studded with flowers. A few remaining foundation stones outline a ruined two-roomed temple with an altar.

We sit down on the grass at the base of two mighty columns and lean into them, letting them bear our weight. We stretch out our legs in their shadows, and as the Sun moves through the afternoon, we move our legs, becoming human sundials, doing nothing more than simply being.

It's peaceful here. The grassy land spreads out at the feet of this temple like a park. The air is still. No car noise is audible, not even the drone of an airplane, and without a breeze to lift it, the hum of the machines in the henequen factory falls early to ground. Orange butterflies flit by. A little *zorro*, or fox, lopes by. Two gray iguanas nearby look like spiky stones. The afternoon heat is intense, and the trees and bushes sweat a cloud of steamy mist. The word that comes to mind to describe this place is Grace, which in its theological definition is the freely given, unmerited favor and love of God.

A touch of Grace lingers in Ak'e like a whiff of flowery perfume.

THE ORIGIN OF the name Ak'e isn't exactly known. Ake (without the accent) is the name of a shrubby plant. Ak'e is the ancient name of the Maya city on the Mexico-Guatemala border now called Bonampak, with its famous murals. Locals say it comes from Maya for *ek'*, or star, which became Ak'e from mispronunciation. Others associate the word with *Ah Keh*, for Lord Deer or the Deer People, and speak of a legend about the white deer that lives here.

According to the story, the old Maya respected the Deer People,

seeing the deer as the body of the Mother Earth and the pheasant as her soul. While they hunted deer to feed their children, they never considered killing the white deer, who is white because she carries a sacred stone inside her—a *sastun*, or quartz crystal, that holds the spiritual vibration of the Deer People.

But one day, a hunter from a distant city was passing through Ak'e and heard talk of the white deer and the crystal she carried. He reasoned that if he could take possession of the stone, he'd know everything there was to know about the Deer People and would always have meat to eat. Acting on his greed, the hunter stalked the white deer, and when he found her in a clearing, took deadly aim on her with his *atlatl*, or spear thrower.

The white deer looked at him. "I see that you have it in your heart to kill me," she said. "Have you brought grass to give me first?"

The hunter kept his aim on the deer's soft side.

"Have you brought fresh bedding for my fawns to lie on?" the white deer asked.

The hunter maintained his deadly aim.

"Then what gives you the right to kill me?" the white deer said, and she disappeared in the blink of an eye.

As it happened, a doe, heavy with pregnancy, walked into the clearing at that moment. The hunter turned his atlatl toward her, took aim, and prepared to launch his spear into her heart. But a voice at his ear stopped him. The white deer stood at his side.

"Spare her," the white deer said, "and you may kill me in her place. You may have the stone you desire, but you must agree to return it to my people in a *k'atun* of twenty years."

The hunter smiled. He unsheathed his knife and slew the white deer. The quartz crystal tumbled from her forehead into his hand. Later he wrapped it with cord and wore it as a pendant around his neck. Then, knowing that he would always have meat, he married two local women and fed his children and relatives very well.

At the end of the k'atun, the white deer came to the hunter in a dream. When the hunter awoke, he called to his eldest son, who was nearing twenty, and placed the crystal pendant around his neck. Then the two of them went into the forest.

In the forest, the hunter and his son soon found a doe and her fawn and took deadly aim on them. But before the men could make the kill, twelve males of the Deer People surrounded them.

"For a k'atun, we have sacrificed ourselves for you," the males said, "and now you must give us the stone."

The hunter laughed, but before he could release his spear, the male deer charged him and pierced his belly with their antlers, and he fell back against a tree. In that moment, a silver cord exited his body at the site of the wound just above his navel, and it rose until it wrapped itself around a tree limb like a vine.

"Father!" the boy said.

"He will die," the male deer said. "And without his cord, he will be forever separated from the Milky Way that would take him home with the ancestors, just as we have been separated from our stone."

The boy felt the crystal against his chest. He knew that if he gave it to the deer, his family would no longer be able to find meat so easily. And yet if he kept it, his father would be a ghost and the link to the ancestors of Time would be broken, and the family would have no one to speak for it in the spirit world.

"I will give you the stone," the boy told the deer, "if you will return my father's cord."

At once, a small female deer, not quite fully grown, came forward. The boy removed the stone from his neck and held it out to her. She put her head against the crystal, and it disappeared. In that moment, the deer turned white.

"What has vanished will be restored," the white deer said, and the silver cord unwrapped itself from the tree limb and re-entered the hunter.

"Now I may die in peace," the hunter said and drew his last breath.

Some say you can still see the white deer in the forest near Ak'e among the Deer People.

BESIDES ITS HOUSE of Columns, Ak'e has another remarkable attribute: It's the place where the god Itzamná is said to have appeared on Earth at the first dawn of this creation. While Ak'e enjoyed a position of influence from perhaps 400 to 800 CE, exactly when Itzamná appeared here isn't known, although his role in creation is depicted in scenes painted on pottery.

Before the beginning of this fourth creation in which we live, water covered the Earth and the sky. There was no Light, no Time, no Place. Only the Absolute Being, in all its infinite aspects, existed. Into this void came the Old Paddler god, rowing across the dark waters in a canoe. Near the constellation now called Orion, he stopped and directed that three stones be set upon the water. The first was the jaguar-throne stone (the kingdom), and the second was the serpent stone (the authority). Itzamná set the third stone, the crocodile stone (the glory). These three stones are now known as the stars Alnitak, Saiph, and Rigel, which the Maya still view as being the hearth, or the womb of the heaven, that is forever linked to the womb of Earth by a cord. In the traditional Maya home, the hearth always has three stones, and it's in the hearth that the afterbirth of an infant girl is buried in order to connect her to the home and the wombs of heaven and Earth.

Once the three stones had been set in the waters, the Maize Lord emerged from their center. He grew into a corn stalk, the World Tree, and even the Milky Way, as he raised the sky and the four corners of the universe became supported by stone columns to keep the sky aloft. Once Place was established, Time could begin. The constellations began their cycles through the sky, and with the heavens in order, the Sun of our solar system could rise. The first day dawned when Itzamná, the Almighty's chief liaison with humanity, revealed his face in Ak'e.

Even now, the four corners of the cornfield correspond to the four corners of the universe, and it's in the cornfield that the afterbirth of an infant boy is placed.

Some traditional Maya still hail each other with the greeting, "Where is your afterbirth buried?" Some believe that the trouble with the world today is that most people don't know where they belong, nor do they remember their ancestors in prayer. Until now, I've never stopped to ponder the whereabouts of the remains (ashes undoubtedly) of the afterbirth that once connected me to my mother. But now I wonder: Does the heart, with its passion and compassion, make any less of a connection?

AS WE LINGER on the House of Columns, the little boy from the doorway of the henequen factory runs toward the old man who is still cutting the grass. The boy's arm is up, and a length of string flies behind him like a glad streamer. The man motions the boy to one of the temple steps, and they sit together in the shade of a lone tree. The old man takes the string from the boy and ties its ends together to form a circle. He loops it over his fingers on both hands to make a square, then threads his fingers through it, pulling it this way and that into various geometrical designs. When my grandma played this game with me, we called it "Cat in the Cradle."

The boy watches intently. After a few minutes, he takes the string and mimics the old man's actions as he learns to form a square, then a series of triangles. His chubby fingers are the loom of life.

I find it odd that I'd think of my grandma here on this temple. Already old when I was born, she's been gone now for more than thirty years. She who traveled the American prairie in a covered wagon when she was a girl would have judged this foreign temple "falderal" and this elective journey we've undertaken as "pure foolishness." And yet I think of her here and now.

As we climb pyramid after pyramid in the realm of the Maya, we're beginning to realize the vastness of the network created by these sophisticated, complex cities—some sixteen hundred in the Yucatán Peninsula alone, inhabited by 5 million people. Many are connected by *sacbeob* (the plural of *sacbé*), but there also seems to be an invisible web here that serves to link us into lucky connections and chance meetings, odd dreams and old memories.

I open my notebook and write:

> *Maybe like the www. links our computers*
> *there's a Universal Web that connects us to everyone*
> *past, present, and future.*
> *Just close your eyes and think, UW.net, and you're in touch.*

The ancient Maya believed that the cords connecting the wombs of heaven and Earth are as real as the stone *sacbé* that connects the cities of Izamal and Ak'e. Of course, just as travelers walked both directions on the *sacbé*, the cords linking heaven and Earth also offer two-way communication. As David and I get up to leave Ak'e's grand temple, I'm left wondering: When I think of my grandma, does she also think of me? ▲

20. Mérida

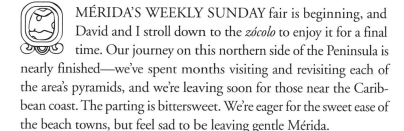

Unity...

MÉRIDA'S WEEKLY SUNDAY fair is beginning, and David and I stroll down to the *zócolo* to enjoy it for a final time. Our journey on this northern side of the Peninsula is nearly finished—we've spent months visiting and revisiting each of the area's pyramids, and we're leaving soon for those near the Caribbean coast. The parting is bittersweet. We're eager for the sweet ease of the beach towns, but feel sad to be leaving gentle Mérida.

This Sunday street fair celebrates life's most basic joys—family and food. Only a few blocks away, in the city's traditional market, *Mercado Luis de Galvéz*, women sell hogs' heads and jicama, tomatoes and roses, baskets and buckets, and a hundred thousand other things. But for this Sunday festival, vendors erect portable booths in the city's three central parks and sell their handicrafts—handmade wooden toys, embroidered clothing, crochet purses, jewelry, honey, and traditional foods. They offer roasted ears of corn-on-a-stick smeared with cream and chile powder, hot crepes rolled around shredded Edam cheese, tamales, tacos, and *panuchos*, or corn tortillas coated with beans, fried, and topped with shredded turkey, lettuce, avocado, and pickled onion.

The Maya market is a tradition that has probably changed very little in two thousand years: Its rhythm is walk a little, talk a lot, eat; walk a little, talk a lot, eat; walk a little, talk a lot, eat, and buy something. Of course, human nature being geared to embracing convenience, the accouterments have changed. Cook fire comes from cannisters of propane, not wood. Portable food stands have metal roofs, not thatch. And people lounge on the ubiquitous white plastic chairs that have overtaken the Earth. While music still comes from traditional pipes and drums or mariachi or salsa bands, now it's blasted from man-sized speakers powered by electrified trees—trees having a dozen or more electrical outlets trailing thin, brown wires that snake across grass and streets in an electrician's nightmare. Puppets' shrill voices are lifted to new heights by the sound system, and the children shriek in delight.

The smell of grilling meat catches David's attention, and he follows his nose to thin strips of pork sizzling on a grill at a taco stand. We sit in the street in front of the Cathedral (traffic is blocked off for the day) and give our order to the *taquero*, or taco server. David wants two *tortas*, lofty white-bread buns stuffed with grilled pork, edges seared and curled with heat. I want a taco of grilled meat on a corn tortilla. The taquero offers a mild, green sauce of tomatillos and avocado.

On Sunday in Mérida, a woman wheels her portable drink stand down the street.

We eat slowly and linger at the table enjoying the shade beneath the dignified, old shade trees—always leafed in this tropical climate—watching a procession of the generations that we rarely see at home except at birthday parties held in restaurants. Young fathers carrying a baby stroll by with their wife, mother-in-law, sister-in-law (pregnant and pulling a toddler along), and frail grandmother-in-law guided by a supporting arm—the other men in the family working here on Sunday or in the States. Babies are dressed like little barons and princesses. Baby girls, ears pierced with pearl or gold studs, wear long, flowered dresses and lacy socks inside new white Mary Janes. Little boys sport pressed shirts and long shorts. Even with precious few pesos, there's always a few cents for an ice cream cone or a helium-filled balloon.

Family here seems at the root of Self in a way that's different than in the States where Self is increasingly defined by a person's expression of creativity. In this place with a history of loss, family is primary. Parents, children, and grandparents leapfrog through Time within a network of cousins, siblings, aunts, and uncles. Even when they're asleep in their graves, they're still present to the family, their photos on the home altar (beside the Virgin of Guadalupe). Family is the future. Family is forever. I open my notebook and write:

*I'm comfortable here in this land of the Mother
and macho men.*

We're still sitting at the table as people line up for tortas and tacos. The taquero circles. He'd never ask us to leave—the generosity and courtesty of the culture doesn't allow for such abruptness. But after a while he directs two young women to the empty chairs at our table. They're fidgity and uncomfortable with us—many of Mérida's people don't have much contact with tourists—and we smile and get up, leaving them the table.

It's only ninety degrees—relatively cool for any day in Mérida—and we decide to walk the two miles from the city center to the Hyatt Hotel for chocolate fudge cake and espresso. A driver of a *calesa*, or Victorian-style horse-drawn carriage, offers us a ride in a buggy pulled by a small dappled horse with a purple feather on its head. We shake our heads no, and the carriage goes on. There's an advertisement for Avis rent-a-car tacked on the back.

Many people here work hard to earn a meager living. We pass women sitting in door jambs selling little plastic bags of pumpkin seeds and peanuts. The candy man offers peanut brittle and other sweets from the wooden tray he carries on his head. Men sell balloons and old-fashioned windmills for kids. They sell plastic whistles that mimic the mewing of a desperate kitten trapped in a box. (Who would buy such a thing!) They hawk Panama hats and hammocks. Polite, good-looking boys offer single cigarettes and little packs of gum.

Those with nothing but advanced age and infirmities simply ask for coins. An old man with rumpled white hair holds out his hat for a peso—one of three men in a row. Yucatecans usually give a few pesos while tourists brush by without making eye contact. Perhaps tourists can't bring themselves to acknowledge those with nothing while they have so much. Perhaps they don't know how much to give—or whether giving a peso will pull them into unwanted contact with the person. But for the needy it's a purely professional activity involving nothing more than the exchange of a coin or two. They remember who gives and on later circuits exempt those who donate.

I try to keep a pocketful of two-, five-, and ten-peso coins, and give them to everyone who asks until the coins are gone. But it's like chips and dip at a party—there's always dip left after the chips are gone, or too many chips. In Mérida, there're always more people with their hands out than I have coins, and my pocket is empty before we come upon a young man with cerebral palsy, his hands too weak to hold the can for donations, which must be taped to his wheelchair. Before we meet an old man with such severe Parkinson's that his coin cup is a moving target. Before we see a man with such a debilitating skin disease that he seems to be melting down to his bones.

Walking toward the Hyatt, we leave them behind in the city center, knowing they'll be there when we return with more coins.

TO STROLL NORTH from the city center is to walk through a timeline of Merida's history. When the Spanish colonists laid out the grid for the city, they reserved the center for those of wholly Spanish origin. Amid existing thatch-roof huts and ruined pyramids, they built stone and stucco homes in the style of the late Middle Ages and Renaissance in Europe. Even now the city has a wealth of magnificent old buildings, although many have been divided into small spaces affordable to video arcades, travel agencies, shoe repairmen and tailors, fabric stores, and little eateries. An entire book of photographs could be done on their door jambs—elegant uprights and lintels carved with trailing vines and flowers—with another devoted to the brilliant colors and patterns of their floor tile. The city is rescuing its once-grand buildings that have fallen into disarray, and men who are genies with concrete are restoring their crumbling facades. The men bring charm to a street by laying fake (cement) cobblestone. They chisel round holes in the sidewalks for spotlights that make the streets inviting at night.

With the city center once reserved for the "whites," others lived in *barrios*, or neighborhoods, where the Franciscan friars built them churches, making Mérida a city of churches: Santa Caterina and Santiago for the local Maya, with San Cristobal for the central Mexicans who accompanied the Spaniards as military auxiliaries. Walking north, we pass the small, welcoming Santa Lucia church, with its deeply shaded courtyard, built for black African slaves and mulattos.

Inland from the Gulf and away from the scourge of pirates, Mérida prospered and grew and became the capital of the Yucatán Peninsula. Politically separate from Mexico City, it was governed by Spanish appointees who became quite progressive under the reforming influence of King Charles III. By 1780, its streets were paved, and highways connected it to Campeche and Izamal. Oil lamps lit its streets, and it had an elegant, broad boulevard where its citizens proudly promenaded on Sundays. Its prosperity encouraged learned men to found intellectual societies and a university. With its style and elegance, the city became the Grande Dame of the Peninsula, and the last of her Spanish governors presented her with a jewel in the form a theater.

The city lost momentum during the War of the Castes when Maya rebels turned on the "whites" in the mid 1800s—"white" being less a descriptor of skin color than a self-identification. Its citizens trembled in fear as outlying towns fell to the rebels. Then refugees from the countryside swamped the city, camping on every inch of available ground. Finally, only Mérida and Campeche held out against the rebels, and as supplies dwindled and Mérida was on the brink of

The church at Tepich was the scene of many battles between government troops and Maya rebels.

heavy with Italian marble and Austrian crystal for the hacendados' grand mansions. Smitten with the sophistication of Paris, they wanted to build new mansions in a more stylish setting than Mérida's city center, and upon securing land on the city's northern edge in 1904, they designed a boulevard reminiscent of the Parisian Champs-Elysees. They named it Paseo de Montejo for the *conquistador* who had founded the city. It became the Paseo for those having lots of pesos.

Paseo de Montejo still has an air of elegance. A parade of trees borders its wide sidewalks, their slender trunks whitewashed so they look from a distance like girls on their way to a party. Set back from the sidewalk, its mansions are rich dowagers surrounded by velvet lawns. Impossibly grand, they're ornate confections festooned with plaster garlands of laurel leaves and rosebuds that number in the thousands. The false columns adorning their walls are topped by false urns draped with plaster fabric. A gallery of faces stares out from under their eaves: the narrow faces of girls, the fat pusses of lions, and the menacing masks of gargoyles. Even the boulevard's modest mansions (an oxymoron?) have wrap-around porches with wicker rockers.

The fabulous houses wear paint the delicate blue of robin eggs or the blush-pink of baby roses. They have state rooms for entertaining, and one has a tower like the mast of a tall ship.

They make a show of having Fortune. Power. Class.

Which must be protected. Tall, black, iron fences with spikes surround the properties (where guards sit, watching), and iron grills bar the windows, the ornate spikes painted white to blend with the lace curtains behind them.

But with the advent of synthetic rope, the demand for henequen declined, and now many of the houses that henequen built are occupied by banks and securities exchanges that can afford their upkeep.

Now money is the Money-Maker.

Today, armored trucks cruise the boulevard alongside horse-drawn carriages. When an armored truck pulls up to a bank, guards wearing flak jackets jump out, one leveling his assault rifle into firing

surrender, the governor sent word to the United States and Cuba offering the Yucatán as the prize for whomever would defend it. But the city was spared when the Maya went home to plant their crops.

Mérida fervently embraced the economic boom that followed. With the flurry of trans-Atlantic crossings between Europe and the Americas during the late 1800s, the international shipping industry had great demand for the thick ropes made from the fibers of the *henequen,* or sisal, plants that flourished in the thin soil of the Yucatán's haciendas. Henequen became a wealth-maker, and it elevated the henequen barons' life-style (if not their bloodline) to the level of royalty. Abroad, the *hacendados,* or land-owners, were familiar figures in Paris where they purchased fine brocades and lace for their abodes back home. Ships laden with rope left the Yucatán for Europe and returned position to cover a second guard heading into the bank. One day we see the second guard emerging from a bank with three clear plastic baggies of pesos. Another day, someone whistles as the heavy truck groans away from the curb, and it lurches to a stop and the guard opens the door for a man running out with two bottles of Coca-Cola.

A decade ago, the Paseo got two new hotels in addition to its upscale Holiday Inn—a traditional-style Fiesta Americana and a modern-style Hyatt. Now a new super-Walmart has also opened on the boulevard that has some of the city's finest mansions.

IN THE COUNTRYSIDE, down-at-heels haciendas are now being bought up by corporations and converted to bed-and-breakfasts charging several hundred dollars for a night's stay. But a few of the century-old factories still process henequen, sometimes in cooperatives run by workers themselves.

We stumble upon a working factory at Hacienda Chunk'anan one day when our friend Fernando suggests we drive out to a remote cenote. We're looking for it down a narrow, rural lane that ends in a village snuggled into the lap of a once-grand hacienda when a man tells us that the cenote is too far for us to reach on foot and that it's too late in the day to arrange to reach it by way of a horse-drawn railcar. Seeing men at work processing the henequen in the old hacienda, David asks to take photos. The jefe welcomes us, and we walk across a field toward the factory, picking our steps among the rusty tracks of narrow-gauge railcars, water puddles, oil spills, and piles of horse dung. The sun-warmed ground emits a peculiar odor of fermenting plant material that, though slightly acrid, isn't at all unpleasant.

Ahead of us, the factory still shows the charm of Times Past—grandly arched doorways and windows and a dignified forty-foot smokestack. But while henequen made the land owners filthy rich, the workers labored in virtual bondage. During the 1600s, the colo-

A henequen plant stands in front of a former mansion, now a museum, on Paseo de Montejo.

nial system of land grants had begun to create vast estates by appropriating lands designated for common use into private hands. These later became haciendas, and by 1845, the Peninsula had 1,105 haciendas occupying hundreds of thousands of acres. The Maya had previously been herded into villages as a means of controlling them, and with the growing demand for henequen and sugar cane usurping more and more community land, they no longer had enough land to grow food for their families. At the same time, the opportunity to glean meat through hunting had diminished as the forests were felled for dyewoods to be exported to Europe. Desperate to feed their children, the Maya moved to the haciendas to work.

Technically the Maya were free men, and yet debt peonage kept them bound in the chains of poverty, which they passed like a dark

Mule power pulls the railcar carrying henequen fiber at this processing plant in the country south of Mérida. Once a privately owned hacienda, it's now a cooperative.

inheritance to their children. They worked and lived on haciendas isolated from towns, which forced them into buying essentials such as salt and cooking oil from the company store. As a result, they always owed more than they could cover. Even if they could get to town, few had any money since they were mostly paid in "chits" good only on the hacienda. Even worse, they were subjected to cruel physical abuse and severe punishment for any small misstep, real or imagined.

In 1845, the Maya found themselves in the possession of firearms when landowners, fearing that Mexico City was coveting their wealth, organized the indigenous into an armed force. A few Maya became involved in a murder plot fostered by a duplicitous "white" politician, and when things got out of control and violence erupted, many Maya rose up in revolt against their oppressors in an attempt to regain their land and sovereignty. In 1847, they sacked the town of Valladolid near Chichén Itzá and the War of the Castes began.

Both the Maya and the "whites" released decades of pent-up fury in the ensuing orgy of bloodshed. Armed Maya rebels attacked town after town killing "whites," who were actually mostly *mestizos*, without regard for women, children, and the elderly. Government troops attacked Maya settlements killing women, children, and the elderly.

And yet, the war was strictly neither one of class nor ancestry since "whites" fought alongside the Maya rebels, and many Maya fought with the government troops.

The rebels and the army struggled mightily for control of the towns of Tepich and Tihosuco near the center of the Peninsula. Finally, the Maya gained control of the Peninsula except for the walled cities of Mérida and Campeche. But then, the flying ants whispered to them that the rains were coming, and they went home to plant corn and beans to feed their children. (Always the children.)

Mexico City sent armed forces to Mérida and Campeche to vanquish the rebels, and in return for the support, the leaders of the Yucatán affirmed their allegiance to Mexico.

Men prepare to load bundles of henequen spears onto a conveyor taking them to the crushing machine.

Yet the War of the Castes continued on for decades in the central and eastern areas of the Peninsula. Treaty dates between the government and the Maya rebels passed with papers left unsigned and the proponents assassinated. Fighting continued to destroy thousands of lives. On one occasion, the rebels once killed fifteen hundred soldiers and took their weapons. Army troops retook territory and captured Maya prisoners—again women, children, and the elderly. Without enough capable hands to work the land, the army executed prisoners so as not to have to feed them. Other Maya were sold as slaves in Cuba with the proceeds from the sales going to buy more guns.

In the forest not far from Tulum, the Maya rebels received what they believed to be a directive from God when a Cross engraved on a tree near a cenote seemed to speak to them. A man named Nahuat

A workman retrieves the henequen fiber from the crusher to send it out to the drying fields.

they reached a peaceful understanding with the government. To this day, many Maya still believe that they won the war. Sometimes, Time offers the most effective defense.

HENEQUEN PROCESSING AT the Hacienda Chunk'anan is now a cooperative with the workmen earning wages for their labor when there's work. While today's shipping industry has little demand for henequen rope, there's a market for mid-weight rope and string made from the strong fibers. The fibers are also used to make the huge bags for chemical fertilizers, conveyor belts, the backing on carpets, and many other items. But first the fibers must be processed.

As trucks come in from the farms, men unload their bundles of henequen leaves that have been cut by hand. Working with the leaves produces many wounds, and the men's arms show a crosshatch of scars accumulated over the years. The henequen plant is a utilitarian relative of the famous blue agave cactus, or century plant, that produces tequila. A type of maguey used by the ancient peoples of Mexico, it has long, spear-like leaves armed with a lethal needle at the tip and tearing spines along both edges. The long fibers that can be braided and woven into rope and cloth are deep inside the fleshy pulp.

David and I follow the henequen spears to the second floor where the crushing machine roars to life as they arrive. In this room of elegant arches, men feed the spears into the jaws of the insatiable crusher, where its brass teeth gnash them to bits, sending green pulp flying. Driven by conveyor belts, the crusher chews the spears as though they were celery, separating flesh from fiber, then spitting out the whole mess. The blenderized pulp goes one way through a hole in the floor to be dumped on the fields, while the long, luxuriant green fibers fall through another hole into small, wooden railcars reminiscent of the old narrow-gauge ore cars used in the gold mines of the Rocky Mountains. Here the paydirt is henequen fiber. Green gold.

spoke its words, and the Cult of the Talking Cross was born. Believing that they were favored by God, the rebels fought to extend their power from Peninsula's center to the Caribbean and down to what is now the Mexico-Belize border. As the war raged, the number of people—estimated at 100,000—was reduced to 10,000 toward the end of the 1800s, as people fled or succumed to drought and the diseases of malnutrition.

In 1900, the government used modern weapons and canons to launch a new assault on these rebels occupying the territory of Quintana Roo, the state now home to modern-day Cancún and Playa del Carmen. Unable to arm themselves with equal firepower, the rebels melted into the forests where they remained for decades.

Finally, as the leadership in Quintana Roo changed, the rebels returned to their Talking Cross and restored its sanctity. In the 1930s,

Standing near the behemoth crusher, I'm caught up in its sounds. Brass teeth make a metallic beat as even as a metronome's—clack, clack—which gains an echo as the sound hits the walls. Clicketty, clicketty, clack, clack is the sound of chewing.

A dozen conveyor belts of varying widths add a chorus of slapping sounds. Whapitty, whapitty, slap, slap.

The leaves' pulverized flesh drops through a hole with a splat. The green fiber drops into a railcar with a plop. Splat. Plop.

The room as elegant as a ballroom rumbles with the rhythm: Clicketty, clicketty, clack, clack. Whapitty, whapitty, slap, slap. Splat, plop. Plop, splat. Clicketty, clicketty, clack. Clack.

The rhythm insinuates itself into my head.

Clicketty, clicketty, clack, clack. Whapitty, whapitty, slap, slap. Splat, plop. Plop, splat. Clicketty, clicketty, clack. Clack.

The organic beat goes on, and I wish Mickey Hart of the Grateful Dead were here to make it into music. Or Peter Gabriel with his *Passion*. Clicketty, clicketty, clack, clack. Whapitty, whapitty, slap, slap. Splat, plop. Plop, splat. Clicketty, clicketty, clack. Clack.

Or Dr. Seuss to make a rhyme: "There's a zusher in the crusher, and a welt in the belt."

Below the crusher on the first floor, a man and a mule wait for the railcars to fill, the mule (pronounced mool-eh) nibbling on tender grass. When a railcar is heaped with the green hair-like fiber, the man clucks softly to the animal, and the mool-eh swivels his ears, finding the man's voice among the industrial sounds. But the animal needs no coaching—he could do this dance in his sleep. He steps backward toward the railcar until he feels his harness being hooked to it. Then he leans into the load, inching the railcar forward on the rusty track. Beyond the building, the shiny, brown mool-eh picks up speed on the worn path beside the track, while the man walks, too, not adding to the burden. At the drying field a hundred yards away, man and mool-eh drop their load of hair, and the mool-eh prances back to the processing plant for another nibble of sweet grass and another dance.

Henequen fibers are hung over clotheslines in the drying field.

In the drying field, men and boys drape the long, green hair over low clotheslines to dry in the Sun. In two or three days, it'll lighten to the pale, yellow blonde of summer hair. California hair.

Once dry, the henequen fibers will be gathered and baled and transported to a different factory to be turned into string and carpet.

The price of the fiber is dropping, making work at the co-op sporadic. There's talk of developing a use for the henequen pulp-waste as a pigment for paint. But more exciting is the news that the thin, dry soil of the Yucatán might be suitable for the blue agave that produces tequila. Traditional growing grounds in the Mexican state of Jalisco have been overworked, and tequila-makers have planted the first few blue agave in the Yucatán. The men are optimistic—today's world seems to need tequila more than rope.

Of course, these men of the co-op will never own elaborate houses like the former hacendados. The floors of traditional Maya homes are dirt or slab concrete, not marble, and light comes from a bare bulb, not a crystal chandelier. But theirs is honest labor that feeds and clothes their children with enough left over, if there's work, to buy them a notebook and pencil for school.

WE'RE EATING LUNCH in the restaurant of our hotel. Every table is full with Méridians in from the suburbs, and a thin man of about fifty—dark-haired, chain-smoking, and drinking beer—sits with two women at a wrought-iron table near the courtyard. Behind them, an old man and his grandson of about twenty are caring for the plants in the courtyard that's not much bigger than a big family room. They're clipping off dead and bruised leaves, and stooping to pick up leaves fallen from the two resident mamey trees.

As his grandson finishes the pruning, the old man pulls a small, push-style lawnmower onto the grass and begins to mow in short bursts that last about as long as his arms are long. The mower is quaint with the soft metallic whir of sharp blades rather than the roar of a power mower. It reminds me of being a kid, watching my dad push a hand-mower across the lawn. Suddenly the chain-smoking man stands up, leans over the courtyard rail, and orders the old man to stop mowing. Tension tightens the old man's features, but he obeys. Flipping the mower handle over, he takes the mower to the far end of the courtyard. In a few minutes, he begins to mow the grass at the far end.

The smoking man explodes out of his chair again, and again he leans over the rail and orders the old man to stop mowing. The old man stops in his tracks, his eyes down, riveted to the lawn.

Anger grips his grandson—his shoulders tighten, his clenched jaw works. He goes over to the old man and urgently speaks to him in a low tone, no doubt trying to convince his grandfather to let him

finish the mowing. The old man moves his hands down in a damping motion that seems to say, "Don't cause trouble, keep your voice down."

The grandson pleads, the old man shakes his head. Soon they are squatting, cutting the grass by hand with short, pruning knives.

The smoking man goes back to his beer.

I can barely contain my chagrin at the unfairness of it all. I want to leap up and grab the lawnmower, and push it over the grass. I could easily finish the job in under ten minutes. I could be done before the smoking man could finish his beer. And even if he started something with me, I'd have the job done before he could involve management.

My body is already on its way. I can almost feel my hands on the mower's handle. But I hold myself back. I want to right the injustice done to the old man and his grandson, who are now forced to cut the grass with kinves. I believe there would be value in my taking action—especially for the grandson. But I hold back because it would embarrass the old man in this traditional culture. I hold back because there'd be a fuss of some sort, and I don't know if it would cost the old man his job.

Instead, I ferociously dip my tortilla chip into the guacamole we've ordered and then spoon on some xnipek, the Maya salsa of diced tomatoes and onions, cilantro and habañero pepper. I chomp down on a chunk of habañero, and the heat explodes in my mouth. On the Scoville heat scale, cayenne registers 8,000 units, jalapeño 25,000, and an orange habañero 210,000. My eyes water, and my nose runs. I can feel the inside of my bottom lip beginning to swell. I fish an ice cube from my lemonade and press it onto the blister, waiting for the fire to go out. But a big blister rises until my lip hangs out like a balloon.

The old man and his grandson finish up their work in the courtyard and leave. On the way out, the grandson drops a rake that skitters over the tile floor in the corridor like a fingernail on a blackboard. A hotel guest picks it up and hands it to him with a smile.

The smoking man lights up another cigarette. I glare at him, wishing my neighbor from home was here with her leaf blower. ▲

21. Muyil

Water...

HAVING LEFT MÉRIDA behind, we're heading toward the Peninsula's Caribbean coast and straight into a rain storm. Night has fallen, and the headlights of our bus flash across roadside puddles like comets. The storm is a stationary front that has been parked overhead for four or five days, the last hair on the tail of the dog that is the rainy season. Technically, it should have ended by now, this first week of December, but Nature is taking its Time. The problem is, people on a week's vacation don't have much Time. Reaching the bus station in the beach-town Playa del Carmen, we're waiting for our luggage to reappear from under the bus when a man beside us grumbles about going home as winter-white as he arrived.

"Where's my trophy sunburn?" he says to his wife as they wait for a bus to take them to Cancún and the airplane home.

"We could go to a tanning booth," his wife suggests.

"No one'll even know I've been away," the man complains.

In possession of our bags, we step from the bus station onto Fifth Avenue and head toward the hotel where we have a reservation. The rain has dwindled to a tropical mist, and Fifth Avenue is filled with tourists out for a night on the town. Once the town's main street,

it's now a brightly lit walking mall offering patio restaurants and shops selling jewelry, striped Mexican blankets, dishes, pottery, clothing, and cigars. A man in the door of his shop calls out, "Come see my junk, I need your money." Maitre d's rush to offer us menus. Tour-salesmen promise good deals on trips to Chichén Itzá, Cobá, Tulum, Cozumel, scuba diving, snorkeling, cenotes, and the drink-till-you're-drunk SunsetBoozeCruise. Women want to braid my hair into tight corn-rows that would only look good on (the young) Bo Derek.

Playa del Carmen was a sleepy fishing village of fewer than a thousand people until 1985 when divers and backpackers discovered its beauty. They came, they saw its beaches and coral reef, and they came back. Again and again. Small hotels and restaurants sprang up to serve them, and the village became a destination for alternative travelers. Word spread, mainstream tourists dropped in from Cancún and Cozumel, and in 1991 the hotel development known as Playacar transformed it from being a funky, laid-back divers' hangout into a sophisticated resort where guests of all-inclusive hotels need never speak a word of Spanish, nor change even a dollar into pesos. Now the city is known simply as Playa, for *beach*, the fastest growing city in Mexico.

Now it's the star of the coast known as the Riviera Maya, seventy-two miles of paradise running from just south of Puerto Morelos (in the direction of Cancún) to Punta Allen, a fishing village south of the ruins of Tulum. In 1998, Playa had 70,000 inhabitants and fewer than 14,000 hotel rooms. With hotel rooms expected to more than double by 2010, its population is soaring as hundreds of families from throughout Mexico move here to work.

And yet the flurry is calmed by the luxurious sea, its waters the soft, blue-green of old turquoise.

By lush rains nourishing the exuberant tropical vegetation.

By the subterranean rivers pouring their waters out of wide cenote-mouths into the sea.

Upon reaching our hotel, we drop our bags in the lobby and immediately step out onto the beach. We dig our toes into sand as fine as face powder beside water as black as jade in the night. Across the dark sea, the waxing Moon is rising up yellow from behind the island of Cozumel, home of the Maya fertility goddess Ixchel.

IT'S EARLY MORNING. I lie warm against David, beginning to awaken, yet not quite knowing where we are until my eyes open on the gray dawn beyond the open window and I hear the sound of waves roaring into the room, endlessly keeping to the rhythm of thrust, then pause; movement, then reflection; action and its consequence.

We've come to the coast to climb its ancient Maya pyramids—mostly smaller pyramids we suspect than those we've seen in rich cities of the interior—and to revel in its exotic beauty. A friend has arranged for us to join an eco-tour going to the ancient Maya city of Muyil this morning, and we're standing outside our hotel at 8:30 am when Eduardo, a guide for the eco-tourism company Eco-Colors, comes to collect us. In his late twenties, Eduardo is tall and lanky with longish, dark, curly hair and a ready smile. Opening the

door of the white van he drives, he introduces us to the others on the tour—three middle-aged men from London, a couple from Montreal, and newlyweds from Mexico City on their honeymoon. Then we're off on the day's adventure.

Eco-tourism, at its most basic definition, is simply nature-based travel, from rafting a river to going on safari. Increasingly, however, the term means responsible travel that conserves the environment at the same time it sustains the well-being of local people. Now, with 500 million people engaging in leisure travel each year, the number of people participating in eco-tourism is growing by 20 to 30 percent a year—with most of them going with a tour company. People crave experiences that are beyond the ordinary but not beyond their comfort zone. They want to feel like Robinson Crusoe for three or four hours, then dine in comfort on fine cuisine. They perceive the value of going with an eco-tourism company as safety (a guide), convenience (reliable equipment), and a clear conscience (no litter). As one of the Londoners tells us, "We want to do something a little more adventurous than just lie on the beach. And besides, we've already got a sunburn."

Driving south from Playa, Eduardo passes the highway going inland to the Maya city Cobá, and then the road to the Maya city Tulum beside the sea. In the town of Tulum, he stops for what he calls the "last civilized bathroom," and everyone but David lines up for the facilities at a pleasant open-air restaurant. That's one perk of tour-going—someone knows where there's a restroom.

I'm on my way back to the vehicle when I stumble on the broken edge of the sidewalk. I feel the sharp pain in my left ankle and hear the twang of muscles, ligaments, and nerves being wrenched out of place (and hopefully settling back). Suddenly, I'm staggering, thrown off balance by more broken sidewalk and loose rocks. As I struggle to stay upright, I see David's face through the window. It's his expression of alarm that keeps me going until I manage to regain my balance.

"Are you hurt?" David asks, opening the door for me.

Muyil's great pyramid has stucco images of herons on its substructure, an indication that migatory birds have been spending winters here for at least a millennium.

I describe the pain and the tearing sound. He groans.

"What do you need?" he asks

I tell him I'll be okay. "It would've been much worse if I weren't wearing my boots."

"Why do you think that happened?" he asks.

"Besides the broken sidewalk?" I say.

He nods. I shrug.

South of Tulum, the highway narrows as it enters a dense rain forest, its sodden trees leaning over the road like gossipy old women. Here the Riviera Maya segues into this pristine stretch of coast known as the Costa Maya, which is on the developers' drawing boards. Settlements here are scarce, accommodations limited, and travelers who come in to frolic in the forest or cenotes return to their hotels before nightfall or drive on south to the cities of Bacalar and Chetumal near the Mexico-Belize border. Then, within minutes, Eduardo is pulling into the archaeological zone of Muyil, and we pile out of the vehicle.

The sky over Muyil is the soft gray of old sweatpants. Rain isn't falling so much as hanging suspended in the air, and we're soaked before Eduardo can offer us thick, yellow rain slickers. With the generosity inherent in the Mexican culture, he offers us water and soft drinks and snacks from a basket brimming with bags of chips and peanuts, bananas, and apples. As we eat and drink, he talks and laughs, trying to build common ground between people from four different countries. Then he leads us into Muyil.

A medium-sized port, Muyil once functioned as a ceremonial center for several smaller ports and fishing villages along this part of the coast. In ancient times, ports were situated on the trade route around the Peninsula from Kin Pech (now Campeche) on the Gulf of Mexico to Belize and beyond, each a day's journey from the next so the Maya trade canoes could hopscotch down the coast from one to another, safely putting in at night. The sea-going canoes reached Muyil through a series of lagoons and channels, and trade goods going to the inland cities of Cobá, and later Chichén Itzá, were transported by way of a *sacbé*.

Like most Maya cities, Muyil was rebuilt several times with newer structures being placed over older ones. Current research of its buildings indicates that it was inhabited from about 100 CE until the coming of the Spaniards. Its important structures were built in 800 CE, with changes being made to them during a period of renewal after 1200. Now workmen are restoring them in keeping with a plan to make the port a major tourist attraction by 2002, drawing visitors south on Highway 307 the 95.8 miles from Cancún.

Eduardo leads us to Palacio Rosa, a structure identified by a sign as 9K, or the Temple Formerly Known as 8. This is the first ancient Maya structure that the Londoners and the couple from Montreal have seen, and they scramble like kids up steps covered with moss as thick as fur, stopping at the low entrance to a small temple on top.

"Go ahead, you can go in," Eduardo assures them. "You might be able to see a bat."

"A bat!" says one of the men, stopping short and not at all delighted.

Wanting them to experience the site at its fullest, Eduardo bounds up the steps to the temple and squats down at its entrance, ready to go in and show them there's nothing to worry about. Just as he sticks his head in, two bats fly out. He ducks, and people screech and jump back.

"Well, there now," Eduardo says, "you've seen a bat anyway."

Bats notwithstanding, the Maya of Muyil placed stucco images of giant herons on the substructure of their great pyramid. Identified by a sign as structure 81-13, this pyramid is the tallest pre-Colombian structure on the Caribbean coast at fifty-two feet. We want to climb it, but it has been closed since Hurricane Gilbert blew through in 1988, after which a woman researcher was killed during a collapse in its interior. Since then, a tomb in it has yielded 264 precious objects including jadite, shell beads, lip rings, ear flares, pendants, rings, flint knives, and a clay incensor. Yet, it's the stucco herons that most impress us—evidence that Muyil's nearby lake and lagoon have provided a winter refuge for migratory birds for at least a thousand years.

BEHIND MUYIL WE encounter the dense forest of the Sian Ka'an Biosphere Reserve, one of the most prodigiously protected natural environments in Mexico. Eduardo leads us down a forest path where we walk through rich, slick mud crisscrossed by tree roots that seem like the forest's nerves. Dampened by mist, the tree trunks are dark-coffee brown, the leaves the saturated green of old lichen. The forest is classified as tropical deciduous and subdeciduous, meaning that some of its trees lose leaves during the dry season, but for now, at the end of the rainy season, it bristles with splendid vitality.

Known to many as simply *Sian Ka'an*, Maya for Place Where the Sky Is Born, the reserve embodies the biosphere concept of establishing measures to ensure a long-term, sustainable environment for all the eco-system's inhabitants from forest to animals to local villagers who hunt and collect firewood within its wilderness. Its 1.5 million acres support a complex biological relationship between seaway and coral reef, wetlands and mangrove swamps, lakes and lagoons, tropical forests and animals, and humans. The reserve is home to a multitude of species such as jaguars, jaguarundis, howler monkeys, and small wild pigs; crocodiles and turtles; deer and anteaters; manatees; and millions of migratory birds that flock to its mild clime to wait out the cold northern winter. It also has twenty-three small, ancient Maya sites.

While tourists can visit the reserve (even camping is allowed), the number is restricted, and EcoColors and other small eco-tourism companies operating here donate part of the tour fees they collect to the local Maya community. EcoColors returns the equivalent of five dollars US per tour-goer to the community, plus hires a local man to accompany each of its groups. It also lends its kayaks to the Maya four days a week so they can earn money directly from tourists.

In the forest, we follow Eduardo single-file on the path without speaking, hoping to catch sight of birds that have made themselves scarce as we tromp on twigs and slide over roots. At a wide place on

Ancient Maya hand-dug this canal to connect Muyil's lake to the lagoon ahead, and then the sea.

the trail, Eduardo points out a *chechen* tree, which has poisonous sap that can raise blisters on the skin of humans and animals—a property the Maya supposedly used against the Spaniards.

"But wherever you find the chechen tree, you also find its antidote, the *chakah* tree," he says, placing his hand on a nearby tree having loose, reddish bark. "The locals call it the 'tourist tree' because it's skin is red and flakes off."

We walk on, and in half a mile or so, the trees give way to a large lake, and we stand beside water as smooth as a pewter platter under the gray sky. For as far as we can see, there's no hint of civilization—no buildings or powerpoles or roads—nothing to indicate that we aren't the very first people to see this lake. Except for the Maya boatman waiting with a *lancha*, or motorboat, to ferry us across the lake.

This is paradise—Nature unfettered. The gray sky is an inverted, alabaster bowl. The huge, gray lake is as fresh as new rain, fed by underground rivers bubbling up from cenotes in its lake-bed. We seem tiny in the gray landscape, gliding across the glassy lake beneath the sheltering sky.

In the distance, low *hummocks*, or islands, covered with spiky grass look like adorable green hedgehogs. On one of them, a white bird lands on a slender reed, sways, but holds steady, the first of the millions of birds that will arrive for the winter—herons, egrets, orioles, ibises, storks, and frigate birds. Hiding somewhere in the distant tall grass and dense trees are the jaguars and deer that call this land home, wild pigs and anteaters, and the crocodiles that are now thriving after their population dipped dangerously low during the craze for crocodile shoes, purses, and belts in the 1950s.

Then, nearing land ahead, the boatman cuts the lancha's speed, and with experience born of a lifetime on the lake, he gently noses the boat into a narrow canal. Barely wider that the boat, it's a quarter of a mile long, a blade of silver water cutting between green banks of razor grass. The canal, according to researchers, was hand-dug by Muyil's ancient Maya between this lake and the lagoon ahead to connect their city to the sea and make it accessible to the trade-canoes. It's an enduring artifact of Maya engineering and enterprise.

The far end of the canal delivers us into the briny water of a lagoon, and then the boat picks up speed again on the open water. On the far side of the lagoon, the boatman take us into another channel, this one some ten feet wide, a natural path to the sea. After a few hundred yards, the boat pulls alongside a dock, and we pile out.

"Okay, this is where you get wet," Eduardo says.

The adventure calls for us to travel down the channel toward the sea, letting the current move us along at two miles per hour to where the boat will pick us up. Wanting to take photos, David stays with the boat, and I watch as he disappears around a bend downstream.

Eduardo passes out bright life vests and offers snorkel equipment to those who want it. He shows us how to slip into the water without stirring the white sediment on the bottom into a dense cloud of invisibility, and one by one we slide from the dock into the water.

The water is surprisingly cold, and I shiver in getting used to it. The current makes it feel very different from a lake or swimming pool, as though the water in the channel is alive, with a will and influence of its own. Leaning back into my life preserver, I play with the current, experimenting with the feel of it. For awhile, I float effortlessly, eyes closed, drifting, surrendering my control to the water on its way through the channel. Lying back like this, I'm a log, flotsam on the cloud-gray water going surely to the sea. I'm Huck Finn in Mexico instead of on the Mississippi, with a space-age life preserver instead of a home-made raft.

Opening my eyes, I have a duck's view of banks alive with mangrove trees so wide and spreading that they seem an impenetrable tangle you couldn't get through if your life depended on it. Their leaves are oval eyes, their multiple silvery gray roots like legs so they look like centipedes dancing on the banks.

At one point, it begins to rain, and drops fall all around me, water into water, surrounding me in silvery stars of splash.

I try paddling and am amazed at my speed in going with the flow. I'm suddenly Mark Spitz, the Olympic swimmer. My effort is redoubled by the current, and I make excellent headway through the channel—like taking the moving walkway at the airport. But then, I'm getting too far ahead of Eduardo and the others, and I lean back into the preserver and let the water carry me at its own speed.

Subtle as a dream, the current wends its way between the banks, racing like a pulse in tight places and lazing through the wider ones, as though demonstrating the mercurial nature of water—nuturing life at times, yet also equally capable of destroying it. Floating along, I'm the water's captive, and it pushes me like a leaf toward the bank and the mangrove roots that would pluck me from the current and hold onto me if given half a chance. But not wanting to get stuck in the flotilla of leaves, I reassert my will and paddle to the channel center.

In a place without mangroves, the current pushes me toward the grassy bank. I stick out my foot to push off of what appears to be white stone. But instead of touching something solid, my foot sinks into the soggy-dog muck of tender soil barely held in place by a thatch of grass roots. Still the current pushes me toward the bank, and I stick out my other foot, directing it lower, seeking something of substance with which to change my direction. But there's nothing but water where the grass overhangs the soil by a foot or more, concealing the deeply concave bank below.

Suddenly, I recall being a kid and watching a horror movie on television about a killer crocodile. I hid then behind the easy chair where my grandma sat, and peeked out to watch a big croc grab a beautiful young woman and drag her down into the water. The huge reptile spun her around and around until she drowned, then it stored her body beneath a bank that was stocked like a pantry with other decaying human bodies ripening until the beast had an appetite for them. I shudder now at the memory, and drawing in my feet, I paddle hard toward the center of the channel.

"A boat is coming," Eduardo calls out from his place at the rear of the group. "Get close to the bank."

The opposite bank is lined with mangroves, and I paddle over and hang onto the tree roots as two boats approach. People bundled in yellow slickers pass silently by.

"Come on in and swim with us," Eduardo says to them, grinning. "You're missing the best part."

They don't answer, they don't smile.

"Why don't they swim?" asks one of the Londoners as the people disappear around a bend.

"That tour company doesn't offer swimming," Eduardo says.

"But why? We're having fun," says the woman from Montreal.

"I think they're afraid of crocodiles," Eduardo says, eyes twinkling.

A man jumps into the channel that connects the lagoon to the sea.

"Really?" asks the woman.

"Really," Eduardo says, trying to stifle a smile.

I assume he's joking, but I don't ask.

DAVID IS WAITING for us in the lancha with the boatman. As Eduardo explains how we'll be getting into the boat, I'm glad David is in the boat and not behind me taking photos.

"Now here's how we're going to do it," Eduardo says, bracing himself against the boat. "Just put your foot on my knee here and I'll give you the boost you need to get up."

The knee we're to stand on is braced against his other knee, which is braced against the boat. The channel bottom is too silty to offer him any support, so it's a water trick.

When it's my turn, I place my hand on Eduardo's shoulder and step as lightly as possible on his knee, not wanting to wrench his joint. I leap up and grab for the side of the boat. I hoist myself up and balance on the edge on my stomach, teetering, about to fall back into the water (which would be funny, I admit.) I toss a leg up and over the edge of the boat, and I can just imagine the view of my backside going up and up, pausing and nearly plummeting down into the water with a splash. But I manage to shift my weight a fraction of an inch and at the last second, I dump myself into the boat. I laugh and take a seat.

When we're all in the motorboat, it heads back up the channel, back across the lagoon, back through the hand-dug canal, back across the lake toward Muyil. A heron flies, flapping its great wings to gain altitude, swooping, soaring, big and proud. Soon he'll have a million companions, happy to be in their protected winter home. Tourist birds, as we are tourists, in the place where the sky is born.

EDUARDO RETURNS US to the restaurant with the "last civilized bathroom" where he supplies us with dinner—I select a delicious grilled fresh fish hot from the fire and a papaya milk shake. Then he's off to Palenque where he'll be guiding people on a two-week bike tour, and we're back in our hotel. While David cleans his cameras, the rhythm of the waves on the beach fills the room—thrust, then pause; movement, then reflection; action, and its consequences—and I get out my notebook and write down the events of the day.

In Sian Ka'an, we stood with Nature in all of its glorious complexity. I think we were good eco-tourists: Guided by Eduardo, we left nothing but our footprints (and not many of those). And our participation benefited the Maya community. In the Human versus Pristine Forest controversy, some would say that we had no business being in the reserve—that Nature should be left untouched, even unseen, by humans, whose very presence impacts it. My view is that we're in relationship with Nature every moment of our lives in a harmonious interchange (although the harmony might not always be apparent). Did we harm the environment? No, but then there *was* the gasoline and sound of the motorboat. Are we enriched from having gone? Yes, although it's probably not important to anyone but us. But then, like a tree, I too am a daughter of Nature, with responsibilities and privileges.

"How's your ankle?" David asks, as he puts his cameras away.

It's swollen and doesn't flex at all, I tell him. "But I'm sure the cold water in the channel helped it a lot."

David wraps my ankle in the elastic bandage we carry with us and gives me Advil, and I consider his earlier question about my frame of mind before twisting it. What I remember is the happy anticipation of going out in a boat on the open water, and I can see no cause for the mishap other than the broken sidewalk. Then suddenly, I remember being carried along in the current, being pushed this way and that by the silty water, and it occurs to me that travel is an act of deliberate adventure, with all of its potential for the unexpected to happen. Even when we imprint each day with our intention for it, much is still out of our control. While we want to believe that we control our direction—and we do to some extent—we're also part of the vast current of Time-Place in which we live. We find ourselves mired in backwaters sometimes and at other times caught in rapids moving too fast. As travelers, we want Sun, and sometimes get rain. We seek fun, and sometimes get circumstances we couldn't have fathomed at the outset. As we navigate the current, our "life preserver" is our desire to attain what we want—and our resiliency to mediate between what we plan (and pray for) and what manifests. I write:

We weave the fabric of our lives
with each surprising new color given to us
by events beyond ordinary control from Time to Time. ▲

22. Cenote

More Water...

AGAIN, THE EVENTS of a water-soaked day happen too quickly to be recorded on the spot and must be stubbornly remembered until I can write them in my notebook. The day dawns cloudy over Playa, and before we leave our hotel room, I slip my notebook into a plastic bag and put it in my backpack. It's harder for David to protect his cameras from the rain. But as we get into the nice, dry Chevy van from the eco-tourism company Alltournative Expeditions, we don't know how hard.

"You're ready?" asks the guide Gavin.

"We are," I say.

We've signed up with Alltournative Expeditions for a trip to a cenote inside the rain forest. According to the *Guinness Book of Records* (1997), the cenote Nohoch Na Chich south of Playa opens into the longest underwater cave system in the world—just forty-two miles of it so far charted by divers—and we're eager to see it. But first the van stops at the exclusive Riu hotel in Playacar to collect the rest of the tour-goers—six Canadian men for whom the trip to the cenote is a stag party. Brad is to be married tomorrow, and his best man, father, uncle, future father-in-law, and sister's boyfriend have chosen a day of

adventure for Brad's last day as a single man. They're in high spirits.

Even though it's starting to rain.

"A little rain can't be that bad," says the groom's father.

Gavin just smiles.

He's still smiling when the van drops us off near Tulum, and with a wink, he goes to get the off-road vehicle that will carry us to the cenote. We all laugh and talk as we wait in a courtyard, swept up in the adventure and ready for fun.

By the time Gavin returns, it's raining buckets.

"Your chariot awaits," he says, coming to collect us.

In the driveway is a mammoth vehicle—a six-ton Mercedes Benz 4 x 4 truck called a Unimog. At twenty feet long and nine feet tall, the Unimog was designed to haul military personnel and supplies in the world's hot spots for agencies such as the United Nations.

"It doesn't go fast," Gavin explains, "but it goes anywhere. And we'll need that capability where we're going."

The thrill of its ruggedness electrifies the men, who declare they're glad to be doing some "real four-wheeling," and the anticipation of going off-road (and the stories they'll take home) lights their eyes.

Gavin prepares to muscle the Unimog over the road's rocks and tree stumps.

The color of dirt, the Unimog looks like an enormous, open sardine can atop big, fat tires. Its stuffed with power and has a complicated-looking gear shift mechanism that can manage more than two dozen speeds. Forget super-sized SUVs. Forget road-hogging Humvees. This is a motorized mastadon.

Forget comfort, too. This particular vehicle has no windshield. Its bare-bones "personnel" area is open except for a black tarp draped over some steel bars, and there's no enclosure to stop the weather from coming in. The only amenities are two hard, bench seats running along both sides, and a steel pipe wrapped with duct tape running down the center between them.

"I'll show you what that bar is for," Gavin promises.

"I can imagine," says one of the men appreciatively.

The first adventure is getting up into the vehicle. Gavin lets down the tailgate and instructs us to step up onto a narrow bar on the swinging gate, then up into the bed of the truck. Both are long steps, even for long legs like mine.

Then there's the choice of seating.

"Sit toward the back and you fly with the bumps," Gavin says. "Sit in the front and you get the wind and water."

David wants the front for taking photos, and I sit beside him. Across from us are Brad's father, father-in-law and uncle, while the younger men take the rear.

When we're settled, Gavin explains the purpose of the center bar: When going over bumps, we're to hold onto it with one hand, and the side of the truck with the other.

"It'll help keep bits of your face off the steel frame," he says.

The men laugh.

"Okay, now," Gavin says, "we're going to have a practice run."

Before he starts the engine, he offers us large, black plastic trash bags to help keep us dry. The younger men refuse them, but David and I take one. It's another one of the great Commandments of Tourism: Never turn down anything you might need later. I get out my knife and cut holes in my impromptu black raincoat for my head and arms. Putting it on, I look like a penguin with pink arms.

Gavin starts the Unimog and drives it onto a dirt service road that parallels the highway. As the mighty truck picks up speed, rain pours in the front of the unprotected personnel area.

"Ready?" Gavin hollers above the engine noise.

"Yeah!" the men call.

Ahead, a deep puddle almost covers the road. The Unimog hits it without slowing, and the water from the puddle joins the rain to become a swill of dirt soup that splashes into the truck. At the same time, the truck bounces hard into a bump, throwing us up off the seats to land with a slap. I thank myself for accepting the black plastic that now keeps me dry.

Gavin slows the truck and hollers back over his shoulder: "Now just one more thing—in the rain forest, the road is very narrow, and when there're branches coming up, I'm going to call out 'branch.' Be careful then, because they can slap you hard. Got that? Branch."

In his South African accent, the word sounds like "brunch."

"Yeah, brunch," the men say, laughing. "We'll watch out for brunch."

Gavin turns onto the highway, and the rain, made torrential by the speed of the Unimog, pummels our faces like steel pellets. Despite not having a windshield, Gavin seems not to notice the rain. A little past thirty, he's muscular and well-built. His sandy hair is a close-cropped cap, his thin nose polished by weather. When he turns to look at us, his hazel eyes shine with delight. He's clearly a man who loves the outdoors.

"Only mad dogs and South Africans go out in the midday rain," David tells him.

Gavin just smiles.

In a few miles, Gavin turns the Unimog onto a narrow rut leading into the jungle toward the cenote *Nohoch Na Chich*, Maya for Big House, and cuts the engine. The rain has let up to a tepid drizzle, and he suggests we roll up the truck's tarp.

"Lucky for you, you've got rain today," he says. "The rain forest is at its best in the rain. And besides, the water helps the truck slide over the bumps."

This seems a good thing since the road ahead appears to be only bumps. Barely wider than the truck's frame, it's the road from Hell with tree stumps protruding from between white rocks that look like the knobby joints of the Earth's skeleton. Gavin starts the engine, and the Unimog grinds forward, rocking from side to side over bumps in the road like a canoe in rough water. We come so close to the trees along the road that I can see the worm-trails in their bark.

"Branch," Gavin calls, and a branch full of sopping leaves slaps the truck's frame, tossing a bucketful of rain on us.

The Unimog seems to leap from stone to stone like a frog after flies.

"Brunch," we sputter, wiping water from our faces.

The forest is magnificent in the rain. The trees' trunks are as dark as the polished wood of a dining room table. Leaves are as big as saucers and vibrantly green. It's as though the artist who painted this scene selected only the most saturated colors on his palette. Brilliant red flowers hang from vines in the tops of trees like Christmas lights. Spiky bromeliads with lush red centers cascade down the tree trunks like feather boas on chorus girls. Strappy-leafed epiphytes snuggle into branches as they prepare to shoot out stems of orchids like rockets.

Gavin muscles the Unimog forward, dropping into a lower gear to finesse the water-soaked trenches, then goosing it up the rocky hills. The truck leaps from stone to stone like a frog after a fly.

"Branch," he says.

A satellite dish gives the Maya in this family compound a window on the world.

"Brunch," we yell.

Then the road narrows impossibly.

"Branch," Gavin warns.

"Log," one of the men says in alarm.

Gavin stops the truck beside a narrow fissure in the forest floor—one of the two-dozen windows into the underground river we'll soon be swimming. Having this grand cenote changed the fortune of the Maya family who owns this land, Gavin tells us. The father of the family homesteaded this small *rancho*, or farm, several years ago, claiming it from acreage set aside for natives of the area. He believed the cenote would be helpful in providing water for the lime trees he planned to plant. The trees grew, and he established a market for the limes. Money from lime sales was used to purchase cooking oil, salt, and clothing

while the family grew most of their food and hunted for meat.

The family's financial situation changed when in the late 1980s, scuba divers began exploring the cenotes and underground rivers in the area. As the Nohoch Na Chich cenote became known, the family began charging divers a hundred pesos to dive. With Alltournative bringing in groups of eco-tourists, the family's income has jumped again. Now a satellite dish in the compound of their traditional, thatch-roofed homes gives them a window on the world.

Gavin stops talking when he spots a leaf cutter that has been hitching a ride on the truck's frame. He takes off a leather glove and coaxes the insect onto his finger. It's a fat green wedge with legs—a cartoon bug.

"Look at it," he says, "isn't it fantastic?"

Suddenly sunshine breaks through the clouds, and its light reflects from millions of wet leaves that glint and sparkle until the forest looks like a mirrored Disco ball. Butterflies as big as a man's hand emerge from hiding, some wearing green-and-brown camouflage while others are wildly, bravely, black-yellow-red. A blue one, a morpho, is the blue of the summer sky. Life shines from every inch of the rain forest, and I remember the words of Henry Wordsworth: "Nature is something that touches the essentials of the heart, making us feel part, not apart."

In the midst of such vibrancy, the spirit can't help but soar.

WHEN WE REACH the Maya family compound, Gavin leads us on foot to the cenote, and we descend two dozen steps into the mouth of the underground cavern. The scene could be from *Jurassic Park*. Long fingers of sunlight probe the depths, making rainbows in the mist. Ferns lift arching, neon-green fronds. Birds flit. Lizards lounge. Dragonflies hot-dog around like miniature helicopters. Beneath it all is the black water of a river flowing into the heart of darkness.

Beside the water, the facilities constructed to serve scuba divers and snorkelers are neat and practical. A large deck of sturdy planks supports a high table for personal gear and a low one for used diving equipment. There's a large dressing room for clothing changes. Bright, new life preservers hang on a clothesline, and snorkel masks lay on a table in a perfect, straight line.

"Okay," Gavin says, getting our attention. "Did anyone put on sunscreen today?"

None of us is wearing sunscreen because of the rain, but if we were, we'd need to wash it off before entering the cenote to keep its oil from polluting the clear water of the cenote. Tour-goers are also advised not to use deodorant or perfume.

"Okay, then, grab a snorkel mask," Gavin says.

Brad's future father-in-law makes no move to get a mask—he tells Gavin that he can't swim.

"How are you with floating then?" Gavin asks, assuring him that the life preserver would keep his head above water.

Brad's uncle isn't too sure about his snorkeling skills.

"You can mostly keep your face out of the water," Gavin says, adding that he's a certified diver. "If at any time you feel you've got to leave, I'll bring you right out."

But beyond offering this reassurance, Gavin doesn't coax. When I ask him about it later, he tells me he figures that people know their limits. He tries to get them to quell their fears enough to swim at least to the mouth of the river. "If they get that far," he says, " I just say, 'Is everyone okay?' and they think 'Yeah, I'm okay.'" His youngest tour-goer was thirteen (the minimum age), the oldest seventy-three. But the adventure is not for people afraid of water or unable to handle the physical challenge. And it's not for people with claustrophobia.

"Okay, who's going?" Gavin asks.

David needs to take photos and elects to stay on the deck. Brad's future father-in-law also stays behind.

Gavin moves to the tasks at hand. He teaches us to spit on the

Snorkelers leap into the cenote Nohoch Na Chich, part of longest underwater cave system in the world.

inside lens of our snorkel masks and rub the saliva over the plastic to prevent fogging. When we put on our life preservers, he double-checks the fasteners and makes sure we cinch up the strap running through the crotch so the vests will keep our heads above water. He hands each of us an underwater flashlight and tells us to familiarize ourselves with it so we can turn it off and on with our eyes closed. I do everything he tells us to do until he instructs us to jump into the cenote.

While the men leap in, I descend the ladder into the cold water.

LIKE MOST INTERESTING women, the Yucatán Peninsula has a past. For eons, the Yucatán lay beneath the surface of the sea, the last stop for the billions of sea creatures that died and drifted down to the ocean floor to be slowly compressed into limestone.

Then, some 150 million years ago, the Earth's fortunes changed, and the sea receded, leaving the Peninsula high and dry. The limestone became exposed to rains that percolated through its fractures, eroding them, enlarging them, and occasionally carving them into great underground cave systems. Under the right conditions, each drop of rainwater that dripped into the subterranean world left an iota of deposit. Very gradually these deposits built up to form stalactites (hanging "titely" from the ceiling) and stalagmites ("mitey" columns) in the grand caverns.

Finally, at the end of the most recent Ice Age, the glaciers melted, and the level of the sea rose, sealing off many of the underwater galleries. Hidden beneath the surface, they've only became visible as the ground has collapsed in places, making a cenote, a Maya portal into the watery Underworld.

Unlike the large, open cenotes at Chichén Itzá and Dzibilchaltún, this one is tucked beneath an overhang of rock, its water open on only one side as though caught in a tipped teacup. As I descend the ladder into the crystal-clear water, little black fish dart around my legs like slender bullets, and the cold—the water is only about 64 degrees Fahrenheit—creeps up my thighs.

"Okay, let's go," Gavin orders, motioning me away from the ladder.

I let go and fall back into the water with a splash, panicky as the cold envelopes me and I struggle to adjust. But then I lean into my life preserver, and am buoyed in the water, and I pull my snorkel mask over my eyes. I know I'm good to go when I can't get a draft of air through the mask.

Gavin is giving final instructions: Don't touch the stalactites—they are millions of years old; stay together; go single file when told.

But in truth, I'm only half listening.

The stone mouth of the cavern lies ahead, behind which is only the darkness of the Underworld. This is where the ancient Maya believed the souls of the dead go, into this cold, dark, watery abyss until the end of Time, when they will rise up and cross the Milky Way to be reunited with the One. It's an enchanted world full of spirits. It's mystical. Mythic.

I'm in awe of floating into the mouth of the Underworld on this river of black water, gliding under the curtain of stone hanging down like a uvula. Behind me at the entrance, I see David standing on the deck, silhouetted by golden sunlight. But as I pass into the dark throat of the cavern, the sunlight grows distant, gold fading to blue on the water's surface, then to gray, then silver.

In the shadowy realm ahead are the people of the Underworld. Stout columns emerge from the water like fat bathers emerging, dripping, from a swim. Delicate stalactites hang from the cavern ceiling like girls on trapezes frozen mid-swing. In one place, a stalactite hovers over stalagmite beneath the water's surface, seeming to reach for it, the points nearly touching but not quite—yearning lovers, Romeo and Juliet in stone, destined never to unite.

Passing through small rooms in the cavern and grand chambers brings a wonderland of sights: fossil sponges of stone, stone seashells the size of a fist, labyrinthine stone brain coral. Star bursts of sparkly, moist points emanate from the ceilings, glistening in the beams of our flashlights, looking like all the stars of Heaven falling in a trail of light.

"What's that brown stuff?" asks one of the men, pointing to a dark spot on the ceiling.

"Bat poop," Gavin says. "Wherever you see that, you'll find bats. Come look."

He paddles under the brown stain and directs the beam of his flashlight up to the ceiling. Brown bats as cute as Beanie Babies open their pink mouths in protest. Squirmy and vexed, they squeal until Gavin drops the beam.

He looks at me. "Did you lose your lamp?"

"No it's here," I say, lifting the lamp dangling from my wrist.

"Well, then, turn it on," he says.

We go ever deeper into the cavern, leaving the light of day for a world born into darkness. At one point Gavin instructs us to switch off our lamps, and pitch black closes down my vision so I can't tell whether my eyes are open or closed. Human eyes never adjust to such darkness, and fish and snakes here are blind as Nature enforces her law of "use it or lose it."

I follow along through the bends and twists in the river. Entering its inner sanctums, I learn its secrets. I hear the song it sings to itself as it sloshes into nooks and crannies, making splishy-splish sounds in the smaller ones, and in the bigger crevices, the hollow wock-wock of a big log drum. It pushes and pulls me in a manner reminiscent of the current in the channel at Muyil under the open sky. It snuggles against me. It lifts me up (with my life preserver), and carries me off as it desires until I protest with a countermove. It learns the terrain of my body, its hills and valleys. It licks the salts from my skin. It molds to me like a second skin—as it would mold to the interior passages of my throat and lungs if given half a chance.

Yet, even deep inside the cavern, the surface makes itself known. Water percolating down through a fissure in the stone dribbles onto my head—warm, like water from a teakettle, as it carries the Sun's energy underground. Roots from trees overhead follow the stones' fractures, seeking moisture to carry them through the dry season, and they hang into the water like thick, brown straws.

Gavin directs his light ahead to a tight tunnel where the cavern ceiling closes down nearly to the water.

"Okay, we're going under that curtain," he says. "Single file."

When my turn comes, I float on my back into the narrow opening, feeling the water rising up into my ears, creeping up on my cheeks, making its way toward my eyes. The limestone drape hangs low over my face, refusing to give me even half-an-inch. But then I'm clear of it and into a small chamber with more low places ahead.

Gavin is counting. . . four, five, six.

"Where's your lamp?" he asks.

"It's here," I say, making no move to turn it on in the comfortable dark. It occurs to me only later that he might be counting light beams as a means of keeping track of his charges.

We pass through two more tight, stone openings, and suddenly we're in a domed chamber. In the beam of the flashlights, the ceiling is as scaly and rough as a crocodile skin. This is the Earth's innards. We've reached the bowels of the dragon.

ONE OF THE men in the group is cold to the bone, and having been in the water for nearly an hour, he shivers uncontrollably—his lips a blue stain across his face. I'm comfortable, protected by my feminine fat. But our journey upriver has come to an end. Gavin turns and leads us silently downstream through the dark water.

Ahead a tiny silver eye winks at the end of the long, black tunnel. It widens as I get nearer. Then, I see its twin—the oval reflection it casts on the water's glassy surface. From inside the river's stone throat, I seem to be trapped on the far side of a mirror, peering into the world of the living, not as one of its bright beings but as a creature of the cold, watery abyss.

"Here come the guppies," David says, sounding far away.

As I near the cenote's entrance, the silver eye on the water's surface opens wide and turns blue, then green with the reflected shapes of bright ferns. Then David's reflection is there, too, his face in the water.

The men paddle swiftly to the ladder, while I hang back, not quite ready to leave this exotic world. Ahead the water picks up the men's movements, and the mirror images waver, then ripple, then fracture into a kaleidoscope of light and color. David lifts his camera, focuses, and shoots several photos. Click, click, click goes his camera as it blinks its mechanical eye, and the cavern picks up the sound and bounces it off the walls and water, distorting it.

"Poink, poink, poink," echos the cavern.

As the men climb the ladder, I revel in the brilliance of daylight and the happy chatter of birds. I'm sad to leave this black water heading toward the sea. It knows me—it has tasted me and borne my weight. I know it, too—its cool fingers, its taste. And yet, I know I'm one of the lucky ones—an escapee from the Underworld, before the end of Time.

DAVID GIVES ME his hand, and pulls me up beside him on the planks of the deck, and I'm suddenly cold and shivering. I place my mask into the neat rows of masks. My life preserver goes onto the clothesline to drip dry. My feet leave behind drops of water brought from the Underworld to be vaporized by the Sun.

Back at the Maya family compound, two women are cooking dinner for us on a traditional hearth of three stones. They send us to sit at a long table covered with red oil-cloth, which they load with platters of chicken seasoned with achiote, rice and beans, tomatoes and pickled red onions. There are warm, handmade tortillas and a bowl of xnipek made spicy by habañero peppers.

As we eat, we all laugh and talk, exhilarated by our adventure. We're happy and eager to share our impressions. We share the camaraderie of a challenge undertaken and met. The food seems especially delicious, and I'm thankful to be eating. I wrap my hands around my mug of hot coffee, reveling in its warmth, and make note of what I'll write in my notebook when I get the chance:

> *The land of the living is warm.*
> *It has texture and brilliance. Thank God.*

"*Dios Botik,*" we say to the women as we leave, thanking them for the meal in the Maya words Gavin has taught us.

Then too soon we're dropping the Canadians off at the Riu and saying goodbye to Gavin. I can't help but hug him, my guide to the Underworld.

IT'S NIGHT, AND in our hotel room I surrender to the bed. I can hear the ocean pounding the shore of this peninsula that was born at the bottom of the sea, and which even now is now undercut by magnificent rivers. This is a land of water. Even the wind mimics the sound of falling water, as it fiddles with the palm leaves.

David is quickly asleep, but I fight sleep, not wanting the day to end too soon. But I can't keep my eyes open. I doze, and the bed becomes a raft and I'm floating. In my sleep, I re-experience the motion of the underground river—not the rhythmic beat of ocean waves, but the sporadic sloshing of a playful current. I open my eyes, and reaffirm that I'm in bed. But even so, my body is recreating the sensation of my experience of the black water. It's like when I was a kid, and I roller-skated for hours, only to feel the friction of the skate wheels on concrete zinging through my feet as I fell asleep. With its own intelligence, my body is remembering the river, and I lie back and go along for the ride.

A legend in the Yucatán says that if you drink the water of a cenote, you'll be forever destined to return to it. As I tuck this extraordinary experience into my memory, I think that I'll never quite leave this land of water. ▲

23. Cobá

Death and Potential...

THE JUNGLE NOW owns the once-mighty city of Cobá. Cobá once tamed the jungle in this area. Gave it what for, and let it know who was boss. Beat it back and put people and cornfields in its place. But all that's changed now. The area's back under Old Management.

David and I enter Cobá on another day of rain (just what the jungle ordered), having driven from Playa del Carmen thirty-eight miles south to Tulum, then turning inland to drive another thirty or so miles to Cobá. Now at midday, we follow a path under tall trees that let barely a drop of rain fall through their canopy.

The jungle here is a living, breathing entity (that exhales the oxygen we treasure). This is not the short, scrubby, dry, and long-disturbed brushy woods of Chichén Itzá. This is rain country, where nearly forty inches of rain fall each year. Where the jungle is a great, green (not so jolly) giant that if it were to pull itself up, would reach the stratosphere. It's dark. Dense. Thorny. With noisy flies, sluggish in the drizzle.

Splashes of yellow and orange here aren't flowers but fungus undermining the wet wood.

Tour-buses pull up and people step out of their air-conditioned space capsules on wheels and walk down a path between the trees in shorts and sandals. The jungle pants, tongue out, watching them, taking inventory: Skin. Blood. Muscle marbled with fat. Hair (indigestible).

Visitors are here, by grace, on a day-pass.

At night they'd be bait. Sweet meat.

The pyramids, once the divas of Cobá's stuccoed plazas, are now precarious stepping stones drowning in a sea of trees. The jungle crashes against them, wearing them down, returning whatever man has made (and man himself) to the Earth.

Walking beneath the tall trees, we're like toothpicks beside fence posts. The whiteness of our skin seems out of place here. In the jungle, the only things white are fragile—a transitory flower and a twenty-four-hour butterfly. Or hidden—snaky, albino roots beneath a fallen log. The forest lets me know how small we humans are, made Big only by our will.

As we walk toward Cobá's great pyramid, we spot a snake at the edge of the path. About as round as my forearm and over four feet long, it lies as still as a tree root in the dirt. The putrid smell of death

rises from it, and we see that its head has been chopped off. A beetle with a back as blue as a peacock feather walks beside it, rolling a ball of organic brown soil down its length. (I can't help but think of Egypt's scarab beetles rolling their precious eggs of dung.) The ball hits a bump and gets away from the beetle. The beetle charges after it, and carefully gets it back on track before resuming the push.

We're bending over, watching, when a man and woman stop to see what we're looking at.

"A snake!" the woman shrieks.

"It's dead!" the man tells her, but she shrieks again and runs off.

David takes the snake's photo and I draw the pattern of its skin in my notebook. After that, my gaze lingers on every fallen tree limb and creeping root, seeing in them the loitering ghosts of serpents.

I HOBBLE ALONG, my ankle swollen against the elastic bandage wrapped around it inside my boot, sore to the touch and unable to flex. It's going to take me awhile to walk the 1.2 miles to the great pyramid.

"You go on ahead," I tell David.

He stops in his tracks. "You know that tricycle-taxi we saw at the entrance? Why not hire it?"

We return to the entrance where a delicate-looking boy stands beside a *trici-taxi*, one of the three-wheeled bikes we've seen throughout the Peninsula, loaded with firewood, a table and chairs, a live pig, a dog, women and children, a washing machine, and the strangest of all, a plain wooden coffin. The boy quotes a price, and I climb in. I feel his legs pumping hard as he gets the trike's wheels going on the damp path, trying to gain momentum. His lungs are its carburetor, his legs its pistons.

At first he tries to keep pace with David's walking, a good gait but erratic as David stops to take photos. Finally David motions the boy to go on, and the trike gains speed. People coming from the pyramid see me flying towards it on wheels and smile and say, "Why

didn't I think of that?"

"Where are you from?" the boy asks.

I tell him and ask his name, which is Luz.

"You speak Spanish," he says.

"*Poquito*," I say. A little.

"Do you speak German?" he asks.

"No, do you?"

"A little," he says. "French?"

"No, do you?"

"A little," he says. "Italian?"

"No, do you?"

"A little," he says.

"But I know three words in Maya," I tell him.

"Which?" he asks, his voice unbelieving.

I recite the words roughly equivalent of thank you, how are you?, and you're welcome. But Luz doesn't comment—we've reached the pyramid, and he's braking the trike, bringing it to a stop for me to get off. As I hobble away, it occurs to me that I've forgotten to ask him if he would wait and take me back.

ARRIVING AT THE pyramid ahead of David, I look up its long staircase with trepidation. The Sun has broken through the clouds, its rays transforming this pyramid called *Nohoch Mul*, or Big Pyramid, into a castle the color of pale, yellow tigers' eyes.

At the height of its power, Cobá was the godfather of trade and commerce on the Caribbean coast. The grand manager of goods and services coming into and leaving the northern Yucatán, it grew large and wealthy and stood unequalled in the area. With ties to Tikal in Guatemala, it was the keeper of Maya orthodox architecture and ceremonies on this New Frontier. The earliest date that has been found at the site is 613 CE, the last one November 30, 780.

Coba's great pyramid—tall, weathered, dignified—is still lord of the trees that surround it.

With four lakes in its midst, Cobá enjoyed fertile land and fresh water that gave it surpluses of corn. But as the city expanded to cover more than forty square miles, it required even more labor and agricultural products than its citizens could provide. As it reached out to farmers in surrounding towns, it became a city of roads. To connect the grand metropolis with its rural suppliers, Cobá built a highway system of sixteen radiating *sacbeob*. Additional regional roads with access and exit ramps linked Cobá to Ixil, some twelve miles away, and to Muyil on the coast. Thirty-five local roads connected the rural and regional roads.

But it was the coming of the Itzá that caused Cobá to build the longest known road in the Maya realm.

When the Itzá moved into the center of the Peninsula aiming to establish a power base, they set their sights on conquering the prosperous little town of Yaxuná at the edge of Cobá's sphere of influence. The king of Cobá considered Yaxuná a strategic location, and to fortify Cobá's claim on it, he commissioned a road to be built between the two cities. As the Itzá advanced toward Yaxuná, Cobá's workmen hurried to quarry, stack, and pack three-quarters-of-a-million cubic yards of rock for the road, the surface of which was two to eight feet higher than the forest floor. They capped its surface with tons of white stone. It became the grandest road in the realm at sixty-two miles long, thirty-two feet wide, and an average of five feet high.

For awhile, Cobá stayed the Itzá, but finally the Itzá prevailed. Cobá went into a slow tailspin from which it never recovered—perhaps because it had overextended its resources in building the road to Yaxuná, or perhaps because it fell victim to the century-long drought that apparently contributed to the collapse of other major cities in the realm. Whatever the reason, the jungle slowly ate Cobá. Now only one percent of the formerly grand city is visible among the trees. If that.

I stand beside the great pyramid, waiting for David to arrive, and we climb together, although he ascends faster. Its steps are not the even steps of Chichén Itzá and Uxmal, which have steps as straight as orthodontured teeth. These steps are rough. No two are the same size or height, and they throw my ankle this way and that, teasing it to the point of pain. I'm compelled to use that wounded foot only for stabilization as I push my weight up step after step with the other leg.

This pyramid is the highest in these parts—more than one-hundred-twenty feet tall. Its body is composed of seven platforms, its stairway thirty-nine-feet wide. But for some reason, its stairs don't raise my usual fear of heights. The dreaded Moth of Fear doesn't awaken and flap in my stomach as it does at Chichén Itzá's pyramid. Perhaps the millions of trees in Cobá seem like a safety net.

At the summit, the pyramid reveals its splendor. Threshold stones leading into its temple have been carved to resemble shells—the sea elevated to the top of the sacred mountain. In a niche above its temple door is a stucco statue of the Diving God, or Descending God, portrayed as a honey bee and called *Ah Muzencab*, or He Who Guards the Honey. He was one of the sky-bearers in ancient Maya mythology, and here his countenance still bears traces of original blue paint.

While the city's other structures have fallen to the jungle, this tall, dignified pyramid is still lord of the trees (with some help from archaeologists). It's still the stately grandfather prevailing over the flood of trees at its feet that covers every inch of ground like the mighty Mississippi overflowing the barrier walls that protect the towns along its path. I wonder if this old-man pyramid still holds a shred of spirit from the Maya who built it.

The yellow of the pyramid notwithstanding, green is the dominant color here. The rain forest is a vast organism of palpitating chlorophyll that seems to come in every shade and hue of green. Emerald, jade, lime, avocado, and olive. The green of grass, apples, peas, pines, moss, mint, and snot.

In the end, the city of Cobá—for all its wealth and power—couldn't withstand the onslaught of the rain forest. It's the nature of the jungle to reduce and recycle, to rot and renew, and it finally bankrupted even the rich godfather Cobá. I write in my notebook:

The jungle—a thing of beauty and betrayal.
Dream-eater.

DAVID AND I sit on the pyramid until nearly nightfall, watching as the trees clamp the falling Sun in their branches and extinguish its light. In the dusk, we slowly descend the steps and walk toward the path leading out. Ahead, there's movement in the shadow of a low wall where Luz is talking with another young man. When Luz sees me, he jumps up and pushes the trici-taxi toward me. I climb on, and he pumps the pedals. As before, David waves him on ahead.

On the path back to the entrance, the older, stockier boy that Luz had been talking to rides his two-wheel bike alongside us.

"Is it true you know words in Maya?" the boy asks.

His forwardness surprises me; in this area of the Peninsula, people normally seem more reserved with strangers.

I tell him it's true.

"Which?" he asks, and listens as I repeat the words I know.

The ride back to the entrance is fast—the boys are like horses going home to the corral for the night. The way is slightly downhill, and Luz peddles fast, taking the rocks and dips hard, racing through patches of mud.

"Do you want to learn three more?" the young man says.

"Are they good words?" I ask, aware of the potential for a prank.

"Yes," he says, and Luz agrees.

"Are you sure?" I persist, but they're steadfast.

They teach me the Maya words for another version of how are you?, alright, and where do you live? I give up on trying to remember the pronounciation and open my notebook to write them phonetically.

When Luz rolls to a stop at the trici-taxi station, I get out of the trike and lean against a tree, trying to keep my weight off of my ankle. The boys are volunteering more words, and they watch me write them

A warning about crocodiles keeps people from swimming in this lake near Cobá.

down—Maya words sounded out in the flat twang of Rocky Mountain English and carefully written on the white, college-rule lines of my Mead notebook.

"In English, how do you say, 'for all day?'" the young man asks.

I turn the page of my notebook and draw a line down the center of a clean page. Then I write the words he wants in English on one side of the line and in Spanish on the other so he can see the translation.

With Luz joining in, the boys want to know how to say "the price includes there and back" and "you can't park your bicycle there." I write the words for them, then teach them to say how are you?, and I'm fine. The between-the-teeth position of the tongue necessary to say "the" is difficult for them, just as I have trouble with the Maya glottal stop for k', which sounds like a hiccup when I say it.

David comes along, and I show him the English I've written for the boys, and the Maya words they've taught me. As we prepare to leave, I rip the English-Spanish page out of my notebook and give it to them.

It occurs to me as we leave Cobá that what we have in common with the people we meet is our ability to share what we know and learn from their experiences. In making ourselves available to others, our lives are enlarged. In discussing conservation, people sometimes tell me they value Nature over humans. They claim to like trees, dogs, birds, and turtles better than 99 percent of the people they meet. Me, I like the stew of everything together—living, compromising, adapting, and finding our place in the harmony of things over the decades, centuries, and eons. Nature is always in flux, and I have a lot of faith in it to bring things back into a place of goodness over the course of its evolution.

Just as we forge our path despite odd turns and strange choices.

And today, I can thank my twisted ankle for putting me in the presence of boys who gave me seven more Maya phrases.

WE STAY THE night in Cobá, rather than try to make it back to Playa on the narrow roads. We get a room in a nearby hotel and go out to watch night blanket the lake. The lakeshore is posted with a "no swimming" sign and another sign showing a crocodile with an open mouth and teeth as sharp as an ice pick. The red clouds of sunset shimmer over the lake, putting it in a pink tutu. The reeds dance in pink water that fades to green as night settles in, then gray on its way to black.

We catch sight of something in the water. Moving. A definite shape. Perhaps a crocodile shape. But it turns out to be a duck, and we laugh at our gullibility—at being kept from wading the bank of the lovely lake by a sign that might be a joke.

As the first star of evening appears—Venus, a sign of love to us and war and sacrifice to the Maya—we notice a log in the glass-gray water.

"Was that there before?" David asks.

"I don't know," I say.

We watch it until night falls, and we can't see it anymore. Then we turn our attention to getting supper.

We go into a little restaurant beside the lake, where David orders *poc chuc*, grilled pork, and I order *pollo pibil*. On the back of the menu, stuffed into the plastic cover, is a grainy, much-xeroxed photo of a big crocodile slithering along the grassy bank of a lake.

"Is *crocodile pibil* on the menu?" David asks, with a grin.

The owner smiles broadly. "If you'd like," he says. ▲

24. Tulum

Quick Time...

OUR HOTEL IN Playa occupies a swath of beach in Old Town midway between the all-inclusive resorts both north and south of town, and just a block from Fifth Avenue where tourists come to eat and strut, see and be seen. Our second-floor room is an airy, square turret with windows on two sides—one overlooking roofs and palm trees, the other offering a grand view of the sea. Ocean winds whip in through the open windows, bringing the roar of the waves, and at night, we can lie in bed and see the lights of the floating-hotel cruise ships on the dark water. The sea—that's what I miss in Mérida.

Playa feels different from Mérida. It's the difference between having both a lock and a safety chain on the hotel door (Mérida), and a door that doesn't lock at all. Between going to a fancy dinner party (Mérida) and a beach barbecue. In Mérida, women wear pantihose; on Fifth Avenue, they wear only inches of fabric tied with narrow strings. Naturally, people look, but it's nothing out of the ordinary.

After the rainstorms have moved on, David and I get up early one morning to watch the Sun rise up out of the water behind the island of Cozumel. Tourists are already walking the hard sand at the edge of the waves, while men from rural villages, who've spent the night on the beach, are sleepy and disheveled. The Sun makes a brilliant debut before sliding up under a bellyband of clouds along the horizon. But true to the old adage, it turns the upper edge of the clouds silver, then platinum, before it emerges to beam a titanium ramp of light across the water, inviting us to climb aboard the new day.

We dress and walk up to Fifth Avenue to join the throngs of people looking for breakfast. The locals mob a food-cart on the street corner near the bus station, hurriedly eating panuchos topped with beans and shredded turkey. Tourists laze in tony coffee shops where muffins are the size of softballs and latte comes in three sizes and costs a half-day's wages for the ordinary Mexican worker.

"What are the muffins?" I ask the girl behind the counter as I order coffee and Diet Coke.

"*Mora azul,*" she says.

I don't understand, and she repeats the words three more times before she gives up and tells me in plain English that they're blueberry. I take one, and a slice of moist, orange-flavored pound cake.

Full of sweets and caffeine, David and I walk down to the pier where the Playa-Cozumel ferry comes and goes twenty hours a day,

At Playa, people can go their whole vacation without ever changing out of their bathing suits.

carrying working people back and forth between the island and the Peninsula, and tourists to beaches that are always whiter on the other side. Men from the Union of Tricicleros-Ixchel rush to meet every boat, loading their trikes with freight such as Zenith televisions, suitcases, elderly women, and little children. Seeing the men, I think of Luz peddling through Cobá.

Having already walked north of town to the deluxe palapa-topped bungalows of the Shangri-la Caribe hotel, we decide to walk south to the hotel zone of Playacar along the white beach. Close-in, the shallow water is the sparkling blue of aquamarine, deepening farther out to lapis lazuli and then indigo. Overhead, white puffs of clouds combine and blow apart then recombine, writing a slow Morse code across the azure sky.

Like most good places on Earth, Playa was inhabited by ancient people. The Maya established their port of *Xaman-Ha,* or Northern Waters, here, and a handful of its small, well-kept structures (designated as A-B) still look over the water toward Cozumel. Just two blocks from the present-day pier, they perhaps served as the departure point for the pilgrims going to shrines on Cozumel, home of the fertility goddess Ixchel. Seeing couples lying nearly naked on Playa's beaches, kissing and caressing, I wonder how many babies are conceived here.

Walking north along the beach, we encounter thousands of bodies in various states of tan, from the fluorescent white of new arrivals from the northern latitudes to people well-bronzed by genetics or days of sunshine. Lounge-chairs are positioned to maximize the body's exposure to the Sun's fiery touch, with bodies and chairs being repositioned every half hour to match the changing angle of the rays. Women undo the tops of their bathing suits, leaving only a (mandatory) Y-shaped patch of latex fabric between them and the atmosphere.

But this is not so much Sun worship as worship of the body. Limbs and torsos are slathered with fragrant oils and lotions of mango, peach, and strawberry. Special water spritzers moisten the face and chest while bronzers baste the midriff and legs, and tanning gels are applied by a companion to spines and rumps. Thick towels cushion the head. Hands are dipped in paraffin wax during beach manicures while feet are pampered by pedicures. No amount of coddling is considered excessive.

A masseur sets up his portable table, and within minutes his sign-up sheet is full and his first client is lying face-down on the white sheet—her blonde hair tossed to one side, bikini top undone. The man dribbles a thin film of sweet oil on his palms, then slowly slides his hands over her back, bottom, and legs—rubbing, massaging, kneading, and rubbing. People sweat even more than is warranted by the Sun's heat as they sneak peeks from behind their beach novels.

A few people dabble at water sports to break the boredom of hard-core lounging. While dare-devils try the new 10,000-foot, free-fall sky diving, others go for wind-surfing, jet-skis, and parasailing. They ride a banana-shaped, yellow tube pulled behind a motorboat. Women improve themselves with classes in water aerobics and beach calisthenics while the men play polite volleyball and smoke Cubans.

Everyone records the vacation days for posterity with point-and-shoots and video cameras. They video the waiter taking their order, then bringing their order, and then they hand him the camera so he can video them eating. They video themselves sunning. They video themselves wading in the sea.

Always the sea—with its Coke-bottle green waters lapping against the white apron of sand under the blue-eyed sky. It makes people feel freer and more beautiful, more loved and loving, as its salt scours away old skin cells and worries.

Returning from Playacar, we stroll the beach fronting Old Town, where the scene changes. Here young men play a rough, intense game of soccer, and local children gambol in the waves. While American girls start their vacation in two-piece suits, those from Europe and South America drop their tops without hesitation, leaving a bikini bottom so small it's only a theory. Their level of comfort with their bodies is such that there's never any adjusting of fabric as they stoop and squat. And as Mexican men stare. Admiring their ease and confidence, American girls drop their tops, too, and hug their knees to their chests as they get used to the idea of baring their breasts.

Bodies here are younger than in the hotel zones and exhibit trendy ideas of beauty: nipples pierced (and permanently erect), and pierced belly buttons, tongues, and lips. Tattoos bloom like vines from out of bathing suit bottoms. Those lacking commitment get fake tattoos that last the duration of the vacation.

In makeshift plywood stalls, young men from dive shops use rapturous terms like bliss, ecstasy, and euphoria to describe diving the coral reef (the second largest in the world) beyond Playa's shoreline. People in wetsuits return at dusk from an entire day spent scuba diving, tired and peaceful and happy.

Mannequins show tourists the corn-row braids that will make them a "10."

Late afternoon is when music happens at the Blue Parrot and Ronnies, where musicians reach their own rapture and listeners lounge on the sand like driftwood floating on a sea of notes. As the Sun drops behind Playa and shadows cover the beach, the skyscrapers of Cozumel still gleam in the sunshine like a mirage.

THE NEXT MORNING, our room is awash in sunlight before six, and by seven we're already at the Playa bus station catching the second-class bus to Tulum. We're early enough to get seats. Later, when the bus drives through town, men waiting on street corners board with their wrenches and hammers, axes and lunch boxes, and stand in the aisle until the bus is cram-jammed. Then, beyond town, the bus scatters them like seeds along the highway, dropping them at the narrow footpaths to hidden ranchos and the wide driveways of lavish hotels. About an hour down the highway, we get off the bus at *Ruinas de Tulum*, stepping down onto sunbaked Earth as hard as stone.

Walking the mile or so to the ancient city, David and I arrive in Tulum before it gets busy. We pay the entrance fee and pass through a tunnel-like passageway in the high, wide wall that surrounds the city's ceremonial center. Directly ahead is Tulum's great pyramid, and we hurry toward it, intent on climbing while it's still deserted. But upon arriving at its steps, we find it closed—climbing has been forbidden since archaeologists decided the structure was wearing too quickly under the stress of millions of feet. So we head to the site's next highest structure, the Temple of the Wind God.

This small, square temple on a cliff offers a view of Tulum that's truly spectacular in its beauty. From here we can see the angular great pyramid atop a distant, sheer, gray cliff that drops fifty feet to the green sea. With its hulking back to the water, it seems the regal commander of this glorious stretch of coast. Something about the cliffs and the rolling, white waves stirs romantic thoughts of fishing boats and sailing ships and the lonely sea and sky—of a castle hard beside the ocean, like Tintagel of King Arthur's tale.

I can imagine the nobles of the powerful inland city Chichén Itzá sweating in their elegant homes, and telling their wives they have to go check on business in Tulum. (Something about trade routes and shipping.) Of course, once they're here, the work takes twice as long as originally anticipated, prolonged by daily dips in a sea like a jewel.

Reveling in the beauty and the breeze, David and I sit down on the footing stones of the wind god's temple and lean against its wall. As the morning passes and the tours arrive from Cancún, Cozumel, and the cruise ships, people squeeze in to sit beside us until we're hip to hip with strangers like blackbirds on a fence.

A man and woman of about fifty with gold-and-diamond jewelry and matching red resort polos look toward the pyramid-castle and smile.

"Don't you just love this place?" the woman says.

"It's the perfect place for a bed-and-breakfast," the man says.

"Oh, let's buy it!" the woman says.

They leave, and another couple takes their place. "When was this city built?" the man asks his wife. "Did the guide say 600?"

"I don't know," she says. "I couldn't understand him half the time. I think he said 1500."

They get up and leave, and another man takes their place. "Factoids," he says to a companion. "That's what the world runs on. A sound-bite to take home to friends."

"More like *bulltoids*," his companion says.

Bulltoid: The Maya were peaceful people.

Factoid: They beat the heck out of each other.

Bulltoid: The Maya became extinct.

Factoid: Drought, deforestation, and the demise of effective leadership all seemed to played a part in the scattering of the ancient Maya, but their descendants are alive and doing well, thank you.

DAVID IS TAKING photos when I go outside the city's thick wall to use the *baño*, or bathroom, and follow signs pointing the way to the rooms for *Caballeros* and *Damas*. In front of the *Damas*, a woman weaving a hammock shakes a small tip container at me as I approach, letting me know I must pay to pee. It must be hard dealing with tourists who are stressed by the heat. Who resent having to give two pesos (less than 20 cents) to use the bathroom, but might not otherwise offer a tip. Who don't have any pesos because their all-inclusive hotel deals in dollars. Who can't distinguish the denomination of the coins even if they get them in change. Who long for the comforts of home for basic needs. I smile and give her the two pesos she asks for. She hands me a neatly folded pillow of toilet paper.

A frisky, happy Tulum dog enjoys a donated tourist breakfast of bagel with cream cheese, with the city's great pyramid on the far cliff.

With Tulum's pyramid closed to climbing, people pile onto its small Temple of the Wind God.

"*Gracias*," I say, "*muy amable*." Thank you, you're very kind.

When I leave, she goes in to flush the toilet with a bucket of water. I put a few more pesos in her tip jar.

"*Gracias, muy amable*," she calls out from inside the bathroom.

Going back into the site, I pause at the entrance to survey the long line of people waiting to pay the admission fee. Tulum lures more tourists than any of the other Maya ruins—more than 600,000 a year. Only eight-one miles south of Cancún, it's an easy day trip by tour bus or rental car, and the site is often packed nearly wall-to-wall with tourists—probably more people than the little city's ancient population. People often visit the ruins in the morning, then go to the ecological parks of Xel-Ha or Xcaret to eat lunch and splash in the cool water during the heat of the afternoon.

"Guide lady?"

A man standing with the ticket-taker guard beside the entrance is offering me his service as a guide. He's about my height—five-foot-seven—and wears a white guayabera shirt having long sleeves against the Sun. A wide straw hat shades his face. His eyes are anonymous behind the small, round, dark lenses of wire-rimmed John Lennon glasses.

"No, thanks," I say.

"Why not?" he says.

For some reason, I hesitate, and in that instant, the guide lifts the yellow cover on a little plastic photo album, its edges tattered and shredding from use and heat. He shows me a night-time photo of the full Moon hovering over Tulum's great pyramid like a UFO.

"Look what you'll be able to see with me," he says, his voice enthusiastic. "The Maya calculated the cycles of planets and Moon—do you know what they called the Moon?"

"*Uj*," I say, making the word sound like the "ou" in you.

The guide's head bobs in surprise, and he looks at the guard.

"Oh, yes, well, there's also a name for the Sun," he says.

"*K'in*," I say, pronouncing the "n" as "m".

He smiles in surprise.

"The wind?"

"*Iik'*," I say, making a sound like "eeeeek."

"How do you know this?" he asks.

"From boys and books," I say, remembering the boys of Cobá.

He shrugs, not understanding.

"How much do you charge?" I ask.

He tells me his fee, and I present a counteroffer.

David and I learned the useful art of bargaining from our friend Buenaventura, a Cakchiquel Maya woman in Antigua, Guatemala. Her method for getting a fair price is to offer half of whatever is asked, knowing that the final negotiation will probably end at 75 percent. I'd prefer a straight fee, without negotiation, but in most cases, the price of goods has been inflated to account for the discount. And especially with beach vendors, the bargaining seems to be part of a process for transferring the ownership of the item, much like transferring a property title at the closing of a real estate deal.

The guide and the guard discuss my offer in Spanish. Here in Tulum, where many American tourists speak no Spanish, they assume I don't understand what they're saying. ("Take it," the guard advises, adding that the sum is more than he makes in a day. "No," the guide tells him. "It's early. I've got time.")

In English he tells me that he can't possibly accept less than his stated fee.

"I have many expenses," he says, tapping his official name badge.

"Like syndicate fees?" I ask, wondering whether guides, like taxi drivers, have union dues to pay.

"Not exactly," he says.

I scan the people in line, wondering whether any of them would want to share his fee with me, but they all seem to be with tours. Yet, I can't quite walk away from the bargaining table. Like a fish lunging after bait, I committed to the project when I showed off by naming the Moon.

"What do you think, Señorita Moon?" the guide says.

"I think I'm old enough to be *Señora* Moon," I say.

"How old are you?" the guard asks.

The first time a stranger in Mexico asked my age, I was puzzled. But by about the fifth time, it occurred to me that they're seeking a comparison. Boys compare me with their mother, men with their wife. I start to reply, but the guide interrupts.

"Wait, let me guess," he says, and he quotes an age a decade younger than I am.

"Exactly," I say.

"I am that age also," he says, and reaches to shake my hand.

"Twins," I say.

"Okay, then," he says, and lowers his guide fee a little. Now he's invested in me, too.

Tulum's great pyramid faces inland toward this altar, its back to the sea.

TULUM MEANS "WALL" in Maya, the guide Gregorio tells me, the name given the city in the early 1900s for its thick wall, although people once called it Stinking Earth for the smell of its swamps. It was a port in the Maya's extensive trade route that extended south to the Colombian coast of South America, and possibly as far north as the Four Corners area of the United States. While the earliest date found here is 564 CE, the city hit its apex between 1200 and 1521, when great sea-going canoes came in heavy with black obsidian and copper from Central Mexico, jade from Guatemala, and flint and pottery from the Yucatán. Among the delicacies were *cacao* beans, for chocolate, considered an aphrodisiac and drunk as cocoa by kings and nobles.

"Before Tulum, it was called *Zama*," Gregorio says. "For dawn. Maya people don't say, 'see you tomorrow,' they say '*zama*,' for 'when it dawns.'"

I can visualize the dawn at Tulum: the newborn Sun ascending from the eastern sea behind the great pyramid. Rising up out of the Earth-mother, and spilling the blood of first light on the water.

"Wait, let me show you something," Gregorio says, flipping through his photo album and presenting a photo. "This is the Sun, Itzamná, rising up into a notch between two buildings here on March 21. Spring equinox."

The photo shows the great solar bulb shining out from between the corners of two structures to the left of the pyramid.

"And here's where it sets on that day," he says, flipping to another page. "Here's the Sun setting into the passageway in the wall that we walked through. This happens at exactly the same moment that the seven triangles of light descend the pyramid in Chichén Itzá."

I look at the photo showing our great star caught, captured, corralled in the passageway through the wall.

"So you see," Gregorio says, "this little city of Tulum—like Ek Balám and Dzibilchaltún and Chichén Itzá—is like a grandfather clock keeping track of the Sun throughout the year."

It's noon, and the straight-up Sun beats down on us where we stand on a little knoll. The breeze from the sea doesn't make it this far, and Gregorio takes off his hat and wipes his brow. His black hair is wet with sweat and hugs his skull like a dark swimming cap. His head is small, his face a delicate oval cut into thirds by sunglasses and a thin mustache. He points to a structure, and as we walk to it—and then others within the wall—he shows me each building, then a close-up photo of it.

There's the Temple of Frescoes (its worn murals now indistinct); the Temple of the Diving God (having wings like a bee); the House of Columns (with its flat-nosed depictions of Chaak looking like an Italian prizefighter instead of the elephant-nosed Chaak of Uxmal). He shows me the great pyramid with its columns like raring serpents remi-

niscent of those on Chichén Itzá's great pyramid. He points out several structures having walls so crooked that the Maya applied a dozen coats of thick stucco to even them out. For decades it was thought that the Maya of Tulum hadn't known how to use a plumb line, but now it appears the buildings were purposely constructed out-of-square.

Finally, Gregorio takes me to a little building beside the great pyramid.

"See that little window?" he says. The tiny opening, barely longer than a hand, is about two-thirds of the way up the wall. "It marks the winter solstice. There's another little opening on the wall opposite it, and the rising Sun shines through that little window at dawn on winter solstice, December 21."

He shows me a photo of a starburst of spiky light breaking through the opening.

"This building that gives birth to the Sun on that date is also the place of the mother goddess, Ixchel," Gregorio says, pointing to a very worn carving of a woman. "See her legs parted, she's giving birth."

In truth, I only see it by applying a good bit of imagination.

"You know, Señorita *Uj,* the ancient Maya had a very different concept of sex than we do," he says, dropping his voice a little.

I feel myself waiting for the punch line, but his face is serious.

"They weren't so prudish as we are," he continues. "Their almanacs are full of drawings of all kinds of sex—have you seen them?—men having sex in every possible position, with both men and women partners. Sex was a celebration of life and the gods and the very act of creation. And fertility was a sacred gift from the goddess Ixchel."

IT'S AFTER ONE when David and I see each other across the crowded plaza. We head to a rock on the edge of the cliff near the great pyramid and sit down together to share a Clif bar, carried so many miles and months from home. We alternate bites of it with nibbles of potato chips—sweet, then salty—savoring the combination in this heat. Between bites, we swig from bottles of water.

High on the cliff, this great pyramid seems like the crest of a stormy, gray wave frozen at its apex. Facing inland, the stones of its formidable back have presented strong resistance against the sea winds and hurricanes that have battered it over the centuries. Yet, if not for its grand angles that are visible from the sea, the Spanish explorers might have sailed on by without taking notice.

In 1517, the *conquistador* Francisco Hernández de Córdoba landed on Isla Mujeres near Cancún where he found gold and statues of women. But rather than sailing south down the unexplored coast near Tulum, he turned northeast and continued on around the Peninsula to Campeche. Still, word of the gold spread in Cuba and Spain.

A year later, the *conquistador* Juan de Grijalva landed on Cozumel and then sailed down the coast where he noticed the hulking shape of Tulum's pyramid rising up above the cliff. He must have known at once that it was the work of man, not Nature, for only man builds in straight lines and angles. Grijalva wrote in his journal, ". . . toward sunset, we saw a burg, or town, so large that Seville would not have appeared larger or better. We saw there a very high tower."

The Maya of the port also displayed flaming torches that were visible at night for miles along the coast.

Tantalized by thoughts of gold, the *conquistadores* fought the Maya for decades for sovereignty over the Peninsula, setting in motion the influences that have made it what it is today.

Now, from where David and I sit on the cliff, the sea below is the blue of faded jeans. Farther out, the color deepens to new-jean indigo, peacock blue, and then the light blue of forget-me-nots. On the horizon, sea and sky merge, making blue on blue. Little swallows fly close overhead, giving us glimpses of their soft little bellies, and stately pelicans glide by, big feet daintily tucked up like landing gear.

Between the cliffs occupied by the great pyramid and the wind god temple beyond is a natural cleft where long-distance canoes once

pulled onto a small, sandy beach. Conga lines of waves roll into it with their promise of fun, and now people throw off their clothes and frolic in the surf. People love Tulum because it's charming and picturesque and small enough to make them think they've explored it all and therefore know it. It's cozy.

And it has the gloriously beautiful sea. Tulum by the sea.

AS DAVID AND I leave Tulum and walk toward the highway and the bus back to Playa, the beat of a small drum and the piercing notes of a pipe catch our attention. In the shopping center in front of the archaeological site, five men are sitting atop a turquoise-colored pole some forty feet tall. The man playing the drum and pipe sits directly over the pole while the others sit around him on a circular bar.

As we watch, the four men on the bar fall backward in unison to swing from it by their knees. They loop yellow nylon rope around one of their ankles, and then drop from the bar. Hanging upside down on the rope, they slowly spiral around the pole. Descending lower and lower with each revolution. Headfirst. The blood rushing to their heads making their faces as red as their tight trousers.

The man still on top of the pole plays a thin tune that, impossibly, never seems to repeat, as the four men spiral around and around the pole, dropping lower on each pass. I count their spirals—each makes thirteen revolutions around the pole so that by the time the four men reach the ground, they have made a total of fifty-two turns.

Then, releasing themselves from the nylon ropes, they pass a hat among the onlookers, collecting tips from those who will give.

These "papantla flyers," as they are called, are performing an ancient ritual in a tradition from the Mexican state of Veracruz, but David and I have witnessed a similar ceremony performed by the Maya of rural Guatemala. There, "flyers" conduct the sacred ceremony once a year—on the winter solstice, December 21, the shortest day of the year—when they spiral down the pole to celebrate the winter Sun's return towards summer.

In the Maya Tzolk'in calendar, four gods each take a turn in carrying the years. Like a relay team, one of the gods carries a year before passing the responsibility for the next year to the next year-bearer. After each of the gods has carried thirteen years, a cycle of fifty-two years has passed, and the spiral of Time has wound down a notch. According to the calendar, this cycle of fourth creation of ours will wind completely down on December 21, 2012. At that point, 5,126 years will have passed since the first day dawned in the year 3114.

Now, as tourists leave and more arrive, the four men climb the pole to repeat their performance. The drumming and piping begin again, and the four flyers spiral down the pole again. Another fifty-two revolutions—in theory, another fifty-two years. When more new people arrive, the men again perform their flight.

"Maybe that's why time seems to be speeding up," David says.

I nod, saying, "They're burning a lot of years in one day."

"I guess that's why there's no slow lane anymore," David says.

On the highway where we wait for the bus to Playa, the first bus flies by so fast that it passes us without stopping.

THE NIGHT SKY visible through the windows of our hotel room is covered with clouds as softly gray as wool batting. David lies sleeping beside me, but I'm content to lie awake and savor the night. The sound of music from a bar drifts in through the window. It's heavy with drums—bom-diddy, bom-diddy, bom, bom, bom—like a tribal dance with stomping feet and thrusting hips. Every now and then, there's a cheer and a command for more. For "take it off." The request probably isn't for the shedding of a sweater.

David stirs. "You awake?" he asks.

"Yeah."

"I was dreaming," he says, and begins to relate his dream.

"It's night, and a large ship enters a bay," he says. "I'm sitting on a cliff above it—you're not there—and I notice its lights. Then I notice a lot of small landing boats coming in from the ship, so I decide to run. I'm running down a wide path through the jungle with some other men, but within minutes men from the boats are already ahead of us—they're bounding along beside us in the brush, and I know they're trying to herd us together so they can ambush us. I finally see them—they're raptors! But they're mechanical—like robots. Everything they do is highly coordinated and completely regulated. They're very well-trained, very disciplined. But they have no soul.

"Then I'm in a house, fighting hand-to-hand against them. The men and I are hitting the robots with sticks and spears. We're winning, but then they begin to replicate in another room. We send in one of our own so that when the robots mate with it, they'll die. But they discover the plot because they're so intelligent.

"Then, just when we're winning the battle, the robots send in hundreds of bats. These bats have huge wings, but they're only an inch thick, and when I spear them, they just turn into ink blots.

"In the end, I cross a river on a wire with three other men, and we think we're getting away. But then we realize that the robots can anticipate our moves and that they're climbing the wire to reach us.

"That's when I woke up. My first thought was of Chichén Itzá."

Another cheer from the bar comes in the window.

"What do you think it means?" I ask.

"I don't know" David says, "maybe it's a metaphor for the Conquest. The Spaniards must have seemed like aliens to the Maya—they had horses and armor and swords while the natives had spears and sticks. Maybe I was picking up that energy." ▲

25. Chichén Itzá

Light Descending...

WE'VE COME BACK to Chichén Itzá for spring equinox, and to the room in the rural hotel where we've spent so many nights. As we eat an early breakfast beside the round swimming pool, I think (as I often have during this journey) of the dark-haired woman who walked ahead of us on the path at Dzibilchaltún last year. I wonder where she's celebrating spring equinox this year—and whether her initiation has brought her the changes she desired. For us, it's been a year of adventure and reflection as we've explored thirteen Maya pyramids. David's exposed film is heavy with images of the pyramids, and my notebooks are full of facts and dreams, memories and impressions. I consider which of my journal entries I would read to the dark-haired woman to describe how we've changed.

When we enter Chichén Itzá at just past eight in the morning, people are already pouring into the park. Turnstiles at the entrance have been removed; admission is free today—it would be impossible to sell tickets to the more than 50,000 people who are expected to arrive here from all over the world for the light-and-shadow spectacle that will take place on the pyramid in the late afternoon. Instead, people pass through a line of guards checking them for inadmissibles.

Here, as in Dzibilchaltún, the stuff of ceremony is banned—drums and flutes, incense and conch shells. Carry-in food is prohibited, too, and guards toss sandwiches, fruit and even packages of crackers into black trash bags along with cans and bottles of soda and beer. ("I hope you're at least going to *give* that food to someone," says a woman about to lose her can of beer.) Only water is allowed in.

Let loose, people hurry down the gravel *sacbé* toward the pyramid, many about to see it for the first time. "Oh, my God," a man says, catching sight of the pyramid. "Will you look at that!" He and the woman with him stop in their tracks and stand looking up at it, eyes lifted to take it in while the current of people parts and rushes on by them like water to the sea.

On most days, tourists fill the park, but today there are more Mexicans, who have come with their families. They spread striped blankets on the grassy plaza, staking out a patch of ground with a good view of the pyramid's northwest side where the spectacle will take place. While the kids take turns holding the family's place in the Sun, the elders retreat to the scant shadows under the nearly leafless trees. They pull loose stones into a circle, and three or four generations

of the family—from toddlers to great-grandparents—sit down on them to wait for the Sun to roll through the day. David and I park our beach-towel near the front of the crazy-quilt of blankets, and wander over to stand in the shade of the pyramid.

THE SUN IS the self-appointed Stage Manager of this show. By mid-morning its white light dazzles, fading the sky to the tired blue of old eyes. For weeks now, it has been vaporizing the impotent clouds, making rain impossible, and the grass in the plaza lies defeated, a trampled carpet of brown. Cornstalks in the nearby fields are tattered mummies. Trees are skeletal, their white branches like bones on an x-ray. The Sun has set the mood: Everything longs for Renewal.

People have come to the great pyramid not to climb it (it's closed to climbing for three days at equinox) but to pay their respects to this stone mountain that will host the phenomenon of seven triangles of light descending it. One young man kneels and kisses the west stairs. People unaccustomed to such open displays of adoration stare and whisper, holding their lips in a half-smile, nurturing amusement as a means of distancing themselves from the goings-on.

But the young man is not alone. A tall, blonde man and woman walk up to the pyramid and place their foreheads against it, eyes closed, hands clasped over their chests, lips mouthing silent words.

A heavyset man bends over and places his cheek on the muzzle of the huge, stone head of the Plumed Serpent that will later be illuminated by the seventh triangle of equinox light while two elderly women ladle out little handfuls of corn and seeds to anyone wanting to offer the grain to the stone snakes.

Men, women, and children plaster their bodies against the pyramid, adoring it with outstretched arms.

"What are they doing?" a young woman asks me in halting, German-accented English.

"I think they're meditating," I say.

"Oh," she says, and she and her boyfriend go and lean against the pyramid among them.

It's apparent that many have come here seeking physical healing. A Mexican man tells a guard that he has prostate cancer, and he and his American wife search among the pebbles at the foot of the pyramid, finally deciding on two. "For luck," the woman says, and the guard looks the other way as she drops them into her purse.

A rail-thin Mexican woman clings to the corner of the pyramid. Her legs are as thin as twigs, her skin sallow, her hair the limp, dull noncolor of the very ill. She squeezes her eyes shut and softly murmurs in Spanish.

A Mexican woman has endured a twenty-four-hour bus ride from Xalapa, in the Mexican state of Veracruz, to be here for the equinox. Her soiled yellow dress is tight across her swollen belly and breasts. "I need some good luck," she tells me. "My husband left me with four children to support, and my mother has cancer."

I wonder whether the pyramid dispenses such luck.

A woman from Wisconsin has convinced three of her friends to make the pilgrimage to the pyramid for spring equinox. "My sister came here once, and she loved it," she tells me. "She was killed in a car crash a few years ago, and I wanted to be here for her today."

The pyramid seems to bask in its celebrity. It's the star of the coming drama. The King. The young Elvis on stage in black leather, cheered and loved and bigger than life. Because of its fame, people feel a kinship with it and freely project onto it their deepest longings. They see it as sacred ground. A work-of-art. A cosmic calendar. A healer. A lifeless ruin. A canvas for the Divine. (While the pyramid is probably thinking, "You can't begin to know who I am.")

Some people have managed to smuggle into the site the tools of ceremony, and despite the rule forbidding incense, the smell of smoldering sage wafts across the plaza—not the pungent aroma of wild sage but a spicy fragrance reminiscent of Thanksgiving turkey and dressing. Half a dozen people from the United States draw faded blankets into a circle and kneel on them. In the center of the circle is a coiled root from a tropical vine, along with an apple, a quartz crystal, and a stone in the familiar shape of the Egyptian pyramids.

The group's leader, a man of about thirty, is dressed in loose, white muslin pants and a white muslin shirt, his thick, cinnamon-colored hair hanging nearly to his waist. He blows a whistle, its sound is barely audible, like the soft whir of a jungle bird. People in the crowd don't pay much attention until one of the young women in the group assumes a yoga pose. Then they grab a second look—perhaps because of her good looks and long, lean, tan legs, or perhaps because her thigh-high dress does nothing to hide a tiny turquoise undergarment.

After a bit, another man in the group stands up. He's thin, with brown-graying hair tied back in a sparse ponytail decorated by a brown feather. He begins to move his arms and hands in wide arcs, and then as the movement involves his body, he sways in what looks to be a form of Tai Chi. Drums not being allowed in the park, those in the circle slap their thighs to make a rhythm. Onlookers gathers to watch, and people whisper and snicker as they comment on the goings-on. If the thin man notices them at all, it doesn't register on his face.

He moves his arms and hands as though stroking, caressing, the air. He makes a quarter turn and repeats the motion until he's performed it in the east, west, north, and south. A wall of wind suddenly comes up and lifts everyone's hair before it dissolves into stillness.

"Did he do that?" a woman asks, with a nervous laugh.

Seeing the onlookers, those in the circle smile and motion them to join in. Several Mexican people step forward, and blankets and bodies are shifted to make the circle larger.

The man in white muslin picks up a yard-long wooden tube and blows into it. The sound is subtle and low—like a distant truck gearing down—and none of the guards seem to notice. One of the women lights a little pile of sage cradled in an abalone shell and walks

People who view the great pyramid as sacred smuggle into the site the props for small ceremonies,

inside the circle fanning its smoke into the faces of the newcomers who close their eyes and breathe deeply of the blessing-cleansing. A guard appears. The man in white muslin quickly rises and goes to speak to him in a soft, resilient voice. By the time he has promised to extinguish the incense, the smoking shell has traveled the circle.

Back in the circle, the man in white muslin begins to sing, and the others join in. "Earth is my body," they sing. "Water is my blood. Air is my breath. Fire is my spirit."

The man shakes a small egg filled with grain or sand, and the blonde woman beside him shakes a long, dry seed pod from a tree.

They sing the refrain over and over and over again like a meditation until everyone within hearing distance can anticipate the next phrase and join in if they want. "Earth is my body. Water is my blood.

Air is my breath. Fire is my spirit." Over and over and over again they sing it, until the chant insinuates itself into the minds of the people who've gathered behind them in an incidental circle.

I find myself scanning the crowd for the dark-haired woman from Dzibilchaltún, wondering if I'd recognize her.

SPRING EQUINOX IS an astronomic event that occurs midway between winter and summer. On March 21 (or March 19 or 20 in some years), the Sun rises due east and sets due west. The ancient Maya called it the "tying of the sky." Like the tying of a birthday package—running the ribbon across the box, preparing it for the bow.

The Itzá positioned their great pyramid to face 17 degrees east of north so that on the equinox, the corners of its platforms create a pattern of light-and-shadow triangles running from its temple to the ground, where the last triangle illuminates the stone head of the Plumed Serpent. Some archaeologists believe the phenomenon is a happy accident unanticipated by the Itzá. Others believe it has a ritual or agricultural meaning. But since the Maya chroniclers wrote nothing about it, no one can say for certain.

During spring and autumn, the pyramid illustrates the changing relationship between the Sun and Earth. In the weeks before spring equinox, the triangles of sunlight begin to form on the pyramid in late February. By March 5, five are visible, growing to seven on March 21, and nine on April 6. In the autumn, seven triangles of sunlight appear on the pyramid on September 22, diminishing to six on October 9. Then the spectacle fades away until spring.

NOW, AT MIDDAY, the Sun has turned up the heat. If the Sun has consciousness, as the Maya say it does, it's intent on impressing the equinox crowd. It seems just ninety-three miles from Earth, instead of 93 million miles away, with its dial set on "broil." Its firestorm of energy radiates off the ground in waves. Its light is a zillion-watt bulb. This is the furnace that burns away the dross. Bare skin flames. Flesh turns pink, rosy, scarlet.

"Everyone earns a badge of courage for being here," a woman says with a laugh, "in the form of a sunburn."

People take shelter in the shadows of umbrellas. Of trees. Of bedspreads and rugs held overhead by arms that grow tired. People drape towels over their heads, but can't stand the heat. They stand in each other's shadows, little behind big. A man and woman set up a small tent, but guards make them take it down.

People slather on sunscreen. They make endless trips to the concession stand for drinks, and because containers are prohibited, they return holding little plastic bags of grape- or lemon- or raspberry-colored liquids that glisten like delicate jewels.

"This is like a purification," a man says. "I'm as drenched as if I'd been in a sweat lodge."

At just past three o'clock, guards begin to tug a rope into place to create a void around the pyramid. They herd people away from it, moving them back behind the rope. Those who have guarded their turf all day protest the people pushing in front of them, and make themselves big in an effort to hold their territory, sticking elbows out and standing with feet wide apart. But still people push in behind the rope until they're packed as tight as molecules.

"What can you do?" asks a man, sighing. "It's hard to justify being rude at what's supposed to be a spiritual experience."

David and I manage to stay put on our beach-towel near the rope. Twenty or so teenage boys from a school group squeeze in front of us, but we're more than a head taller than they are so we don't mind. Cloaked in precious youth, they fake-punch and wrestle each other and sneak drags off of Marlboros, bending low to keep their chaperones from seeing.

Still the Sun is too high for the spectacle to begin. More sunscreen. More water. People who want to go out to use the toilet apologetically step on fingers and toes.

"The portable toilet I just visited was made in Wisconsin," a woman says, returning to a space held by her husband. "I'm glad to know my state could contribute."

FINALLY, IT'S TIME for the drama to begin. The great pyramid knows its role. On cue, it permits a hint of a shadow to form near its summit on the west balustrade of the north staircase.

"Look, it's starting," someone says, and as the news crackles like wildfire through the crowd, 50,000 eager faces turn to the pyramid.

A slender, dark-haired girl of about sixteen and her father squeeze into an iota of space beside me. The girl smells of flowery perfume.

"What's the time?" I ask her.

She holds out her wrist, and I look at her watch—its face is a chubby angel with a little cupid mouth and curly red hair. The cherub's pudgy, white arms point to 4:05.

The spectacle unfolds slowly. In the beginning, the Sun is a force that illuminates the entire staircase wall while a sliver of fragile shadow hides in the corner where the wall meets the pyramid. But as the solar disk slowly sinks in the west, the pyramid's platforms block its light, and the shadow emerges from the crevice.

Emboldened by its foothold, the shadow overtakes the light inch by inch. Shadow advances into territory once occupied by the retreating light, climbing the wall, drinking the warmth on the stones.

As the day fades into history, the light loses even more ground. It climbs ever higher on the wall, scrambling ahead of the advancing shadow. When the light has receded to the top of the wall beside the temple, it forms its first triangle of light.

Ecstatic onlookers whoop.

By mid-afternoon more than 50,000 people have packed the main plaza waiting for the light show.

The watch angel points to 4:25.

In the perfect harmony of the equinox, the Sun has ruled the day for twelve hours, and now the night will be king. Now, its champion—the shadow—advances up the wall, a dark sponge absorbing the liquid gold. It seizes more and more ground once held by the light until it corners the light at the top of the wall, pushing it into two, then three, then four perfect triangles.

The crowd cheers.

Finally, the light occupies only a tiny bit of the top edge of the wall, where it pulls itself up into five distinct triangles, with the hint of two others forming above the dark shadow.

Then, nudged by the shadow into completion, the light forms seven white triangles. Linking at their corners, they form a chain of

Young visitors turn toward the setting Sun as the triangles of light fade from the pyramid.

In describing the phenomenon, people give it a personal interpretation. Some see it as Divine Mercy revealed in the white light descending to Earth and humanity.

To others, it's order created from chaos by the Sun cycling through Time.

It's the Plumed Serpent representing the Time-Place of our universe as the union of spirit and matter.

To some it portrays the magical number thirteen depicted as seven triangles of light floating above six points of shadow.

To others, it's simply a sign of future rains to grow corn.

Because the light seems to continue north from the pyramid to the Cenote of Sacrifice, it represents Heaven redeeming the Underworld.

It's Itzamná, making a yearly appearance.

It's spring and the promise of renewal.

It's the New Year.

A man behind me says, "God so loved the world that he gave his only begotten S-U-N." He spells the last word.

Two women glare at him, their faces tight with frowns.

light descending the pyramid from the temple to the ground, with the seventh triangle spotlighting the head of the Plumed Serpent. They look like a lightning bolt hurled from the temple to Earth. Or like the geometric pattern on a serpent's spine, undulating and sinuous.

The watch angel points to 4:45.

Conch shells emit long, low, powerful notes that herald the phenomenon of seven triangles of light victorious above the shadow. A woman throws back her head and utters the piercing howl of a lone wolf.

"The hair on the back of my neck is standing up," says a man.

Reveling in the spectacle, people lift their open palms toward the pyramid, hailing it, hoping to receive a surge of energy from the sacred moment. They honor the harmonious yoking of the light (spirit) and the shadow (matter) that produces this phenomenon.

THE PHENOMENON FADES from the pyramid. A dozen young people turn away from it and hold their palms up to the dying Sun. Now, with the end of the day approaching, I find myself speed-reading the faces of the crowd as I search for the dark-haired woman from Dzibilchaltún. I find myself mentally telling her about our odyssey throughout the Peninsula and the things I've written in my notebook. I'm mentally explaining to her how our visits to thirteen great pyramids of the Maya have changed us. In this moment, she has become my internal reader for whom I write the entries in my journal, and I want her to understand me. I want to tell her that our journey has somehow been an initiation like hers.

But I don't see her.

Triangles of light appear to descend the K'uk'ulkan pyramid from temple to ground where the final one illuminates the head of the Plumed Serpent.

As night falls on this celebration, I pull out my notebook and sit down on the grass in front of the pyramid. It seems appropriate on this first day of spring to consider the changes our journey has wrought in us. Physically, these months of being outdoors have made us much stronger and more agile than we once were. (We even sleep in the fresh air in this culture of open windows.) I feel at least an inch taller than when we first arrived, as though the heavy yoke of pouring myself into work outside my natural interests has lifted from my shoulders, leaving my spine long and flexible.

Then there's the sense of self-reliance that has taken root and flourished in us as we've learned to trust our intuition in making decisions in the face of the Unknown. Without a script (a Day-Timer) prescribing our day's activities, we've come to rely on our ability to respond to events from the basis of what we truly want rather than from what is expected of us.

Now, instead of struggling to find a way to express our creativity through words and photos as we did when we began our odyssey, I write and David takes photos from a place of believing that our view of the world is unique, and should be honored in its expression. Ironically, I think that it's my growing awareness of everyone else's unique value that has rekindled this sensitivity that I had feared lost. In learning to appreciate others without judgment, I've begun to allow my own self-expression without censure. I see that in accepting others, I can express myself. I no longer feel that I'm a glass eye.

David and I have come to see that our desires and choices drive our lives. It seems such a simple concept that I can't believe I didn't fully realize until now that we have a hand in all of our conditions.

Ultimately, we're always choosing to do what suits us best from moment to moment, based on the multitude of factors that makes us who we are, and also the larger current of events that sometimes pitches us headlong into situations we didn't anticipate. We've experienced this in our long journey to the pyramids where we've had the freedom to make choices and see what they bring.

Finally, David and I laugh a lot more than we did before we began this odyssey. While some of our issues seem large to us, I don't think we take things as seriously as we once did.

As I sit here at dusk surveying the magnificent pyramid of the Itzá, the sky in the west is a deep, vibrant coral as the Sun says its goodbyes. In the east, a full Moon is rising up over the Warrior's Temple to cast its own silvery triangles of light upon the pyramid during the night. Most of the equinox crowd have gone on—only the maintenance men remain, gleaning empty plastic water bottles and candy wrappers from the dry grass that has been trampled to bits. In my remaining moments in the park, I write:

> As the Sun turns the season
> the human Will can turn the wheel of Fate
> through choice.
> We can put ourselves in a new place,
> onto a deliberately chosen path.
> But then, making personal history isn't easy.

Then the guards clear us out of the plaza, and behind us, the pyramid falls dark. ▲

26. Chichén Itzá

Heart...

 IT'S MIDMORNING TWO days after the spring equinox. We've stayed near Chichén Itzá so we can climb its pyramid one last time before we leave the Yucatán Peninsula, ending our journey to the Maya pyramids. When we enter the park, the plaza is already filled with tour-goers, and we overhear a guide telling his tour group about the significance of the pyramid's nine platforms. He raises his hands and claps his cupped palms together, and the sound of the concussion bounces off of the pyramid.

"Did you hear that?" he asks. "Nine echoes for the pyramid's nine platforms. Count them."

He claps his hands again, and his people count the echoes.

"Now you try it," he says.

They slap their palms together.

"Again," he says. "Again."

When they're all clapping, he sweeps his hat off and takes a low bow. "I, and the pyramid, thank you," he says.

The lecture over, the people hurry to climb the pyramid

Instead of climbing with them, David and I turn and walk into the trees in front of the pyramid into an area we haven't explored.

Where the plaza gives way to the moldering jungle, we come upon a narrow, but well-traveled path, its dirt moist and the color of port wine, and compacted by countless feet. We follow it, marveling at the hundreds of carved stones that lay alongside it, the handiwork of ancient Maya. Among the stones is the work of modern man (and woman)—plastic bottles discarded where their last drops were consumed, tattered bits of toilet tissue, and torn plastic bags.

Following the path several hundred feet into the forest, we enter a clearing and come across the broken body of a snake. The serpent's slender body is barely two feet long, its back the color of coffee, its belly ocean-coral pink. Its head is narrow, delicate, and jaw-down on the ground, as though it has dozed off mid-slither. But a few inches from its head, its spine is broken—someone traveling the path apparently had a hoe or machete in hand to destroy this poor creature. In the agony of its death, the reptile twisted, looping once, forming half of a figure 8—half of the symbol for infinity. (I wonder, what *is* half of infinity?) Two long, stringy, red fibers of nerve now hang out of the snake's body where the tail has been severed. The scales of its rosy-hued belly are stretched over the bulge of its last meal—possibly a small rodent, now rotting.

"Too bad," I say.

At the sound of footsteps, David and I look up and see a boy of about twelve running toward us, his plastic sandals smacking the moist dirt. His presence doesn't much surprise us—there's no place in the Yucatán Peninsula where someone doesn't see everything that goes on and then talk about it for an hour. But this wildly grinning boy rushes in and snatches up the snake. He grabs it just above the amputated tail, lifts it over his head, and swings it around like it's a lasso. The velocity stretches the snake's body out straight-arrow, and David and I jump back to avoid its head as it whizzes by our faces. Then the boy lets go, sending the reptile flying. For a few seconds, the snake is airborne before it drops into the trees. The boy, still grinning, runs off in the direction he came from.

"How weird," I say.

"When snakes fly," David says.

I look at him, not understanding.

"You know, like the saying, 'when pigs fly.'"

Our desire for going farther down the path has dampened, and we turn around and head back to the plaza. We stop just short of the sunlit grass.

"You ready to climb the pyramid?" David asks.

I look at it ahead, its bleached-bone stones shimmering in the noon-day Sun.

"You go ahead," I say, "I'd like to sit under the trees with my notebook. I'll come in a bit."

"You'll come up alone?" he asks, surprised.

I nod. "But watch for me, okay?"

As he goes off to climb, I sit down on a smooth stone beside a tree and pull my notebook from my backpack and let my mind wander. Above the pyramid, the clouds blow apart and recombine—flowing, then clotting, then flowing again like coagulated blood in a wound. To my left is the Warrior's Temple with its carvings of jaguars and eagles eating human hearts. According to archaeologists, if the Itzá did actually perform the ritual of taking a human heart, they sacrificed their victims on the Warrior's Temple, and I catch myself envisioning how the ritual might have occurred.

IN THE TIME of the ancient Maya, the first day that Venus reappeared in the west as the evening star was a day ripe for sacrifice and war. Knowing from their almanacs that this day was coming, the shamans of Chichén Itzá had prepared to sacrifice a captive—a young noble from Izamal—to the gods. They had painted their faces blue, like the gods are blue, right up to their blood-matted hair. They had fasted and ritually altered their consciousness through alcohol enemas and hallucinogens, and their faces hung slack. Like masks.

The young man to be sacrificed had refused the mind-numbing alcohol he was offered to blunt the pain he would soon suffer. The eldest son of a noble family, he understood that with no choice but to die, the giving of his life with courage would greatly honor his family and ancestors. The handsome young man had bravely suffered the torture the shamans had inflicted on him. He had clenched his teeth against screams of pain when they tore out his fingernails. He had silently borne the disgrace of nakedness as his genitals were exposed when he was bound over to sacrifice.

Being led up the temple stairs to his death, he breathed in the pungent cloud of copal incense that billowed forth as if to greet him. He offered no struggle as he was laid out over a stone, face up, his arms stretched out so his chest rose up like a mountain. He felt terror surge at being so vulnerable. So naked. So close to entering the unknown. But he willed it to drain from him into the stone beneath him.

A blue-faced shaman lifted a knife of razor-sharp black obsidian over the young noble's chest. With the precision born of practice, he plunged the blade between the young man's ribs and ripped a wide cut. He plunged his fingers into the open chest and grasped the beating heart. Gripping it in his vise-like fingers, he tore it away from the body, severing arteries and veins with quick cuts. Then he held the hot, still-beating heart up to the Sun.

For a moment, the young man's heart beat valiantly on, in tune with its own internal rhythm. It beat on as though the young man's life-blood still filled it. It pumped in vain. Until it wound down.

The young man's mother and father had known from the Venus almanac that this day would be their son's last among the living. Barred from attending his sacrifice, they sought comfort in their belief that those brave men who die in sacrifice do not languish in the Underworld (till the End of Time) but rise directly to The One. But even this didn't quiet their torment over their son's suffering. Flesh of their flesh. Spirit fostered by their spirits. Beloved.

While the young man's father went to try and collect a bone or two from his child's body for the family altar, his mother placed a flower on the altar for her boy. She wept as she remembered the creator's ancient command that the Maya give blood to the gods through self-sacrifice—and not through taking another's life, as the shamans now did.

"If a man must be sacrificed," she said, "why must he be my son?"

THE SUN HAS shifted, and I get up and stuff my notebook in my packback and walk toward the pyramid. David sees me and waves.

As I put my foot on the first step of the steep staircase that stretches nearly ninety-feet above me, the Moth of Fear awakens and flutters in my stomach. Suddenly, a memory from my childhood flickers into my mind: I was about seven years old. It was a Sunday afternoon in summer and my parents had gone out leaving me at home with my grandma, who lived with us. I was out in the backyard, climbing the big weeping willow tree. I climbed higher than I ever had before—up into the slender yellow branches at the tree-top that bent under my skinny little-girl body. Frightened, I looked down through the tangle of branches to where the ground seemed to swirl and buck.

"Grandma," I yelled.

My grandma came out of the house and stood beside the tree trunk, lifting her wrinkled face.

"Call the fire department," I said.

My grandma disappeared into the house and returned with a kitchen chair, which she placed against the tree trunk. She left again and came back with a blue bowl full of apples and a paring knife. She sat down in the chair, and slowly began to peel each apple, making one long peeling that spiraled its whole length. She was old even then, so she had lots of Time in the pocket of her blue plaid house dress.

As she peeled, I inched my way down from the top of the tree until finally I stood in the crotch of the big branches only a few feet off the ground. My grandma stood up, and I shimmied down the trunk until my feet touched the chair. Then I sat in the shade of the tree and ate the apple slices my grandma gave me.

I've never gotten over that fear of heights—even fly-overs on the freeway scare me. Driving them, I feel faint and become afraid I'll loose control and drive over the edge and die. And now as I stand with my foot on the pyramid's stairs, the Moth is starting its war-dance in my stomach. Up top, David waits for me, just as my grandma once waited beneath the weeping willow, and it occurs to me that I've been held too long in bondage of fear. Climbing—or taking any risk (even quitting your job to write)—is a matter of faith. Faith in yourself, and your ability to handle conditions you can't begin to control. Now I ask myself, which do I choose—faith or fear?

I put my foot on the second step. The Moth stretches its wings, preparing to fly. I put my foot on the third step. The Moth makes itself larger. I don't make any grand declaration of my intention to climb. I simply begin the process. I put my foot on the fourth step.

There are ninety-one steps, and I know that counting them all will swamp me. So I decide to count to thirteen—just thirteen, I can handle that—for as many times as it takes me to reach the top.

"Five, six . . . ten, eleven . . . ."

The Moth grips my stomach. Still, I climb.

"One, two, three, four..."

The Moth flaps. I concentrate on the rhythm of my feet and hands.

"One, two, three, four ..."

I keep my eyes on the step in front of my face, climbing straight rather than on the zigzag course David takes. I hear voices ahead of me—people are coming down the steps—and I wonder what would happen if they were to fall down the steps onto me. "You'd die," the Moth whispers, and flies up into my chest. My heart pounds.

"One, two, three, four..."

The Moth rises up into my throat. My breath comes hard, but I force myself to move hands and feet, hands and feet, hands and feet.

"One, two, three, four..."

My thigh muscles are burning, and I want to sit and rest for a moment, but I don't think I can bear seeing the ground so far below. I keep going, concentrating on the rhythm of my hands and feet, moving, moving.

"One, two, three, four ..."

The Moth threatens to fly up into my brain, and I can't think. I'm auto-pilot now, totally dependent on my body to climb the steps.

"One, two, three, four ..."

There's no thought, only counting.

"... eleven, twelve, thirteen."

Then David's outstretched hand is in front of me. I reach for it, it's warm and strong around mine.

I'm breathless and wobbly, but I'm on the summit. In a moment of courage, I stand and look down the steps I've climbed. I know then that while the Moth of Fear might grip my stomach at times, it has lost its power over me. I take out my notebook and write:

It's fear that fortifies our faith.
Fear is neutralized by taking action.

I think of my grandma, whom I loved so dearly in my childish way, and ask myself why she has come into my thoughts so many times in so many places during this journey. It occurs to me that a grandmother offers a special place of acceptance. Like the Maya believe their ancestors are their link to the Divine, a grandmother is a link to the integrity of the Self. The Self is always there waiting to be rediscovered. Constant. Enduring. Knowing.

THE SUN SINKS toward the trees with their long shadows. David and I sit on the pyramid platform sipping the water we've carried up and nibbling peanuts and M&Ms, as we look out to the horizon—that luminescent circle where the sky meets the Earth with us in its center. Down in the plaza, the guide we saw earlier is talking to a family with two children who look to be about ten years old. He gestures toward the pyramid, then claps his hands. The children's faces light up with delight as the concussion of his clapping reverberates off the pyramid. They clap their hands, and the guide takes his hat off and bows low. They laugh.

Only a handful of people are on the pyramid at this late hour. There's a young Asian couple and a lone man doing Tai Chi at the entrance to the temple and a man whose long brown hair hangs over a T-shirt printed with a grizzly bear on the front and a soaring eagle on the back.

As we sit, a big bird flying toward us from the west catches our attention. It's much larger than the birds darting past the pyramid after bugs—even larger than the black vultures circling high in the sky looking for a lunch of decay. This big bird—an eagle or possibly a hawk—has great, broad wings that catch the air currents to rise without effort. It's majestic in flight, as though it owns the sky. As it flies near, we see feathers the brown of warm chocolate and yellowish legs pulled up to its body. There's a glint in its bright eye.

The bird flies by the north side of the pyramid, only a dozen yards out from us and not much higher. David and I jump up.

Late in the day, tour-goers climb down and head off to their hotels leaving the pyramid mostly deserted.

"Look," I say, to the man with the grizzly-eagle T-shirt. "It's an eagle. Like on your shirt."

He looks at me, not the bird. "Don't speak English!" he yells with a heavy accent, and I'm confused by his response until I reason that maybe that's all the English he knows.

The bird circles the pyramid, and we circle with it, watching it until it disappears into the Sun.

"Oh, we forgot to make a wish," I say, disappointed at remembering too late the Native American belief that the eagle is a sacred messenger—like Itzamná's Fire Macaw—that will carry your prayer to the Divine. "Oh, I wish it would come back."

The man with the eagle shirt goes down, and then the others, leaving us alone on the pyramid. We're looking at the horizon, when we catch sight of a big bird coming toward us again from the west.

"Would it actually be circling?" David asks.

The eagle glides past the north side of the pyramid again. This time we whisper our fondest desires and splash a few drops of our water on the pyramid in offering. The great bird circles the pyramid before it again disappears into the glow of the Sun.

The guide who was earlier clapping his hands in the plaza arrives breathless at the top of the stairs.

"What about that bird?" he says.

"Did you see him circle?" I ask.

"He heard me call him," the guide says with a smile. "When I'm leading a tour, I always clap my hands softly like the baby eagle, and then loud for when the little eagle grows up. Well, that's him."

We all laugh.

THE SUN HAS begun its rapid slide into the Underworld, and we're standing on this ancient pyramid in that mystical moment between day and night. The scent of rain is in the air, and then rain is falling from a dark-gray curtain of clouds in the east.

"Are you ready to go down?" David asks.

Suddenly, a burst of golden sunlight hits the rain cloud and a rainbow arcs across the sky. Lady Rainbow, to the Maya. Ixchel.

"Wow! Let's go," David says.

I know he wants to take a photo of the rainbow over the pyramid, and I don't want to hold him up.

"You go on," I say. "I can do it myself this time."

He runs down the stairs and has shot a roll or two of film before I reach the ground. The rainbow is beginning to fade, and we sit on the grass watching it disappear.

The ancient Maya believed in a universe in motion—a universe forever driven between light and dark, life and death, day and night, thrust and reception, light and heavy. According to the creation story told in the *Popul Vuh*, it was into this driven universe that we humans came. The creator made the first True Humans to be perfect, giving them the ability to clearly see through all the dimensions of Time-Place. But the jealous gods protested, and giving in to them, the creator blew a mist into eyes of the new humans. That's why we can see only a little way into the future, and must take action without being able to truly foresee all the consequences we will cause.

But unbeknownst to the jealous gods, the creator also gave us the unerring vision of a single eye, the heart. The mind—with its reasoning nature—comprehends the world with two eyes, the right and left, which do not see things in exactly the same way, and therefore present a dual view. Even so, we put our trust in the appearance of the world. But our heart knows only the single path.

I remember when we began our journey, and I didn't know what to write on the first page of my new notebook. Now I know:

Our heart always tells us our fondest desire.
It's never wrong.
Even when appearances seem to go against its wisdom. ▲

27. Afterword

More...

OUR JOURNEY TO thirteen Maya pyramids isn't really over—even as I type these letters into the computer at home, we have airline tickets that will take us back to the Yucatán Peninsula. It has taken nearly two years to compose these chapters of words and photos, with more details being added as we revisited old sites and visited new ones. As a result, the photos and observations in this book cover five years—from late 1996 to 2001.

Many things have transpired since we began our odyssey. In a way, we've been part of the pyramids' history as we've documented and photographed some of the dramatic changes they've undergone—David's early photos of a nondescript, tree-covered mound can now be compared with his most recent photos of the fully excavated pyramid with huge masks. Ek Balám's major pyramid went from being a grassy hill to being a magnificent work of art. Oxkintok went from having one reconstructed pyramid to having three. The huge stones in Izamal's Kinich Kak Mo pyramid have been reappearing from the rubble. And early in this sojourn, we were lucky to be able to climb pyramids now closed to climbers.

As for Mérida, the city grows more beautiful with each passing year as city officials restore and renew its buildings and streets.

Looking back, David and I could never have foreseen the ways in which we would change as a result of our journey. As David says, we were as *verde*, or green, as a new sprout when we began. Some challenges haven't been easy—financing ourselves as we uprooted from one patch of life to plant our dreams in another has taken nerves of steel. On the creative level, we've had to sustain a vision that only we could see as we worked at writing and selecting photos for this memoir of our odyssey. Personally, we've had to reach inside and find strength in ourselves and each other that we didn't know we had.

But then, making personal history isn't comfortable.

The wonders we've experienced on our journey have been worth the risks we've taken. We've experienced the freedom to write and take photographs as we've always dreamed of doing. We've enjoyed perfect moments of sitting on the summits of pyramids together, awash in a sense of peace so profound that we seem to be in harmony with the very nature of our surroundings. I don't know if this is what is meant by the word bliss, but for me, a Western woman traveling in the Yucatán, it's close enough.

We couldn't have done this alone. We've met many wonderful and helpful people during our five years of traveling in the Yucatán. They've been an integral part of our journey, and we would like to acknowledge and thank all of them, as well as friends in the States whose kindnesses we'll always remember.

We thank the management and entire staff of the Hotel Caribe and its two restaurants, El Rincón and El Mesón, where we spent many evenings discussing things and laughing until nearly closing time—these lovely people have always made us feel that we have a home in Mérida. We thank the three Sanchez brothers, the lovely Carmen, and the smiling waiter at Hotel Dolores Alba in Chichén Itzá—the hotel's peaceful atmosphere and wonderful cenote pool always make us want to stay there forever.

We especially thank Donna Rudolph for her guidance, generous help, and invaluable information about the state of Quintana Roo. We thank the Riviera Maya Trust and Ernesto Parra Calderón for familiarizing us with the wondrous stretch of the Yucatán Peninsula that is the Riviera Maya. We thank Mary Carmen Camargo of Xcaret Ecological Park in Playa del Carmen, Gavin Greenwood of Alltournative Expeditions in Playa del Carmen, and Kenneth Johnson and Eduardo Patiño of EcoColors in Cancún for showing us some exquisite sights.

We thank the directors and staff of Mexico's National Institute of Anthropology and History (INAH); the archaeological sites throughout the Yucatán Peninsula are truly a gift to the world's people.

We especially thank Jorge Gamboa Patron, Director of Mexico Tourism Promotion Board in Los Angeles, for his help and advice.

From the Office of Tourism in Mérida, we thank Saul Ancona and Ana Argaez. Thanks to Fernando Cárdenas for his translations.

For their generous gift of knowledge, we thank the authors David Freidel, the late Linda Schele, Michael Coe, Peter Mathews, Anthony Aveni, and Dennis Tedlock, all of whom have poured years of experience in Maya studies into books that fill us with wonder. Thanks to Maya elder Hunbatz Men for his kind sharing of knowledge.

For their long days of driving and friendship, we thank our *taxistas* Fernando Córdova Murcia and Manuel Sosa. Fernando has sold his taxi and is studying the national lottery until he takes his next step. Manuel upgraded his taxi from a '89 Dodge Dart to a '90 Ford Escort, and we've come to understand that he's truly a philosopher.

We thank all of the people who've guided us through Maya sites in the Yucatán Peninsula, whether formally or through simply sharing their experiences and insights. We thank the many people who lovingly shared their favorite recipes with us, especially the grandmother Lupita (who makes wonderful handmade tortillas that we coat with honey while the Yucatecans sprinkle them with chile). We sincerely thank all the descendants of the Maya who have shared their views.

We thank Meigen Thomas for her insight and suggestions and Jennifer Caragol for listening to ideas. We thank Greg Kitsock for his proofreading. We thank Carolyn Turrentine of Via Travel in Boulder, Colorado, whose wizardry has always put us on the right airline flight for nearly twenty years.

We thank David Z. Levin for his reading of the book, and Catherine Roy and Mary Bell-Nyman for keeping an eye on the big picture for us.

We thank the librarians at Longmont Public Library for their willingness to get the books we need.

We especially thank Ray and Velma Raleigh, and our banker John Benedetti for helping us to keep going.

We greatly value our long-time friend Lola Bravo of the Red Cabbage Café in Puerto Vallarta, Jalisco, Mexico, who encouraged us in her famous Pacal Room, when this odyssey was only an idea.

Finally, we acknowledge the little ones—Lily, Theo, Frank, Popo, and Gumby. A finer group of imps cannot be found. ▲

28. Recipes

La Comida...

WE COULDN'T BEAR to leave the traditional foods of the Yucatán, so we set out to bring a few favorites back with us as recipes. In doing so, we found that our interest in *la comida*, the food, of the Yucatán created an amazing bridge that took us into people's lives, values, and traditional cooking methods dating back to ancient times.

People in the Yucatán love to talk about food. In describing the dishes they enjoy, they are transported across the years to happy times spent with the family. Talking about *albondiguitas*, little meatballs, or how their mother made *sopa de lima* or *pollo pibil* makes their eyes shine. In relating recipes, old women labor to make us understand the vegetables and seasonings they use, going to great lengths to show us the *epazote* bush whose mint-like leaves are used to de-gas beans, and the small tree having *achiote* seeds that are ground for a paprika-like chile seasoning for chicken and pork. Then there are the chile peppers—what an array of sizes, shapes, and degrees of heat! Perhaps no other people are so in love with food, except possibly the Italians.

The typical foods of the Yucatán are surprisingly hearty for such a tropical clime—perhaps because historically they have transmitted a feeling of well-being even if the family had little else. They aren't at all the dishes we tend to think of as "Mexican" cooking, but an integration of traditional Maya and Spanish cuisine. Yet, some of the staples in modern meals have their roots in the culture of the Preclassic Maya—cocoa and corn, for example. The ancient Maya flourished on a diet of corn (domesticated by 3000 BCE), and there are still easily two dozen different terms for the types of beverages and doughs made from this essential food. The *cacao* bean, or cocoa bean, which the Spaniards took to Europe where it was used for chocolate, comes from the Maya region in the state of Tabasco where men still carry cocoa to work (mixed with corn-flour) for the "coffee" break. In ancient times, Maya nobles drank cocoa flavored with chile pepper as an aphrodisiac, possibly because of the energy it imparts. Other staples were avocado, banana, yam, black beans, and squash, which was domesticated as early as 8000 BCE. *Pepitas*, or pumpkin seeds, are still an essential element of ritual in some Maya ceremonies. Meat was deer, turtle, wild pig, rabbit, armadillo, turkey and pheasant.

For us, the challenge has been to translate oral recipes given to us as a "little bit" of this and that into actual amounts. But it's been a labor of love, because to know people, you must know their food.

Xnipek

Grandmother Lupita explained this salsa as she patted dough for tortillas.

5 ripe tomatoes, diced
1 small onion, diced
5 springs fresh cilantro, diced (or to taste)
1 habanero chile, seeded and diced very finely*
2 tsp juice from limes—or sour oranges if you can get them

Mix ingredients and refrigerate 1 hr before serving.

* Place on the side unless you're used to very hot chiles.

Salsa Verde

Taco stands offer this thin salsa to be drizzled over meat in tacos.

10 tomatillos, peeled (or canned, which require no more cooking)
boiling water to cover
3 cloves garlic
3 sprigs fresh cilantro
salt to taste

Cook tomatillos 5 min., drain, reserving liquid. Blenderize everything, adding in liquid as needed to make the sauce very thin.

A variation: roast 2 serrano chiles, peel, seed, dice and add before blending.

Red Pickled Onion

This tart garnish is the traditional complement to turkey and pork.

2 red onions, diced
5 peppercorns
2 tsp juice from limes or sour oranges
salt

Pour boiling water over the onion, let sit for 10 min., drain. Add lime juice, peppercorns, and salt and let pickle for at least 1 hr.

A variation: slice onions, then cut the rounds in half for a pretty garnish.

Shaved Radish

Serve as a garnish on the plate to clean and refresh palate.

10 firm, cold radishes

Grate radishes on the coarse side of grater to make curls. Serve cold.

Sopa de Lima (Chicken Soup with Lime)

Instructions for this traditional soup come from Lupita's kitchen. Some cooks add tomato, but she doesn't, making a lovely, full-bodied meal-in-a-bowl.

1 chicken cut into pieces
2 cloves garlic
1 medium onion, diced
1 large green bell pepper, diced
2 large limes, squeezed (retain juice) and diced into 1/2-in. pieces
1 large lime sliced thin
1 tsp dried oregano
1 dried laurel (bay) leaf
1 dozen tortillas, cut in half and then into 1/2-in. strips
oil enough to fry the tortilla pieces

Place chicken in 2 qts. water, bring to a boil, cover and simmer 45 min. In a small frying pan, sweat garlic, onion and bell pepper in oil. Add to the chicken 30 min. into the simmer with the diced lime, lime juice, oregano, bay leaf, and salt to taste. When chicken is tender, remove from bones and shred, then return meat to soup. Fry tortilla strips in oil, drain. To serve, place tortilla strips in bowl, ladle in soup, garnish with sliced lime. Serves 6.

Sopa de Lentejas (Lentil Soup)

A very old man now, Mario shares this recipe from his childhood.

1 cup lentils, rinsed
1 qt. water
1 small onion, very finely diced
1 carrot, coarsely grated
1 stalk celery, very finely diced
1 bay leaf and a pinch of dried thyme
2 Tbsp butter or margarine
1 tsp salt
1/2 lb. pork or turkey sausage, removed from casing (optional)

Bring lentils, water, bay leaf and thyme to boil, then simmer for 30 min. Meanwhile, in a small frying pan, sweat onion, carrot and celery in butter and reserve. Lightly brown sausage, making crumbles of it. Add vegetables and sausage to the lentils and simmer 30 more min. Serves 6.

Cream of Cilantro Soup*

This delicately flavored, softly green soup is a perfect starter for an elegant meal.

15-20 springs of cilantro, chopped very finely
1 small onion, finely diced
1 green bell pepper, finely diced
1 large carrot, finely grated
2 cloves of garlic, finely diced
2 stalks celery, finely diced
1 bay leaf
1 stick butter or margarine
3 Tbsp flour
2 cubes chicken or vegetable bouillon
2 qts. whole milk (or substitute 1 qt. half-and-half for 1 qt. milk)

Saute onion, pepper, carrot, garlic, celery and bay leaf in butter until soft. Slowly add flour, stirring constantly (be careful not to burn flour.) Slowly add 1 qt. milk, stirring constantly as it thickens. Add cilantro and 1 qt. milk. Blenderize lightly. Return to gentle heat for 5 min. Serve hot. Serves 6.

Cilantro, Mexican parsley, is also called coriander, especially in it seed form.

Panuchos (Turkey Tostadas with Beans)

These nutritious "meals to go" are served on street corners throughout the Yucatán. Eat them at breakfast for an energy-sustaining meal. Kids love them.

1 cup black beans, cooked and mashed (see *Frijoles Negro*)
2 cups turkey breast, shredded (use leftovers or deli-roasted turkey breast)
1/2 cup red pickledonion slices (see Red Pickled Onion)
1 avocado, sliced thinly to make 12 slices
12 corn tortillas
1/2 cup oil

Spread bean paste over all the tortillas. Heat oil in large frying pan. Swiftly fry the tortillas for 2 min., bean-side up, then set on paper towel to drain. Place shredded turkey on tortillas, topped by red pickled onion and avocado.

Salbutes (Turkey Tostadas)

These are made in the same way as *Panuchos*, except without beans. A variation: serve with shredded lettuce and diced tomato.

Fresh food is prepared on the spot for the weekly "Mérida en Domingo" street fair.

Recado Colorado (Achiote Paste) *

This traditional Maya seasoning can be compared to chile powder except that its taste is distinctive and rather than being dry, it's semi-moist. Most rural households grow the bushy trees from which the red seeds (annatto) come. Achiote is easy to make and keeps in the refrigerator for three months.

2 Tbsp annatto seeds
3 cloves garlic, peeled
1/2 tsp ground cumin
1/2 tsp oregano
pinch of black pepper
2 pinches of ground allspice
2 Tbsp lime juice, or a combination of lime and vinegar

Crush the annatto seeds with a mortar and pestle or between wax paper with a rolling pin. Add the garlic and spices and crush to make a paste. Conserve in an air-tight container to use in making Pibil and other meats. * Adapted from *Yucatán Cookbook, Recipes & Tales* by Lyman Morton.

Cochinita Pibil (Pork Roasted in Banana Leaves)

Pibil is the term for the Maya tradition of cooking meat in a pit heated with burned wood and hot rocks. These recipes for roasted pork and roasted chicken come from Armando, a waiter in an Italian restaurant, who cooks meat pibil-style in his backyard for his wife to serve in her luncheonette. While people still cook special meals in a pit, for convenience the oven works as well. This dish uses three of the four main secrets of Maya cooking—the slow-cooking of meat in banana leaves and the use of achiote paste and citrus juice. Traditionally, the juice of a sour orange is used, but since there's no equivalent in the U.S., lime juice can be substituted, or half-and-half lime and orange juice.

5 lbs. pork for roasting
3 tsp achiote paste
3 tsp juice of lime or sour orange
salt
banana leaves or parchment wrapper or aluminum foil

Dissolve achiote paste in the lime juice. Rub the achiote/lime mixture onto the pork, salt, and let sit, covered, in the refrigerator all day or night. To cook, place pork in banana leaves, parchment wrapper or foil and place in a heavy baking pan. Slow roast in oven at 350 degrees for 3 hrs. Serve accompanied by *xnipek*, warm red pickled onion, beans, and warm tortillas so people can roll their own tacos. Serves 8 with leftovers.

Pollo Pibil (Chicken Roasted in Banana Leaves)

1 large chicken (4 lbs. or more), split in half lengthwise
1 small onion, thinly sliced
3 cloves of garlic, sliced thinly
3 Tbsp butter or oil
3 tsp achiote paste
3 tsp juice of lime or sour orange
salt
banana leaves or a parchment wrapper or aluminum foil

Dissolve achiote paste in lime juice. Rub chicken with achiote/lime mix and salt. Sweat onion and garlic in butter or oil. Place 1/2 chicken in one wrapper, place 1/2 chicken in another wrapper. Spread the onion, garlic, and oil mixture over each, and place in heavy baking pan. Roast for 1 hr. in 350 degree oven. Cut chicken halves into quarters. Serve with white rice and a vegetable. Serves 4.

Puchero con Tres Carnes (Chicken, Pork and Beef Stew)

This rich stew, the traditional Sunday meal in Mérida, is Spanish in origin. This recipe is adapted from Lupita's kitchen—hers is so good that the owner of a nearby restaurant often sends a waiter over to get some for his dinner.

2 chicken breasts, boneless and skinless
1 lb. pork, cut into 1-in. pieces
1 lb. beef, cut into 1-in pieces
3 cups yellow or zuchini squash, roughly cut into 1-in. pieces
3 carrots, roughly cut
3 small potatoes, roughly cut
1 cup garbanzo beans, cooked (canned)
1/2 small cabbage, sliced thin
3 small onions, roughly cut
3 cloves garlic, sliced
1 bay leaf
1/2 tsp dried oregano
pinch of dried cumin
pinch of powdered coriander seeds (cilantro)
pinch of black pepper
salt
3/4 cup small pasta such as fideos

Place meat, garlic, bay leaf, oregano, cumin, coriander, black pepper and salt in pot, and add water to cover. Bring to boil, then reduce heat and simmer for 30 min. Add squash, carrots, potatoes and onions, and simmer for another 30 min., adding water as necessary. Add cabbage, cooked garbanzos and fideos, and simmer for 10 min. Flake the chicken meat into bite-size chunks. Let stand for one hr. if possible to mix flavors, warming as needed to serve. Serves 6-8.

Frijol con Puerco (Pork and Beans)

This rich dish for bean-lovers uses the traditional black bean. A secret of Maya cooking is the epazote leaf, a mint-like herb known in the U.S. as pigweed, ironweed, and wormseed, which is used to de-gas beans.

1 lb. dried black beans, washed and soaked for several hrs.*

2 qts. water

3 *epazote* leaves **

1 1/2 lbs. pork, a lesser quality meat having bones adds flavor

1 large onion, diced

3 cloves garlic, sliced

oil

salt (add salt toward end of cooking—if added early, the beans get tough)

In a heavy pot, brown the pork a little in oil. (Don't burn.) Add soaked beans, water, *epazote*, onion and garlic, and bring to a boil. Simmer until beans are soft—about 1 1/2 hours. Add salt to taste. Remove pork, cut meat from bone, and add meat back into the beans. Serve in a bowl accompanied by fresh, chopped cilantro, chopped onion, xnipek, diced habanero chile, and grated radish. Serves 4-6.

* For a speedier meal, use 2 No. 2 cans of black beans (called *frijole negro*), and a good cut of pork cut into 1/2-in cubes. Brown the pork a little, add a little water, and simmer 20 min. Add beans, etc. and simmer 10 min.

** We can't get *epazote* leaves, so I substitute a pinch of dried oregano and cumin. Beans that are adequately soaked and cooked rarely cause gas.

Frijoles Negros Colado (Black Beans in a Pot)

These are wonderfully tasty, make them ahead for use during the week.

1 lb. black beans, washed and soaked for several hrs.

2 qts. water

epazote

1 large onion, diced

3 cloves garlic, sliced

Put everything in a pot, bring to a boil, then simmer until beans are tender—about 1 1/2 hrs. Mash a little with potato masher. Serve with tortillas and rice. Or put them in a bowl and drizzle on a mix of half yogurt and half sour cream. (If you can't get *epazote*, make sure the beans are well cooked.)

Estofado a la Mexicana (Mexican Beef Stew)

The desk clerk in a hotel we once we stayed in Playa del Carmen took us home one evening to visit, and his wife fed us this stew and shared the recipe.

3 lbs. beef stew meat

1 large onion, minced

2 cloves garlic, minced

1 green bell pepper, chopped

1 cup tomato sauce

1 Tbsp vinegar

1 tsp dried orégano

1 Tbsp chopped chile chipotle (canned) may be used)or your favorite chile

2 Tbsp flour

oil

Place meat in heavy kettle with a little oil and brown lightly. Sprinkle in flour and continue to brown for 2-3 min. stirring constantly. (Don't burn.) Add onion, garlic, and green pepper; pour tomato sauce over all, then add vinegar, orégano, salt, and chile chipotle. Cook on top of stove, covered, approximately 1 1/2 hours, or until meat is tender. Serves 6

Filete de Res a la Plancha (Grilled Beef Steak)

This recipe and the two that follow are served in Yucatán restaurants more than homes, and present a very nice meal with rice and black beans.

6 good steaks of 1/2 lb. each (such as rib eye)

2 tsp achiote paste

2 tsp juice of lime or sour orange

4 limes cut into wedges

Dissolve the achiote in the juice, then rub each steak with the mix and let sit for at least 1 hr. in the refrigerator. Grill the steaks. Serve with red pickled onion, black beans and corn tortillas. Garnish with lime wedge. Serves 6.

Pechuga de Pollo a la Plancha (Grilled Chicken Breast)

Follow the above recipe using 3 large, split chicken breasts.

Filete de Pescado a la Plancha (Grilled Fish Fillet)

Follow the above recipe using 6 fish filets (3 lbs. total) of a succulent but mild fish.

Filete de Guachinango al Mojo de Ajo (Red Snapper with Garlic)
This is a wonderfully flavorful, easy, low-fat way of preparing fish.
2 lbs. fillet of red snapper (or other fine-textured, mild fish)
10-12 cloves of garlic, peeled and crushed
3 tsp lime juice
1 lime, sliced
oil

Heat a minimum of oil in a heavy frying pan that has a tight-fitting lid. Place the fillets into the pan and immediately reduce heat. Distribute the garlic over the fillets, drizzle lime juice over the fillets, place lid on pan, and simmer about 5 min. (without turning) until fish is flaky. Serves 4.

Poc-Chuc (Grilled Pork)
This excellent dish is served in most traditional restaurants.
8 (4 lbs.) center-cut pork-chops, thin cut
4 Tbsp juice of lime or sour orange
Marinade meat in lime for 1 hr. Grill, and serve with beans, red pickled onion and tortillas.

Albondiguitas (Little Meatballs)
These excellent little meatballs can be made ahead and refrigerated for 2-3 days.
1 lb. ground round beef
1/2 lb. ground lean pork
1 egg, beaten
1 medium onion, finely diced
1 cup fine bread crumbs
2 Tbsp chopped chile chipotle (canned may be used)
1/4 cup tomato sauce (or ketchup)
1/2 tsp oregano
salt to taste
oil

In a large frying pan, sweat onion and chile in oil. In a bowl, combine all other ingredients and mix well. Mix in the cooked onion and chile. Shape into little balls 1-in. in diameter and brown in oil. Transfer to a covered skillet and simmer 5-10 min. Makes 70 meatballs.

Flan (Custard)
This dessert custard from Spain is served in most restaurants in the Yucatán. At home, people mostly have candied fruit for dessert or helado, *ice cream. Aside from having the right bowls, it's easy to fix.*
1 8-oz. can sweetened evaporated milk
1 8-oz. can evaporated milk
1 cup whole milk
8 eggs
1 Tbsp vanilla
2 1/2 cups sugar

Whip milk, eggs and vanilla together and set aside. Caramelize sugar by heating in pan until it liquifies and turns brown. Pour a little of the caramel into the bottom of 8 small (4 oz.) bowls, then fill with the milk-egg-vanilla mix. Steam for 45 min. Cool 1 hr. To serve, pool the remaining caramel on a dessert plate, and then upend the flan onto it. Serves 8

Sangria
Mix the juice from 4 lemons and 1 orange with 1/2 cup sugar. Strain, add one large (4/5 quart) bottle of red table wine. Serve in tall glasses, half-filled with crushed ice. Makes 8 servings.

Liquados (Blenderized Fruit Drinks)
1 lb. fruit, i.e, melon, banana, pineapple, watermelon, papaya, or strawberries and ice. Place the fruit in blender and whirl with ice until you like the consistency.

Cocoa
Cocoa is the drink of Maya kings and nobles, but not in the overly sweet, commercial form of today. To approximate the ancient drink, you will need Mexican chocolate (available in grocery stores), which is pressed into rounds, lightly sweetened and flavored with cinnamon or vanilla. Dissolve the cocoa into hot milk or water and whip it with fork until it froths. For variety, add a sprinkle of ground nutmeg to the finished drink. Or if you're daring, add a sprinkle of cayenne pepper. ▲

29. The Authors

Commencement de la Fin...

 VICTORIA THOMAS, WRITER, and David Björkman, photographer, are a husband-wife team that first came together in 1982 when a magazine sent them on assignment into the Darien Jungle of Panama to document a New York Explorer's Club Expedition to the Chagres River (Flag #172) and find Choco Indian Chief Antonio Zarco, who taught the original U.S. astronauts jungle survival in case their space capsule landed in the tropics. When they returned to Panama the following year on another assignment, Chief Zarco joined them in marriage (which a U.S. judge later formalized), and the Zarco women painted designs on Victoria's face with black juice. They neglected to mention that the facial art was impervious to soap and water and would fade only with time—about three weeks.

Together they went on to cover the conflicts in Central America, including Guatemala, where they had a helicopter shot out from under them in the highlands north of Nebaj. In Nicaragua, they crossed the border at night to spend thirty days in the jungle with the southern Contras led by Eden Pastora, former Sandinista hero, Commandante Zero.

On assignment to cover the drug war in Los Angeles, they accompanied the LAPD and the LA County Sheriff's Department on busts of crack houses run by the Bloods and the Crips. As they pursued stories and photos, they've gone into the field with mercenaries, bounty hunters, repo men, SWAT teams, survivalists, mountain men, body guard trainees and anti-terrorism experts. Their work has appeared in magazines in more than twenty countries.

At the same time, they managed successful careers in book and magazine publishing.

In 1996, after visiting the Pyramid of the Sun at Teotihuacan, near Mexico City, they were so awed by the sophistication of this ancient culture and the immensity of the pyramids that by September of that year, they had severed all of their publishing contracts, and set out on the first of two trips to Egypt to spend several weeks visiting the Old Kingdom pyramids built in 2450 BCE. Upon returning to their home near Boulder, Colorado, they began to feel a pull in a new direction, and decided upon an extended journey to the Maya pyramids in Mexico's Yucatán Peninsula. Fascinated by the complexity of the Maya culture and the land, they spent five years writing and photographing there. *Books of Stone* is a result of those experiences, and they're working on a second book of travels to other pyramids. ▲